FCST 3

Family Development over Life Course

Compiled by Dr. Olena Nesteruk
Family & Child Studies Department

Second Custom Edition for Montclair State University

Excerpts taken from:

The Expanded Family Life Cycle: Individual, Family, and Social Perspectives, Third Edition
Edited by Betty Carter and Monica McGoldrick
Family Interaction: A Multigenerational Developmental Perspective, Fourth Edition
by Stephen A. Anderson and Ronald M. Sabatelli

Learning Solutions

New York   Boston   San Francisco
London   Toronto   Sydney   Tokyo   Singapore   Madrid
Mexico City   Munich   Paris   Cape Town   Hong Kong   Montreal

ISBN 10: 0-558-49470-6
ISBN 13: 978-0-558-49470-4

Contents

Chapters 4, 13, and 14 taken from: *Family Interaction: A Multigenerational Developmental Perspective*, Fourth Edition by Stephen A. Anderson and Ronald M. Sabatelli

Chapters 9-12 taken from: *The Expanded Family Life Cycle: Individual, Family, and Social Perspectives*, Third Edition edited by Betty Carter and Monica McGoldrick

1

Families Past and Present

The Life Course Revolution

Arlene Skolnick

Many of us, in moments of nostalgia, imagine the past as a kind of Disneyland—a quaint setting we might step back into with our sense of ourselves intact, yet free of the stresses of modern life. But in yearning for the golden past we imagine we have lost, we are unaware of what we have escaped.

In our time, for example, dying before reaching old age has become a rare event; about three-quarters of all people die after their sixty-fifth birthday. It is hard for us to appreciate what a novelty this is in human experience. In 1850, only 2 percent of the population lived past sixty-five. "We place dying in what we take to be its logical position," observes the social historian Ronald Blythe, "which is at the close of a long life, whereas our ancestors accepted the futility of placing it in any position at all. In the midst of life we are in death, they said, and they meant it. To them it was a fact; to us it is a metaphor."

This longevity revolution is largely a twentieth-century phenomenon. Astonishingly, two-thirds of the total increase in human longevity since prehistoric times has taken place since 1900—and a good deal of that increase has occurred in recent decades. Mortality rates in previous centuries were several times higher than today, and death commonly struck at any age. Infancy was particularly hazardous; "it took two babies to make one adult," as one demographer put it. A white baby girl today has a greater chance of living to be sixty than her counterpart born in 1870 would have had of reaching her first birthday. And after infancy, death still hovered as an ever-present possibility. It was not unusual for young and middle-aged adults to die of tuberculosis, pneumonia, or other infectious diseases. (Keats died at twenty-five, Schubert at thirty-one, Mozart at thirty-five.)

Reprinted from *All Our Families: New Policies for a New Century,* edited by Mary Ann Mason, Arlene Skolnick, and Stephen D. Sugarman (2007), Oxford University Press.

1

These simple changes in mortality have had profound, yet little-appreciated effects on family life; they have encouraged stronger emotional bonds between parents and children, lengthened the duration of marriage and parent-child relationships, made grandparenthood an expectable stage of the life course, and increased the number of grandparents whom children actually know. More and more families have four or even five generations alive at the same time. And for the first time in history, the average couple has more parents living than it has children. It is also the first era when most of the parent-child relationship takes place after the child becomes an adult.

In a paper entitled "Death and the Family," the demographer Peter Uhlenberg has examined some of these repercussions by contrasting conditions in 1900 with those in 1976. In 1900, for example, half of all parents would have experienced the death of a child; by 1976 only 6 percent would. And more than half of all children who lived to the age of fifteen in 1900 would have experienced the death of a parent or sibling, compared with less than 9 percent in 1976. Another outcome of the lower death rates was a decline in the number of orphans and orphanages. Current discussions of divorce rarely take into account the almost constant family disruption children experienced in "the good old days." In 1900, 1 out of 4 children under the age of fifteen lost a parent; 1 out of 62 lost both. The corresponding figures for 1976 are, respectively, 1 out of 20 and 1 out of 1,800.

Because being orphaned used to be so common, the chances of a child's not living with either parent was much greater at the turn of the century than it is now. Indeed, some of the current growth in single-parent families is offset by a decline in the number of children raised in institutions, in foster homes, or by relatives. This fact does not diminish the stresses of divorce and other serious family problems of today, but it does help correct the tendency to contrast the terrible Present with an idealized Past.

Today's children rarely experience the death of a close relative, except for elderly grandparents. And it is possible to grow into adulthood without experiencing even that loss. "We never had any deaths in my family," a friend recently told me, explaining that none of her relatives had died until she was in her twenties. In earlier times, children were made aware of the constant possibility of death, attended deathbed scenes, and were even encouraged to examine the decaying corpses of family members.

One psychological result of our escape from the daily presence of death is that we are ill prepared for it when it comes. For most of us, the first time we feel a heightened concern with our own mortality is in our thirties and forties when we realize that the years we have already lived outnumber those we have left.

Another result is that the death of a child is no longer a sad but normal hazard of parenthood. Rather, it has become a devastating, life-shattering loss from which a parent may never fully recover. The intense emotional bonding between parents and infants that we see as a sociobiological given did not become the norm until the eighteenth and nineteenth centuries. The privileged classes created the concept of the "emotionally priceless" child, a powerful ideal that gradually filtered down through the rest of society.

The high infant mortality rates of premodern times were partly due to neglect, and often to lethal child-rearing practices such as sending infants off to a wet nurse* or, worse, infanticide. It now appears that in all societies lacking reliable contraception, the careless treatment and neglect of unwanted children acted as a major form of birth control. This does not necessarily imply that parents were uncaring toward all their children; rather, they seem to have practiced "selective neglect" of sickly infants in favor of sturdy ones, or of later children in favor of earlier ones.† In 1801 a writer observed of Bavarian peasants:

> The peasant has joy when his wife brings forth the first fruit of their love, he has joy with the second and third as well, but not with the fourth. . . . He sees all children coming thereafter as hostile creatures, which take the bread from his mouth and the mouths of his family. Even the heart of the most gentle mother becomes cold with the birth of the fifth child, and the sixth, she unashamedly wishes death, that the child should pass to heaven.

Declining fertility rates are another major result of falling death rates. Until the baby boom of the 1940s and 1950s, fertility rates had been dropping continuously since the eighteenth century. By taking away parents' fear that some of their children would not survive to adulthood, lowered early-childhood mortality rates encouraged careful planning of births and smaller families. The combination of longer lives and fewer, more closely spaced children created a still-lengthening empty-nest stage in the family. This in turn has encouraged the companionate style of marriage, since husband and wife can expect to live together for many years after their children have moved out.

Many demographers have suggested that falling mortality rates are directly linked to rising divorce rates. In 1891 W. F. Willcox of Cornell University made one of the most accurate social science predictions ever. Looking at the high and steadily rising divorce rates of the time, along with falling mortality rates, he predicted that around 1980, the two curves would cross and the number of marriages ended by divorce would equal those ended by death. In the late 1970s, it all happened as Willcox had predicted. Then divorce rates continued to increase before leveling off in the 1980s, while mortality rates continued to decline. As a result, a couple marrying today

---

*Wet-nursing—the breastfeeding of an infant by a woman other than the mother—was widely practiced in premodern Europe and colonial America. Writing of a two-thousand-year-old "war of the breast," the developmental psychologist William Kessen notes that the most persistent theme in the history of childhood is the reluctance of mothers to suckle their babies, and the urgings of philosophers and physicians that they do so. Infants were typically sent away from home for a year and a half or two years to be raised by poor country women, in squalid conditions. When they took in more babies than they had milk enough to suckle, the babies would die of malnutrition.

The reluctance to breast-feed may not have reflected maternal indifference so much as other demands in premodern, precontraceptive times—the need to take part in the family economy, the unwillingness of husbands to abstain from sex for a year and a half or two. (Her milk would dry up if a mother became pregnant.) Although in France and elsewhere the custom persisted into the twentieth century, large-scale wet-nursing symbolizes the gulf between modern and premodern sensibilities about infants and their care.

†The anthropologist Nancy Scheper-Hughes describes how impoverished mothers in northeastern Brazil select which infants to nurture.

is more likely to celebrate a fortieth wedding anniversary than were couples around the turn of the century.

In statistical terms, then, it looks as if divorce has restored a level of instability to marriage that had existed earlier due to the high mortality rate. But as Lawrence Stone observes, "it would be rash to claim that the psychological effects of the termination of marriage by divorce, that is by an act of will, bear a close resemblance to its termination by the inexorable accident of death."

The New Stages of Life

In recent years it has become clear that the stages of life we usually think of as built into human development are, to a large degree, social and cultural inventions. Although people everywhere may pass through infancy, childhood, adulthood, and old age, the facts of nature are "doctored," as Ruth Benedict once put it, in different ways by different cultures.

The Favorite Age

In 1962 Phillipe Ariès made the startling claim that "in medieval society, the idea of childhood did not exist." Ariès argued not that parents then neglected their children, but that they did not think of children as having a special nature that required special treatment; after the age of around five to seven, children simply joined the adult world of work and play. This "small adult" conception of childhood has been observed by many anthropologists in preindustrial societies. In Europe, according to Ariès and others, childhood was discovered, or invented, in the seventeenth and nineteenth centuries, with the emergence of the private, domestic, companionate family and formal schooling. These institutions created distinct roles for children, enabling childhood to emerge as a distinct stage of life.

Despite challenges to Ariès's work, the bulk of historical and cross-cultural evidence supports the contention that childhood as we know it today is a relatively recent cultural invention; our ideas about children, child-rearing practices, and the conditions of children's lives are dramatically different from those of earlier centuries. The same is true of adolescence. Teenagers, such a conspicuous and noisy presence in modern life, and their stage of life, known for its turmoil and soul searching, are not universal features of life in other times and places.

Of course, the physical changes of puberty—sexual maturation and spurt in growth—happen to everyone everywhere. Yet, even here, there is cultural and historical variation. In the past hundred years, the age of first menstruation has declined from the mid-teens to twelve, and the age young men reach their full height has declined from twenty-five to under twenty. Both changes are believed to be due to improvements in nutrition and health care, and these average ages are not expected to continue dropping.

Some societies have puberty rites, but they bring about a transition from childhood not to adolescence but to adulthood. Other societies take no note at all of the changes, and the transition from childhood to adulthood takes place simply and without social recognition. Adolescence as we know it today appears to have evolved late in the nineteenth century; there is virtual consensus among social scientists that it is "a creature of the industrial revolution and it continues to be shaped by the forces which defined that revolution: industrialization, specialization, urbanization . . . and bureaucratization of human organizations and institutions, and continuing technological development."

In America before the second half of the nineteenth century, youth was an ill-defined category. Puberty did not mark any new status or life experience. For the majority of young people who lived on farms, work life began early, at seven or eight years old or even younger. As they grew older, their responsibility would increase, and they would gradually move toward maturity. Adults were not ignorant of the differences between children and adults, but distinctions of age meant relatively little. As had been the practice in Europe, young people could be sent away to become apprentices or servants in other households. As late as the early years of this century, working-class children went to work at the age of ten or twelve.

A second condition leading to a distinct stage of adolescence was the founding of mass education systems, particularly the large public high school. Compulsory education helped define adolescence by setting a precise age for it; high schools brought large numbers of teenagers together to create their own society for a good part of their daily lives. So the complete set of conditions for adolescence on a mass scale did not exist until the end of the nineteenth century.

The changed family situations of late-nineteenth- and early-twentieth-century youth also helped make this life stage more psychologically problematic. Along with the increasing array of options to choose from, rapid social change was making one generation's experience increasingly different from that of the next. Among the immigrants who were flooding into the country at around the time adolescence was emerging, the generation gap was particularly acute. But no parents were immune to the rapid shifts in society and culture that were transforming America in the decades around the turn of the century.

Further, the structure and emotional atmosphere of middle-class family life was changing also, creating a more intimate and emotionally intense family life. Contrary to the view that industrialization had weakened parent-child relations, the evidence is that family ties between parents and adolescents intensified at this time: adolescents lived at home until they married, and depended more completely, and for a longer time, on their parents than in the past. Demographic change had cut family size in half over the course of the century. Mothers were encouraged to devote themselves to the careful nurturing of fewer children.

This more intensive family life seems likely to have increased the emotional strain of adolescence. Smaller households and a more nurturing style of child rearing, combined with the increased contact between parents, especially mothers, and adolescent children, may have created a kind of " 'Oedipal family' in middle class America."

The young person's awakening sexuality, particularly the young male's, is likely to have been more disturbing to both himself and his parents than during the era when young men commonly lived away from home. . . . There is evidence that during the Victorian era, fears of adolescent male sexuality, and of masturbation in particular, were remarkably intense and widespread.

Family conflict in general may have been intensified by the peculiar combination of teenagers' increased dependence on parents and increased autonomy in making their own life choices. Despite its tensions, the new emotionally intense middle-class home made it more difficult than ever for adolescents to leave home for the heartless, indifferent world outside.

By the end of the nineteenth century, conceptions of adolescence took on modern form, and by the first decades of the twentieth century, *adolescence* had become a household word. As articulated forcefully by the psychologist G. Stanley Hall in his 1904 treatise, adolescence was a biological process—not simply the onset of sexual maturity but a turbulent, transitional stage in the evolution of the human species: "some ancient period of storm and stress when old moorings were broken and a higher level attained."

Hall seemed to provide the answers to questions people were asking about the troublesome young. His public influence eventually faded, but his conception of adolescence as a time of storm and stress lived on. Adolescence continued to be seen as a period of both great promise and great peril: "every step of the upward way is strewn with the wreckage of body, mind and morals." The youth problem—whether the lower-class problem of delinquency, or the identity crises and other psychological problems of middle-class youth—has continued to haunt America, and other modern societies, ever since.

Ironically, then, the institutions that had developed to organize and control a problematic age ended by heightening adolescent self-awareness, isolating youth from the rest of society, and creating a youth culture, making the transition to adulthood still more problematic and risky. Institutional recognition in turn made adolescents a more distinct part of the population, and being adolescent a more distinct and self-conscious experience. As it became part of the social structure of modern society, adolescence also became an important stage of the individual's biography—an indeterminate period of being neither child nor adult that created its own problems. Any society that excludes youth from adult work, and offers them what Erikson calls a "moratorium"—time and space to try out identities and lifestyles—and at the same time demands extended schooling as the route to success is likely to turn adolescence into a "struggle for self." It is also likely to run the risk of increasing numbers of mixed-up, rebellious youth.

But, in fact, the classic picture of adolescent storm and stress is not universal. Studies of adolescents in America and other industrialized societies suggest that extreme rebellion and rejection of parents, flamboyant behavior, and psychological turmoil do not describe most adolescents, even today. Media images of the youth of the 1980s and 1990s as a deeply troubled, lost generation beset by crime, drug abuse, and teenage pregnancy are also largely mistaken.

Although sexual activity and experimenting with drugs and alcohol have become common among middle-class young people, drug use has actually declined in recent years. Disturbing as these practices are for parents and other adults, they apparently do not interfere with normal development for most adolescents. Nevertheless, for a significant minority, sex and drugs add complications to a period of development during which a young person's life can easily go awry—temporarily or for good.

More typically, for most young people, the teen years are marked by mild rebelliousness and moodiness—enough to make it a difficult period for parents but not one of a profound parent-child generation gap or of deep alienation from conventional values. These ordinary tensions of family living through adolescence are exacerbated in times of rapid social change, when the world adolescents confront is vastly different from the one in which their parents came of age. Always at the forefront of social change, adolescents in industrial societies inevitably bring discomfort to their elders, who "wish to see their children's adolescence as an enactment of the retrospectively distorted memory of their own. . . . But such intergenerational continuity can occur only in the rapidly disappearing isolation of the desert or the rain forest."

If adolescence is a creation of modern culture, that culture has also been shaped by adolescence. Adolescents, with their music, fads, fashions, and conflicts, not only are conspicuous, but reflect a state of mind that often extends beyond the years designated for them. The adolescent mode of experience—accessible to people of any age—is marked by "exploration, becoming, growth, and pain."

Since the nineteenth century, for example, the coming-of-age novel has become a familiar literary genre. Patricia Spacks observes that while Victorian authors looked back at adolescence from the perspective of adulthood, twentieth-century novelists since James Joyce and D. H. Lawrence have become more intensely identified with their young heroes, writing not from a distance but from "deep inside the adolescence experience." The novelist's use of the adolescent to symbolize the artist as romantic outsider mirrors a more general cultural tendency. As Phillipe Ariès observes, "Our society has passed from a period which was ignorant of adolescence to a period in which adolescence is the favorite age. We now want to come to it early and linger in it as long as possible."

The Discovery of Adulthood

Middle age is the latest life stage to be discovered, and the notion of mid-life crisis recapitulates the storm-and-stress conception of adolescence. Over the course of the twentieth century, especially during the years after World War II, a developmental conception of childhood became institutionalized in public thought. Parents took it for granted that children passed through ages, stages, and phases: the terrible twos, the teenage rebel. In recent years the idea of development has been increasingly applied to adults, as new stages of adult life are discovered. Indeed much of the psychological revolution of recent years—the tendency to look at life through psychological lenses—can be understood in part as the extension of the developmental approach to adulthood.

In 1976 Gail Sheehy's best-selling *Passages* popularized the concept of mid-life crisis. Sheehy argued that every individual must pass through such a watershed, a time when we reevaluate our sense of self, undergo a crisis, and emerge with a new identity. Failure to do so, she warned, can have dire consequences. The book was the most influential popular attempt to apply to adults the ages-and-stages approach to development that had long been applied to children. Ironically, this came about just as historians were raising questions about the universality of those stages.

Despite its popularity, Sheehy's book, and the research she reported in it, have come under increasing criticism. "Is the mid-life crisis, if it exists, more than a warmed-over identity crisis?" asked one review of the research literature on mid-life. In fact, there is little or no evidence for the notion that adults pass through a series of sharply defined stages, or a series of crises that must be resolved before passing from one stage to the next.

Nevertheless, the notion of a mid-life crisis caught on because it reflected shifts in adult experience across the life course. Most people's decisions about marriage and work are no longer irrevocably made at one fateful turning point on the brink of adulthood. The choices made at twenty-one may no longer fit at forty or fifty—the world has changed; parents, children, and spouses have changed; working life has changed. The kind of issue that makes adolescence problematic—the array of choices and the need to fashion a coherent, continuous sense of self in the midst of all this change—recurs throughout adulthood. As a Jules Feiffer cartoon concludes, "Maturity is a phase, but adolescence is forever."

Like the identity crisis of adolescence, the concept of mid-life crisis appears to reflect the experience of the more educated and advantaged. Those with more options in life are more likely to engage in the kind of introspection and reappraisal of previous choices that make up the core of the mid-life crisis. Such people realize that they will never fulfill their earlier dreams, or that they have gotten what they wanted and find they are still not happy. But as the Berkeley longitudinal data show, even in that segment of the population, mid-life crisis is far from the norm. People who have experienced fewer choices in the past, and have fewer options for charting new directions in the future, are less likely to encounter a mid-life crisis. Among middle Americans, life is dominated by making ends meet, coping with everyday events, and managing unexpected crises.

While there may be no fixed series of stages or crises adults must pass through, middle age or mid-life in our time does have some unique features that make it an unsettled time, different from other periods in the life course as well as from mid-life in earlier eras. First, as we saw earlier, middle age is the first period in which most people today confront death, illness, and physical decline. It is also an uneasy age because of the increased importance of sexuality in modern life. Sexuality has come to be seen as the core of our sense of self, and sexual fulfillment as the center of the couple relationship. In mid-life, people confront the decline of their physical attractiveness, if not of their sexuality.

There is more than a passing resemblance between the identity problems of adolescence and the issues that fall under the rubric of "mid-life crisis." In a list of themes recurring in the literature on the experience of identity crisis, particularly in adolescence, the psychologist Roy Baumeister includes: feelings of emptiness, feelings of vagueness, generalized malaise, anxiety, self-consciousness. These symptoms describe not only adolescent and mid-life crises but what Erikson has labeled identity problems—or what has, of late, been considered narcissism.

Consider, for example, Heinz Kohut's description of patients suffering from what he calls narcissistic personality disorders. They come to the analyst with vague symptoms, but eventually focus on feelings about the self—emptiness, vague depression, being drained of energy, having no "zest" for work or anything else, shifts in self-esteem, heightened sensitivity to the opinions and reactions of others, feeling unfulfilled, a sense of uncertainty and purposelessness. "It seems on the face of it," observes the literary critic Steven Marcus, "as if these people are actually suffering from what was once called unhappiness."

The New Aging

Because of the extraordinary revolution in longevity, the proportion of elderly people in modern industrial societies is higher than it has ever been. This little-noticed but profound transformation affects not just the old but families, an individual's life course, and society as a whole. We have no cultural precedents for the mass of the population reaching old age. Further, the meaning of *old age* has changed—indeed, it is a life stage still in process, its boundaries unclear. When he came into office at the age of sixty-four, George [H. W.] Bush did not seem like an old man. Yet when Franklin Roosevelt died at the same age, he did seem to be "old."

President Bush illustrates why gerontologists in recent years have had to revise the meaning of "old." He is a good example of what they have termed the "young old" or the "new elders"; the social historian Peter Laslett uses the term "the third age." Whatever it is called, it represents a new stage of life created by the extension of the life course in industrialized countries. Recent decades have witnessed the first generations of people who live past sixty-five and remain healthy, vigorous, alert, and, mostly due to retirement plans, financially independent. These people are "pioneers on the frontier of age," observed the journalist Frances Fitzgerald, in her study of Sun City, a retirement community near Tampa, Florida, "people for whom society had as yet no set of expectations and no vision."

The meaning of the later stages of life remains unsettled. Just after gerontologists had marked off the "young old"—people who seemed more middle-aged than old—they had to devise a third category, the "oldest old," to describe the fastest-growing group in the population, people over eighty-five. Many if not most of these people are like Tithonus, the mythical figure who asked the gods for eternal life but forgot to ask for eternal youth as well. For them, the gift of long life has come at the cost of chronic disease and disability.

The psychological impact of this unheralded longevity revolution has largely been ignored, except when misconstrued. The fear of age, according to Christopher Lasch, is one of the chief symptoms of this culture's alleged narcissism. But when people expected to die in their forties or fifties, they didn't have to face the problem of aging. Alzheimer's disease, for example, now approaching epidemic proportions, is an ironic by-product of the extension of the average life span. When living to seventy or eighty is a realistic prospect, it makes sense to diet and exercise, to eat healthy foods, and to make other "narcissistic" investments in the self.

Further, "the gift of mass longevity," the anthropologist David Plath argues, has been so recent, dramatic, and rapid that it has become profoundly unsettling in all post-industrial societies: "If the essential cultural nightmare of the nineteenth century was to be in poverty, perhaps ours is to be old and alone or afflicted with terminal disease."

Many people thus find themselves in life stages for which cultural scripts have not yet been written; family members face one another in relationships for which tradition provides little guidance. "We are stuck with awkward-sounding terms like 'adult children' and . . . 'grandson-in-law.' " And when cultural rules are ambiguous, emotional relationships can become tense or at least ambivalent.

A study of five-generation families in Germany reveals the confusion and strain that result when children and parents are both in advanced old age—for example, a great-great-grandmother and her daughter, who is herself a great-grandmother. Who has the right to be old? Who should take care of whom? Similarly, Plath, who has studied the problems of mass longevity in Japan, finds that even in that familistic society the traditional meaning of family roles has been put into question by the stretching out of the life span. In the United States, some observers note that people moving into retirement communities sometimes bring their parents to live with them. Said one disappointed retiree: "I want to enjoy my grandchildren; I never expected that when I was a grandparent I'd have to look after my parents."

2

Development of Families Across Time

Family Development Theory

John and Natasha Morrison were looking forward to their retirement in a few years. Their eldest daughter, Tamara, was just finishing law school and was pregnant with her first child. John Jr., their only son, was doing well in college and planning a career in communications. Their youngest daughter, Kamika, would soon be graduating from high school. With her college tuition safely tucked away in an education IRA, they were hoping to take retirement in their early sixties. As a couple with active professional careers and three children, they had often dreamed of an extended vacation but had been too busy to take one. They planned to take a grand world tour when they retired.

Natasha's parents, who lived nearby and saw the family regularly, came to visit for Father's Day. The family sat around the picnic table out back and reminisced about the changes in their lives over the years. When the children were young, they all had the same kinds of activities and friends. Now it was as if they were all in their own separate worlds. It was difficult to find time together because each person was so busy and focused on his or her own life. John and Natasha were worried about John's father, who lived 500 miles away and was in poor health. Tamara and her husband were busy getting ready for their first child and establishing their professional careers. Johnny was beginning to show signs of seriousness about a girlfriend for the first time in his life. Kamika was hardly ever at home anymore, staying busy with her friends and after-school activities. She was particularly interested in dance and recently had made a new friend, Matt, who also wanted to be a dancer.

Everyone gathered around the table to watch John open his Father's Day presents. Kamika seemed very excited. "Daddy, I have the greatest surprise for you!

Reprinted from: *Exploring Family Theories* by Smith, Hammond, Ingoldsby, and Miller (2009), Oxford University Press.

You'll be so excited. I'm so very sure! I'm going to go to New York to be a dancer! I've been accepted into a little company in New York where they will train me, and Matt and I are moving there in a month! Isn't that just great?"

History

Family development theory emerged in the late 1940s, corresponding with the development of the field of family science. It was one of the first family-focused theories, with a separate identity from psychology or sociology. Psychology-based theories, with their narrower emphasis on individuals, did not fully explain what happened in families with competing individual needs. Sociology-based theories, focused on society and culture, were too broad in their analysis. Thus, family development theory originated from the critiques of these two perspectives.

Evelyn Duvall and Ruben Hill (1948) pointed out that families were social groups that were influenced by developmental processes, in the same way that individuals were. Like individuals, families experienced life cycles, with clearly delineated stages, each of which required the accomplishment of specific tasks. But families needed to be studied as a dynamic unit, not as a collection of individuals. According to family developmental theorists, the family life cycle had two major stages—expansion and contraction. During expansion, children are born and raised, whereas during contraction, children leave the family home. This "cycle" of expansion and contraction gave rise to the term *family life cycle* (Duvall 1957).

In 1948, Duvall and Hill first presented their version of the family life cycle in which they identified tasks that would be accomplished by both parents and children. These tasks were grouped into eight stages of development across the family life cycle. Later versions of the theory went beyond the demarcation of stages and tasks and began to focus on changes within the family over time, including transitions and social roles. Duvall later codified these in a textbook, *Family Development*, first published in 1957. Updated and republished many times (Duvall 1957 and the revised editions 1962, 1967, 1971, 1977), this was one of the most widely used textbooks on the subject for the next thirty years. Thus, Duvall's eight stages of the family life cycle are the best-known stages of the family development theory.

Other theorists, building on the foundation laid by Duvall and Hill (1948), worked to expand these concepts. In 1964, Roy Rodgers (1964) developed a version of the theory with twenty-four different stages, but its complexity overshadowed its usefulness. Rodgers (1973) further expanded the concept of family interaction by focusing on three dynamics across the family career. He emphasized that families were influenced by institutional norms, by the expectations that arise from the family itself, and by the expectations that arise from the individuals within the family. In contrast, Joan Aldous (1978, 1996) suggested that family development should be considered in only four stages, because families are often in several stages of parenting at the same time. She further recommended the use of the term *family career*, rather than *family life cycle*, because families did not return to the way they had been at the beginning of their lives.

In the 1970s and 1980s, some family scholars criticized family development theory because it lacked scientific testability. In 1973, Wesley Burr, a renowned theorist and researcher, reviewed many of the major issues in family studies, including the family life cycle. In his book Burr (1973) wrote: "It has not yet been proved that the family life cycle will turn out to be a very useful concept in deductive theories" (219). His concern with the theory was that the concepts and variables were not well defined and so could not be properly tested in empirical research. Addressing these concerns, James White published a book in 1991 entitled *Dynamics of Family Development: A Theoretical Perspective* in which he outlined specific testable propositions and variables for family development theory. White is considered one of the major proponents of family development theory today.

At about the same time, a new variant of family development theory—life course perspective—was being described. The life course perspective went beyond the life cycle view by including additional variables such as multiple views of time (ontogenetic, generational, and historical), micro- and macro-social contexts, and increasing diversity over time (Bengtson and Allen 1993).

Basic Assumptions

Families undergo stages of development, just like individuals. Family development theory focuses on the developmental stages of the family as well as the individual. Transitions from one stage to the next are usually related to changes in individual development. For example, newly married couples, couples with preschoolers, couples with teenagers, and couples whose children have moved out of the home clearly are in different stages of development and have different tasks to accomplish. Family stress is usually greatest at transition points between developmental stages.

There are tasks associated with each stage of development. This concept is taken from psychologically based developmental theories (e.g., Havighurst 1948). Tasks are defined on the basis of normative expectations. Each stage is delineated by a set of tasks that must be accomplished to prepare adequately for the next stage of development. Failure to complete a task does not necessarily preclude moving to the next stage of development but may limit a family's optimal functioning at the next level. For example, parents who pay too much attention to raising their children and not enough to their own relationship may find that they encounter problems with their relationship after the children leave home.

Development is reciprocal. The individual development of each family member influences other family members as well as the overall development of the family. The family's development influences the critical periods of individual development as well. Because there is reciprocity in the interaction of the family and individual development, it is necessary to consider them in concert.

Families must be viewed in multiple levels of analysis. Family development theory requires that family life be considered in the multiple contexts of the society, the family, and the individual. The social context and/or historical period influence both the processes within the family and the developmental issues encountered by individuals within the family.

Families should be viewed over time.   One of family development theory's core assumptions is that families ate not static but change over time. This "change over time" is the primary focus of the theory. How and when families change, what they accomplish at different points of time, and why they change can be known only if one studies families over time.

Primary Terms and Concepts

Family

Duvall (1977) proposed that the family is composed of "interacting persons related by ties of marriage, birth, or adoption, whose central purpose is to create and maintain a common culture which promotes the physical, mental, emotional, and social development of each of its members" (5). The dynamics of the family may change over time, dependent on the needs of the individuals, the relationships between them, and the impact of society on the family. These variables determine the components of the developmental tasks and are dependent on the family "tempos and rhythms."

Normative Events

Rather than focusing on crises in families, family development theorists focus on the things that happen more normatively with the passage of time, such as marriages, childbirth, developmental and educational milestones.

Stages

Probably the most unique aspect of family development theory is its focus on the stages of the family life cycle. These stages are periods of "relative equilibrium in which consensus about the allocation of roles and rules of procedure is high" (Hill 1986, 21). In the model developed by Duvall and Hill, stages are the result of major changes in family size, changes in the developmental age of the oldest child, or changes in the work status of the breadwinner (Hill 1986).

Each stage of development is related to behaviors or tasks that would normally be expected to occur during that stage. Norms govern both group and individual behavior, often defining the roles that people play. It is important to note that these norms are socially defined and change over time as cultural mores change. So, too, static norms regulate behavior and expectations within a particular stage, while process norms regulate timing and sequencing of expectations and behaviors.

Tasks

The concept of tasks in family development theory is derived from a similar concept of tasks, as defined by Havighurst (1948, 1953), in individual developmental theory. According to Havighurst, developmental tasks occur at particular points in development in response to either physical maturation or cultural pressure or changes. The individual must respond by developing new abilities, roles, or relationships. If the challenge of development is met positively, then the individual will be happier and have more success with later stages of development. If not, then, as with other stage theories of development (e.g., Erikson and Piaget), we would predict that the individual would be less successful.

Using this model, Duvall and Hill (1948) incorporated specific tasks for each of the eight stages of the family life cycle. These tasks focus on what the family, as a unit, must accomplish, while taking into account the individual needs of the parents and children. For example, Duvall (1957, 1977) outlined the tasks (as an individual) that a child would have to achieve to develop optimally. She further linked those individual tasks to the tasks that the family must achieve as it assimilates the individual child into its unit. Thus, when a newborn moves into the toddler stage, the family must create a safe physical environment for the toddler to explore. Later, when a young adult enters into the launching phase, the family's task is to provide a secure base but recognize that the young adult's reliance on the family may be more economic than physical. Each stage of development requires the family to change and accommodate the needs of the children as they age (Duvall 1977).

Timing

When something happens has an impact on family life. In other words, it makes a difference to the family when a child is born, or when someone retires, or when someone moves out of the house. This is particularly apparent when there are multiple events occurring at or near the same time. So, too, social prescriptions exist about *when* individuals and families are to engage in particular behaviors or accomplish certain tasks. Pressure exists for family life events to occur "on time" rather than "off time" (Neugarten, Moore, and Lowe 1965). The life course perspective theorists introduced the concept of different qualities of time into family development theory. *Ontogenetic time* refers to the time one recognizes as one grows and changes through one's own lifetime (one's personal awareness of time—like an "internal clock"). *Generational time* refers to how one's time is experienced within one's social group (as in one's family or in a cohort). *Historical time* refers to how time is experienced in the social context or greater historical period (e.g., living during the Great Depression in contrast to being a baby boomer; Bengtson and Allen 1993). Thus, one can experience one's adolescent period as a unique stage in one's developmental history (ontogenetic). But it might matter whether that adolescence was experienced during the turbulent Vietnam era or the late 1990s (historical). Similarly, it might make some difference if one becomes a first-time parent at the age of seventeen or at the age of forty-four (generational).

Change

Something changes when it undergoes a transformation from one state to another. (For example, John and Natasha Morrison's experience of family, noted at the beginning of this chapter, will be different when the last child, Kamika, graduates from high school and moves to New York, leaving them with their home all to themselves.) Family development theory proposes that family relationships are not static but rather change over time. Catalysts for change can be either internal (such as biological growth) or external (through interaction with the environment). The nature of this interaction is reciprocal—that is, the organism both elicits and responds to stimuli in its environment.

Change comes with varying levels of acknowledgment and acceptance by family members. Individual changes become the catalyst for family change, causing shifts from one family stage to another. Changes in personal roles within the family are often the result of individual changes and transitions from one stage to the next.

Transitions

One cannot study change without studying transitions. Transitions are the processes that form a bridge between the different states when something changes. In family development theory, transitions are the shifts in roles and identities encountered with changes in developmental stages (Hagestad 1988). (For John and Natasha Morrison, their experience of moving into the middle years may be dependent upon their sense of success in their parenting roles as well as the degree to which they nurtured their own marital relationship in previous stages.) Ease of transition is dependent on the resolution of the stages beforehand, or the degree to which the stage is perceived to be a crisis. As families shift from one stage to the next, their roles, behaviors, and tasks are reallocated in accordance with their new stage. Some families move easily from one stage to the next and some do not. Depending upon how prepared they are for the new stage, families will respond to the change as either a crisis or as an opportunity (Rapoport 1963). Some developmental transitions, such as when one's child begins school, are easy to recognize. Other transitions, such as identifying exactly when a child becomes an adolescent, are more difficult for the family to pinpoint and to accommodate. Furthermore, crises can create critical transitions—that is, those that occur in addition to normally expected transitions, such as an unexpected pregnancy. Focusing on transitions helps us to understand what families go through as they move from stage to stage (Duvall 1988).

Common Areas of Research and Application

The Family Life Cycle

Evelyn Duvall's eight-stage model (see table 1) is the most well-known version of the family development theory. As with all stage theories, there are specific tasks associated with each stage. The chart provided by Duvall and Miller (1985)[1] provides a delineation of those eight stages.

Stage 1: Establishment phase—courtship and marriage.   Stage 1 is known as the *establishment phase* because couples are focused on establishing their home base. There are many tasks associated with the establishment phase of relationships, and as in individual developmental models, the accomplishment of future tasks relies heavily on the successful negotiation of the previous stage's tasks. If couples can blend their individual needs and desires, find workable solutions to conflicts, and maintain

good communication and intimacy patterns, then they are better able to handle the tasks associated with the next stages.

In the United States, the establishment phase generally begins with some form of courtship. Courtship is the personal preparation for marriage consisting of three general tasks. Duvall (1977) lists these tasks as (1) readying oneself for the roles of husband

Table 1

Stage-Sensitive Family Developmental Tasks Through the Family Life Cycle

Stages of the Family Life Cycle	Positions in the Family	Stage-Sensitive Family Developmental Tasks
1. Married Couple	Wife Husband	Establishing a mutually satisfying marriage Adjusting to pregnancy and the promise of parenthood Fitting into the kin network
2. Childbearing	Wife-mother Husband-father Infant daughter or son or both	Having, adjusting to, and encouraging the development of infants Establishing a satisfying home for both parents and infant(s)
3. Preschool age	Wife-mother Husband-father Daughter-sister Son-brother	Adapting to the critical needs and interests of preschool children in stimulating, growth-promoting ways. Coping with energy depletion and lack of privacy as parents
4. School age	Wife-mother Husband-father Daughter-sister Son-brother	Fitting into the community of school-age families in constructive ways Encouraging children's educational achievement
5. Teenage	Wife-mother Husband-father Daughter-sister Son-brother	Balancing freedom with responsibility as teenagers mature and emancipate themselves Establishing postparental interests and careers as growing parents
6. Launching Center	Wife-mother-grandmother Husband-father-grandfather Daughter-sister-aunt Son-brother-uncle	Releasing young adults into work, military service, college, marriage, and so on with appropriate rituals and assistance Maintaining a supportive home base
7. Middle aged Parents	Wife-mother-grandmother Husband-father-grandfather	Refocusing on the marriage relationship Maintaining kin ties with older and younger generations
8. Aging Family Members	Widow or widower Wife-mother-grandmother Husband-father-grandfather	Coping with bereavement and living alone Closing the family home or adapting it to aging Adjusting to retirement

Source: Duvall, and Miller, 1985 *Marriage and Family Development* 6th ed. Boston Allyn and Bacon: Copyright © 1985 by Pearson Education. Reprinted by permission of the publisher.

or wife, (2) disengaging from close relationships that might compete with the marriage, and (3) reprioritizing, so the couple's interests are more important than those of the individual. The degree to which one is successful at addressing these tasks during courtship predicts success during marriage.

Individuals thinking about forming a couple need to learn about each other's desires, dreams, expectations, and style of living. They need to find out more about each other's habits and hobbies, ways of interacting with their friends and families, and likes and dislikes, from foods to movies to household decorations. In addition to these pragmatic considerations, couples also have to develop intellectual and emotional communication patterns, patterns of behaviors and preferences, and a jointly workable philosophy of life and set of values. Some couples, frequently encouraged by clergy or marriage educators and counselors, participate in a marriage preparation program in order to be certain that the most important issues have been discussed.

Once these topics are explored, the marriage ceremony is an outward and clearly demarcated symbol of status change for couples. It receives both legal sanction and public recognition and, in many instances, religious validation. Before cohabitation became more common, the marriage ceremony also signaled the end of individuals living separately.

The new marital tasks for the couple include developing systems for acquiring and spending money, establishing daily routines, and creating a satisfying sex life. Both partners must also create new and appropriate relationships with relatives and old friends while establishing new friendships as a couple.

Many of the tasks associated with early marriage focus on the establishment of a home suitable for children. Some of these tasks include developing family-planning strategies, agreeing on the timing of pregnancy, arranging for the care of the baby, acquiring knowledge regarding parenthood, and adapting the home to accommodate children. It used to be that couples did not have much control over when they became pregnant. Today, however, couples can use contraceptives to choose the "best" time to become pregnant. But with this choice comes the responsibility for the couple to determine, and to agree, when the so called "best" time is.

Stage 2: Childbearing families—families with infants. The arrival of an infant brings about a new set of tasks for the family to face. The family must expand both physically and emotionally. New roles of "father" and "mother" appear. The couple must now negotiate how they will share the new responsibilities of caring for the child and must reallocate previously assigned household responsibilities.

Infants are completely dependent on their parents for food, clothing, shelter, and medical care. Parents ate also responsible for nurturing their infant's cognitive and emotional needs. Infants require a safe and stimulating environment, which can include car seats, diapers, cribs, and toys. The couple might have to expand their household space by moving to a new home or rearranging their current space and how they use it.

All of this, of course, costs money, which places an additional financial demand on the family. These stressors can be damaging to the couple's relationship, so the couple must continue to practice effective communication strategies to maintain a strong bond. They should also remember to pay attention to their own relationship while they attend to their infant's needs.

Stage 3: Families with preschool children.

In families with more than one child, it is not uncommon for the firstborn to be only a few years old when the next child is born (Glick 1977). In addition to adapting to the even greater physical needs of two (or more) children, the family must also adjust to the individual differences and temperaments of the children. Preschoolers need structure in their play and activities, and they benefit from intensive parental involvement. Infants also need a lot of physical attention, with diaper changes and feedings, as well as emotional and cognitive nurturing.

Just as in Stage 2, there are the issues of additional physical space and additional financial demands. The more children there are, the more difficult it becomes for the couple to meet their own developmental needs and continue to grow as a couple. Despite the demands on the resources of time, energy, and money, the couple still needs to spend time together doing such things, for example, dining out once a week or twice-yearly vacations away. Regardless of the activity, it is just as important to the relationship to spend some time focusing only on their marriage as it is to focus on their roles as parents.

Stage 4: Families with school-aged children.

School is the first public social system that children encounter outside the immediate family. This is significant because families give up some authority over their children to the school. Their parenting skills and their children's behaviors are judged in this public forum. School represents an expansion of the family to other social systems that influence the family in significant ways.

The child's individual development drives the family at this stage. Trying out new activities is a major task of the school-aged child. Families with school-aged children must provide for their children's activities outside of school, which often include sports, music, and religious and social interactions. Parents must work to develop relationships with teachers, religious leaders, and parents of other children. They must develop strategies for accomplishing tasks around the home, particularly if schedules require the parents and children to be away from home more frequently (e.g., evening ball games and weekend birthday parties) and find ways to appropriately delegate family tasks to various family members. Parents must also determine what the appropriate expectations are for their children (who may be at different developmental stages) for helping around the house, developing responsible behavior, watching television, or listening to music. While it is relatively easy to recognize appropriate music for a preschooler, it is more difficult to figure that out for a ten-year-old. And ten-year-olds bring additional issues to the families because they are influenced by their friends and by television. Because these issues require parental decisions, R-rated movies may be prohibited in one ten-year-old's household but may be allowed at her friend's house. One reason for this may be that as their children's physical autonomy increases, many parents increase their level of parental monitoring.

Stage 5: Families with adolescents. As in Stage 4, individual development drives the family in Stage 5. Adolescence is a time of rapid physical (sexual), cognitive, and psychosocial change. According to Erik Erikson, adolescents need to achieve their own identities separate from their families, and they do so by "trying on" different identities until they find one that "fits" (identity achievement). If identity is not achieved, then the adolescent will remain in a confused state without a cleat sense of self (role diffusion). Parents must allow adolescents to establish their own separate identities, which sometimes may be in conflict with the family's values and ideas. Duvall (1957) states that open communication helps parents and adolescents learn from each other and helps to bridge the generations.

The adolescent may express a need for more space, both physical and emotional, more freedom to choose activities, and more activities to do, along with the need for more money to do those things. In addition, many adolescents and their parents have concerns about their futures, including the cost of tuition for college or technical training.

Adolescents are able to share more of the responsibilities of family living, perhaps cooking meals, making repairs around the house, or looking after younger children. This enables many parents to work longer hours and earn more money without having to spend money on child care for the younger children. Thus, families can find ways to develop cooperative and symbiotic interactions.

Stage 6: Families with young adults—the launching stage. When we look at the *launching stage*, we see the beginning of the cycle of contraction of the nuclear family—that is, when family size begins to shrink as the children grow up and move out of the home. This stage begins when the oldest child leaves home and ends when the last child has left. Obviously, this may take some time if there are many children or if the children are widely spaced.

Whenever one member leaves the family, the family must adapt, and this includes reallocating responsibilities, duties, and roles among the family members who remain at home. At times, there is a reallocation of physical facilities and resources, such as when bedrooms are shifted after the oldest child moves away. More frequently, there is a reallocation of financial resources, because the oldest child's move may entail tuition, room and board at a university, a large wedding, or supplementing the oldest child's finances until he or she "gets situated."

As the children leave the physical home, communication patterns change. Daily casual communication around the dinner table gives way to a phone call once a week. The nature of the communication also changes. It moves from conversation about everyday events to crisis management and questions about how to cope with being on one's own. When good communication patterns have been established in previous stages between parents and children, young adults can rely on their parents to support them during the launching stage.

With launching comes an ever-widening family circle where friends and new family members enter into the family setting. From a roommate who visits on Thanksgiving to a potential life partner, young adults' relationships bring a new dimension into the family structure. Similarly, their new interactions may also bring divergent life philosophies into the family. Reconciling these differences can bring about major family changes.

Stage 7: The middle years.   The middle years refers to the time after all the children have launched but before the parents retire. In the 1950s, when this theory was first developed, couples generally had their children in their early twenties, and those children were launched by the time the parents were in their middle to late forties. The couple had about ten or fifteen years to accomplish the tasks of the middle years.

One of those tasks is ensuring security for later years by increasing retirement accounts. The couple must reallocate household responsibilities once again, as now they are no longer serving as "shuttle services" for their busy teens. They need to work to maintain a comfortable home but may look for a smaller one that requires less maintenance and space, given that their children have moved out. Although the children are not physically there, emotional ties still exist, of course, so parents must develop new methods of extended family contacts, which can include increased phone contact, e-mail, or visits. Their children begin to have children during this stage, and now the couple can begin to develop relationships with their grandchildren.

So what is a couple to do when they stop being caretakers of their children? For many couples, this is a major transition, as they have just lost the job of parenting that they had for twenty to twenty-five years. Those couples who neglected their own couple relationships during their child-rearing years, expending their energies raising and supporting a family, are at risk during this time. When the children are gone, they may realize that they are no longer really acquainted with their partner. Now, couples might look to this time as an opportunity to renew their relationship with their partner and become more involved in community life by pursuing political office, volunteer work, or mission work. They may also simply indulge themselves, for example, by eating out more frequently, because it is "just the two of them." Most important, the couple must work to maintain their own communication, as they consider what they want to accomplish during the remainder of their lives.

Stage 8: Aging family members.   According to Duvall (1957 [rev. ed. 1977]), this last stage "begins with the man's retirement, goes through the loss of the first spouse, and ends with the death of the second" (385). This stage includes the task of adjusting to retirement, including the reduced income that retirement frequently brings. If there is illness or physical limitation, couples may seek a new home arrangement that is more satisfying or safe, such as a retirement village, long-term care facility, or moving in with one of their children. All such transitions require a shift in household routines.

Aging adults continue to spend time with their adult children and their grandchildren. Some of these couples may need to care for their elderly relatives as well as their grandchildren. The "sandwich generation" faces many challenges as they deal with their multiple responsibilities.

As the couple ages, they encounter death of family and friends more frequently. Older relatives die, and then friends of their own generation whom they may have known for years, or even decades, begin to die. As they face bereavement, the couple must prepare for their own death and the death of their partner. The family cycle is complete when the last partner dies.

The Family Career

Aldous (1978, 1996) built on the concept of the family life cycle but noted that not all families followed the cycle from beginning to end, as in the case of divorced or remarried families. She preferred the term *"family careers"* to indicate that families followed stages that were somewhat predictable but not cyclical in nature. Moreover, she combined Duvall's (1957) stages of parenting into one stage because parents often were in several stages of parenting at the same time (depending upon the ages of their children). Thus, Aldous's family career had only four stages—the establishment of the marital relationship, the parental role, the return to the couple relationship, and the aging couple.

Aldous's model did not focus exclusively on the family, however, but went further to include dimensions of family interdependency and social networks. For example, in addition to her analysis of the family career, she also considered the parent-child career and the sibling career, and how these interactions changed over the life span of the family. Expanding on the sibling career, Cicerelli (1994) indicated that the sibling relationship was, for many individuals, likely to be the longest bond experienced in their lifetime.

The Dynamics of Family Development

White (1991) and his colleagues (Rodgers and White 1993; Watt and White 1999) expanded the family development theory to provide a more contextualized perspective. The stages of family development are driven not only by the ontogenetic development of the individuals but also by the contexts in which the development occurs. These changing contexts make the family development stages dynamic rather than static. This perspective still takes into account stages over time but recognizes that, in this social context, all families do not follow the exact same path at the exact same time (White 1991). Understanding the family as a dynamic process encourages researchers to see fluidity and interrelationships between the process of development, the individual, and the context of the development (Fuller and Fincham 1994).

Interestingly, Watt and White (1999) found that the family development perspective created a structure for analyzing how computer technology pervades family life. Through each family developmental stage, computers serve as inexpensive tools for education, recreation, and communication. For example, computers impact mate selection by creating a "space" for cyberdating. Computers assist newly married couples with financial planning and career enhancement. When children leave the home, computers can help parents fill the "empty nest" with e-mail or allow them to pursue educational and occupational interests.

It is not enough, according to White (1991), to simply note that computers are used differently in each stage, but use must also be studied based on the context. For example, are boys more likely to use computers than girls? Does this create a hierarchical status in the family? What might be the effect of spending long hours on the computer? How is family life affected? And—more to the point of development theory—does it matter to the family *when* those hours are spent? Is there a different effect if a young adult, early in his or her married career, spends hours on the computer, compared with an older retired adult? These are all interesting questions to consider.

The Life Course Perspective

Bengtson and Allen (1993) expanded the theory with the "life course perspective," which addressed some of the issues not addressed in the "life cycle perspective." The life course perspective incorporated changes over time (and over the life course), identified three different "kinds" of time (ontogenetic, generational, and historical), and included the social context in which the changes occurred. They also highlighted an additional component—the meanings that individuals attach to the changes throughout their life course.

The life course perspective has a number of advantages over the family life cycle perspective in that it takes into account primarily the complexity of family and individual change over time. Each element of the theory adds richness to our understanding of how families exist in time, space, context, and process. It enhances our understanding of the social meanings that people give to their own developmental and family life (Bengtson and Allen 1993).

Let us look at widowhood as an example. As individuals, we mourn the deaths of those we love in a multitude of ways. Thus, we have an *individual response* to death. Now let's put it into a *time context*. Is the death of a spouse experienced differently depending on how old one is? Is grieving affected by our age? (Some people believe that as one ages, death is easier to accept, although it is difficult to gather hard data on that fact.) What about *family context*? Is the death of a spouse processed differently if the children are grown? Is the death processed differently if the spouses spent most of their time together (as in a family-run business) versus less time together? Next, let's consider the *social context*. Is the death processed differently if both partners worked and neither was totally dependent on the other for family income? Finally, let's consider the "meaning" associated with death. Is the death processed differently if the death is the result of a long illness? Is it different for those who ascribe religious meanings to death and "eternal life"?

Following the life course perspective encourages us to consider the multiple social contexts of family development, just as we know that many social contexts influence us individually. Although our families are our primary socialization agent, we are also influenced by our peers, our schooling, our faith systems, our government, and our culture. The diversity of that culture also should be included in any analysis of the life course, as the differences of our ethnic, racial, geographic, and religious heritage play out in our families and in our lives (Bengtson and Allen 1993).

Carter and McGoldrick Model

Family development theory has found support in family therapy, particularly when it defines family more broadly (e.g., remarried families, multigenerational families, gay and lesbian families) and is expanded to include varied developmental trajectories. Carter and McGoldrick (1999) analyzed the individual, from a therapy perspective, in terms of his or her place in the larger context of the family life cycle. Their model is based upon developmental stages, but it also encompasses different levels—the individual, family, and social context—within those stages. As a therapeutically focused model, the emphasis includes how problems or symptoms develop in individuals and families over time, particularly in response to major life transitions.

At the individual level, it includes a focus on such things as individual temperament, class, and genetic makeup as well as change over time. The family level of analysis might include an exploration of family secrets, expectations, emotional climate, patterns of relating, ethnicity, and negotiation skills. Both the individual and the family issues are always considered within the larger sociocultural context (e.g., existence of homophobia, racism, or classism), and how this changes over time.

Carter and McGoldrick provide an example. The birth of a child is naturally a taxing event on a couple, producing "the normal stresses of a system expanding its boundaries at the present time" (Carter and McGoldrick 1999, 7). If there was excessive turmoil in the family of origin for one or both of the parents, then there might be heightened anxiety for the couple as new parents. Relational distress might also arise if there is a mismatch between the temperaments of the parents and the new child. Finally, additional disorder might be introduced if the child is born during a time of political upheaval, such as when the parents might be refugees living outside their own country.

The model is useful in exploring life cycle stressors and how these interact with family stories, themes, triangles, and roles over time. It further emphasizes a balance between connectedness and separateness, as individual identity is understood in relation to significant people, relationships, and contexts.

The Systemic Family Development Model

Most recently, a new model has been proposed that incorporates aspects of family systems theory, family stress theory, and a multigenerational perspective of family development theory (Laszloffy 2002). It addresses two perceived shortcomings in the original theory: the assumption that all families develop similarly (universality) and the bias toward a single generational experience/focus of the life cycle (labeling a stage, for example, the *launching stage* emphasizes the parental experience whereas naming it *launching* and *leaving* acknowledges this multigenerational interchange). The systemic family development (SFD) model proposes, just like other developmental theories, that families experience transitions and shifts in family roles. Unlike other theories, though, which attempt to generalize patterns of family development over time, SFD states that each family's developmental pattern is unique. An analysis of a family must account for the combination, specific to the family being analyzed, of all of the factors influencing the family, including socioeconomic status, race, religion, gender, sexual orientation, politics, and sociocultural values. Laszloffy describes the family as a layer cake, with each layer representing a generation within the family. Each layer is at a different stage within the family cycle (aged adults, parents, adolescents, preschoolers, and others), having to deal with its own issues and developmental tasks. Laszloffy argues that in order to fully describe the family, one must study the interrelationships between the layers and describe the complexities that result from the family dealing with emerging stressors.

From a systems perspective, families are process oriented. While there is a great deal of variability in the timing and type of family stressors they encounter, all families experience stressors and the need to change and adapt. Therefore, even normative developmental transitions cause stress for the family unit. The family's response to its stressors will vary according to its resources, as predicted by stress theory. The more difficult the transition is, the more intense the stress. If the family has many resources, and the developmental transition is normative (and therefore expected), it will be easier to handle the transition. When the family successfully negotiates the transition, stress is relieved, and the family returns to stability.

The SFD model provides a way for family scholars to view the family in multiple developmental cycles concurrently while respecting the various social contexts (e.g., race, ethnicity, and socioeconomic status) that influence development. It allows us to investigate the influences across generations as well as within generations. It may also prove to be an important research tool because scholars can use the same theory to explain a family both at a point in time (a cross-sectional view, or the vertical slice of the cake) and over a span of time (a longitudinal view, or a layer of the cake).

Critique

A primary criticism of family development theory is that it best describes the trajectory of intact, two-parent, heterosexual nuclear families. For example, Duvall's (Duvall and Miller 1985) eight-stage model was based on a nuclear family, assumed an intact marriage throughout the life cycle of the family, and was organized around the oldest child's developmental needs. It did not take into account divorce, death of a spouse, remarriage, nonmarried parents, childless couples, or cohabiting couples. In so doing, it "normalized" one type of family and invalidated others. Today's family experiences and structures are more varied. For example, launching comes later in life for many families and is less complete than when Duvall first described these stages (Qualls 1997). Similarly, Dykstra and Hagestad (2007), in examining the impact of being childless on older adults, expose the way in which parenthood is deemed to be a critical "organizer of the life course and a major factor in social integration" (1275) in family development, disadvantaging those who do not have children, whether by choice or circumstance. Slater and Mencher (1991), too, acknowledge the exclusion of lesbian families from most family life cycle models and the need to afford such families rituals which delineate important markers of family life and connect them to larger society.

Family development theory was also criticized by many as being only descriptive but not heuristic (research generating). Critics said it lacked a sense of usefulness as a theory because it had little predictive power. It described only one particular kind of family (middle class, heterosexual, lifelong couples and their children), and it did not provide much insight into what governed their patterns of behavior (Bengtson and Allen 1993; Burr 1973; Falicov 1988). In fact, in the early 1980s, some researchers pronounced it a "minor" theory (Holman and Burr 1980). Because of these criticisms, White (1991) worked to formalize the theory in a more scientific way, with testable propositions that could be used to predict family functioning.

Mattessich and Hill (1987) worked to expand the theoretical structure, but it was still deemed too descriptive and broad (Aldous 1990). In other words, the theory suffered from trying to explain too much and so could only explain things simply so as to avoid being overwhelmingly complex. Further, while family development theory described the stages of the family life cycle, it did not describe the relationship between the stages or how they formed a total pattern of the family's development (Breunlin 1988).

In addition, early renderings of family development theory failed to include family identity factors such as race, socioeconomic status, ethnicity, and family structure (Bennett, Wolin, and McAvity 1988; Dilworth-Anderson and Burton 1996; Winton 1995). Bengtson and Allen's (1993) development of the life course perspective specifically includes these factors and lends itself to testable hypotheses. Carter and McGoldrick's (1999) family therapy perspective actually includes even more family identity structures (e.g., stepfamilies, divorcing families, never-married families, multigenerational families) and ethnic and racial differences. Laszloffy's (2002) systemic family development model broadens the theory's scope to include not only families of different structure, race, ethnicity, and sexuality but also multiple generations of families at the same time. The continued viability of family development theory will depend upon its ability to incorporate diverse families and varied family experiences.

Application

1. Using the scenario of the Morrison family at the beginning of the chapter:
   a. Identify the different life cycle stages represented by the Morrison family. Note the different tasks that each must accomplish.
   b. Identify the assumptions in the scenario.
   c. Analyze the tasks that each family member must accomplish in terms of different social and personal constraints. Can some tasks be avoided altogether? Must some tasks be addressed within a limited time frame?
   d. Indicate how the concept of change can be seen in this vignette. How do you think the family might cope with these changes?
   e. Indicate how this family provides examples of the effect of social changes.
2. Think of an intimate relationship either you or people close to you have been in. How has being in the intimate relationship changed this person? What kinds of changes have you noticed? What kinds of changes are noticed by your family and friends? Can you identify any of the establishment tasks in this relationship?
3. Draw a picture of your family at the time you entered it; when you were in elementary school; when you graduated from high school; your family as it is today; and your family as you expect it to be five years from now.
   f. How did your family change over time?
   g. Compare and contrast your drawings and reflections with others in class.
4. In the Sample Reading, White (1991) concluded that women in full-time dual-earner relationships are less satisfied with work–family balance than are males. In light of what you know about family development theory, why do you think this is?

Note

1. The edition that Duvall edited with Brent Miller was the last edition of Duvall's *Family Development* textbook. She died in 1998.

References

Aldous, J. 1978. *Family careers: Developmental change in families.* New York: Wiley.
____. 1990. Family development and the life course: Two perspectives on family change. *Journal of Marriage and the Family* 52: 571–583.
____. 1996. *Family careers: Rethinking the developmental perspective.* Thousand Oaks, CA: Sage.
Bengtson, V. I., and K. R. Allen. 1993. The life-course perspective applied to families over time. In *Sourcebook of family theories and methods: A contextual approach,* ed. P. G. Boss, W. J. Doherty, R. LaRossa, W. J. Schumm, and S. K. Steinmetz, 469–499. New York: Plenum.
Bennett, L. A., S. J. Wolin, and K. J. McAvity. 1988. Family identity, ritual and myth: A cultural perspective on life cycle transitions. In *Family transitions: Continuity and change over the life cycle,* ed. C. J. Falicov, 211–234. New York: Guilford.
Breunlin, D. C. 1988. Oscillation theory and family development. In *Family transitions: Continuity and change over the life cycle,* ed. C. J. Falicov, 133–155. New York: Guilford.
Burr, W. R. 1973. *Theory construction and the sociology of the family.* New York: Wiley.
Carter, B., and M. McGoldrick. 1999. *The expanded family life cycle: Individual, family and social perspectives.* 3rd ed. Needham Heights, MA: Allen and Bacon.
Cicerelli, V. 1994. The sibling life cycle. In *Handbook of developmental family psychology and psychopathology,* ed. L. L' Abate, 44–59. New York: Wiley.
Dilworth-Anderson, P., and L. M. Burton. 1996. Rethinking family development theory. *Journal of Social and Personal Relationships* 13: 325–334.
Duvall, E. M. 1957 and the revised editions 1962, 1967, 1971, 1977. *Family development.* New York: Lippincott.
____. 1988. Family development's first forty years. *Family Relations* 37: 127–134.
Duvall, E. M., and R. L. Hill. 1948. *Reports of the committee on the dynamics of family interaction.* Washington, DC: National Conference on Family Life.
Duvall, E. M., and B. C. Miller. 1985. *Marriage and family development.* 6th ed. New York: Harper and Row.
Dykstra, P. A., and G. O. Hagestad. 2007. Roads less taken: Developing a nuanced view of older adults without children. *Journal of Family Issues* 28: 1275–1310.
Falicov, C. J. 1988. Family sociology and family therapy contributions to the family developmental framework: A comparative analysis and thoughts on future trends. In *Family transitions: Continuity and change over the life cycle,* ed. C. J. Falicov, 3–51. New York: Guilford.
Fuller, T. L., and F. D. Fincham. 1994. The marital life cycle: A developmental approach to the study of marital change. In *Handbook of developmental family psychology and psychopathology,* ed. L. L'Abate, 60–82. New York: Wiley.
Glick, P. C. 1977. Updating the life cycle of the family. *Journal of Marriage and the Family* 39: 5–13.
Hagestad, G. 1988. Demographic change and the life course: Some emerging trends in the family realm. *Family Relations* 37: 405–410.
Havighurst, R. J. 1948. *Developmental tasks and education.* Chicago: Univ. of Chicago Press.
____. 1953. *Human development and education.* New York: Longmans and Green.
Hill, R. 1986. Life cycle stages for types of single patent families: Of family development theory. *Family Relations* 35: 19–30.
Holman, T. B., and W. R. Burr. 1980. Beyond the beyond: The growth of family theories in the 1970s. *Journal of Marriage and the Family* 42: 729–742.
Laszloffy, T. A. 2002. Rethinking family development theory: Teaching with the systemic family development (SFD) model. *Family Relations* 51: 206–214.
Mattessich, P., and R. Hill. 1987. Life cycle and family development. In *Handbook of marriage and the family,* ed. M. B. Sussman and S. K. Steinmetz, 437–469. New York: Plenum.
Neugarten, B., J. Moore, and J. Lowe. 1965. Age norms, age constraints, and adult socialization. *American Journal of Sociology* 70: 710–717.
Qualls, S. H. 1997. Transitions in autonomy: The essential caregiving challenge. *Family Relations* 46: 41–46.
Rapoport, R. 1963. Normal crises, family structure and mental health. *Family Process* 2: 68–80.

Rodgers, R. 1964. Toward a theory of family development. *Journal of Marriage and the Family* 26: 262–270.

_____. 1973. *Family interaction and transaction: The developmental approach.* Englewood Cliffs, NJ: Prentice-Hall.

Rodgers, R. H., and J. M. White. 1993. Family developmental theory. In *Sourcebook of family theories and methods: A contextual approach*, ed. P. G. Boss, W. J. Doherty, R. LaRossa, W. R. Schumm, and S. K. Steinmetz, 225–254. New York: Plenum.

Slater, S., and J. Mencher. 1991. The lesbian family life cycle: A contextual approach. *American Journal of Orthopsychiatry* 61: 372–382.

Watt, D., and J. M. White. 1999. Computers and the family life: A family development perspective. *Journal of Comparative Family Studies* 30: 1–15.

White, J. M. 1991. *Dynamics of family development: A theoretical perspective.* New York: Guilford.

Winton, C. A. 1995. *Frameworks for studying families.* Guilford, CT: Dushkin Publishing.

3

The Beginning of Family: Mate Selection

The Mate Selection Process in the United States

Bron B. Ingoldsby

Sarah and Joseph are members of a Hutterite colony in Montana. The Hutterites are theological cousins to the Amish, but they live communally and do allow modern technology for business purposes (Ingoldsby, 2001). There are more than 40,000 Hutterites, mostly in the Plains states and in Western Canada. As is typical, Joseph is in his late 20s, but Sarah, at 20 years of age, is younger than most Hutterite brides. They have known each other for many years but have never "dated" in the sense that dating is known in the outside world. Their interactions have been mostly group activities in this or neighboring colonies as well as simple everyday interactions.

Once it was known that Sarah and Joseph desired to marry, they received the necessary permission from their parents and the church leaders, and then a date was set. Hutterite marriages are always on Sunday and usually in June or November. On the afternoon of the day before, the couple traveled to each home of the extended clan communal farm that makes up their colony, offering schnapps to each adult and receiving a blessing in return.

That evening at about 9 o'clock, everyone gathers in the dining hall for the Shivaree. There are crepe paper decorations, and in a reversal of the typical process, the men serve the refreshments. The evening consists of singing from the hymnal, usually in German but occasionally in English. The minister picks most of the songs, but sometimes the teenage girls will begin a song. At around 11 o'clock, a gift (candles) is unwrapped while a colony elder tells jokes culled from Reader's Digest. *The adults then head for bed while the young people continue singing past midnight.*

Reprinted from *Mate Selection Across Cultures*, edited by R.R. Hamon and B.B. Ingoldsby (2003), by permission of Sage Publications Inc.

The regular church service runs from 8:30 to 10:00 on Sunday morning, with the minister reading one of the standard sermons in German. Quite a few people are missing because there is a flu bug going around, and even the bride and groom are feeling a little under the weather. After a prayer, the wedding ceremony immediately begins. Joseph and Sarah are seated about halfway back, on the aisle and on separate sides. In Hutterite services, the men sit on one side and the women sit on the other, with the youngest in front. Joseph and Sarah come up to the front, holding hands and with her shoulder a little behind his.

The ceremony was written long ago and consists of questions concerning love and loyalty for the bride and groom to respond to as well as counsel. Part way through, Sarah, looking faint and nauseated, has to run out, but the preacher continues the ceremony until asked to stop. Sarah returns, and they are allowed to finish while sitting in chairs. They are declared husband and wife and then return to their regular seats in the congregation. There is no kiss or exchange of rings. After a final wedding song and blessing, they lead the group outside, where children wait with glitter and cameras.

While Joseph and Sarah rest in the afternoon, colony members visit the trailer that has been refurbished for them to look at the wedding gifts and cake that have been given to them. There is an evening dinner with more singing, and with that reception the festivities are over. The next day, Joseph and Sarah—the happy couple (happy because they are in love)—return to their normal work assignments in the community.

The wedding ceremony described above may not seem typical to the reader. However, diversity is the norm in the United States. It is the most diverse nation in the world. Nearly every race, ethnic group, and religious and political persuasion is represented. It is probably safe to say that every situation described in this text also occurs in the United States. As a result, any generalization can be an overgeneralization, and many will find that what they read in this chapter is not typical of their own experience. With that caveat in mind, in this chapter I do my best to describe the couple formation process.

Historical Context

Courtship in America began with the Colonial Puritans. European colonizers to the New World brought with them their Calvinist values on marriage, child rearing, and patriarchy. But the relative scarcity of women on the frontier increased their value and resulted in a modification of some customs. In addition to the many domestic chores, women could engage in just about any income-generating activity so long as it could be seen as helping the family (Ingoldsby & Smith, 1995).

Marriage was essential for a comfortable life, and courtships were brief. Because the Puritans were opposed to nonmarital sex, singlehood was viewed with suspicion. Single men were often forbidden by law to live alone or were taxed for the privilege. It was even forbidden for couples to ride off with sinful intent (Queen, Habenstein, & Quadagno, 1985).

In general, a young man would receive permission from the father of the woman he was interested in, and could then begin a courtship. Dating began with engagement. The woman could veto her parents' choices, but couples rarely married if the parents did not approve. It was hoped that love would develop over time, but dowries

Hutterite Couple on Wedding Day

were often more important than romance. Marriage was a civil ceremony, with banns (the forerunner of today's wedding announcements) being posted about 2 weeks in advance (Ingoldsby & Smith, 1995).

Given the ban on premarital sex, the custom of *bundling* was most interesting. Fuel was expensive, so it was difficult to keep homes warm during winter nights. The suitor would often travel a considerable distance after a day's work to visit with his intended at her home during the evening. As a result, the woman could allow a favorite to get under the covers of her bed with her. The man and woman were to keep their clothes on, and a board might be placed in the middle to separate them. Church leaders opposed the practice, and parents typically stayed in the same room where the bundling occurred. The young woman controlled the practice, which allowed for a certain amount of physical closeness in an otherwise strict society. In spite of the controls and punishments (e.g., fines, public whippings), about one third of couples confessed to premarital relations during this time period (Ingoldsby, 2002).

People needed to get on with the work of adult life. Courtships, as mentioned before, were not long. In general, partners had known each other most of their lives, having met in the neighborhood or at church. The custom of chaperoning young people in their activities never developed in New England (Cate & Lloyd, 1992).

Even though the foundation of marriage was primarily economic, the ideas of love and personal fulfillment were developing as well. Men and women needed each other for simple survival and child rearing. This was especially true for the poor. However, friendship and love were beginning to be seen as increasingly important (Bulcroft, Bulcroft, Bradley, & Simpson, 2000).

Throughout most of the 1800s, men and women were divided socially into separate spheres of activity. This made it more difficult for young men and women to get to know each other. The rituals of courtship became more formal, with engagement announcements, rings, wedding ceremonies, and gifts all becoming more common (Cate & Lloyd, 1992; Murstein, 1974).

Economics continued to be the dominant force in determining mate selection. Men looked for brides who could contribute to their particular business enterprises as well as domestic tasks and child rearing (Bulcroft et al., 2000). Along with this, romantic love grew in importance. Women in particular desired stable love relationships based on communication. It was also women's responsibility to control the amount of physical affection in their relationships, and petting became less acceptable than it had been in the past (Cate & Lloyd, 1992).

Mate selection and marriage were transformed by the Industrial Revolution of the mid-1800s. Family life became more conjugal and private, and love emerged as the keystone for marriage (Bulcroft et al., 2000). The period from this point until World War I is known as the Victorian Era. During this time, men and women were even more separated by their respective spheres, and sexuality was feared and controlled (Ingoldsby & Smith, 1995).

Courtship customs for the middle and upper class were very formal, with women receiving "callers." The man would request to visit the young woman in her home, and the rules of etiquette would let him know whether he was welcome to return. The partners' going off together to private places was frowned on, and parents kept a close eye on the couple until the relationship was close to marriage. Young people of the working class had to meet in public because their homes were not large enough to provide the necessary balance of privacy and chaperonage. By the end of this time period, the wealthy had begun to emulate the working class as they became attracted to the idea of "going out" for pleasurable activities together (Cate & Lloyd, 1992; Whyte, 1992).

Dating—relatively informal and unchaperoned activities—was the established vehicle for courtship by the 1920s (Murstein, 1974). Going to dances, movies, and "out to eat" were the staple activities. Because these occur in public and cost money, control of male-female interaction shifted from the women to the men. The automobile provided young people with unprecedented mobility and privacy and also contributed to a rise in sexual activity. Romantic love was firmly entrenched as the basis for marriage, and love and sex were promoted by the media. Although there was increasing pressure for women to provide physical pleasure to men in return for the money they spent on dates, the majority of young women had intercourse only after engagement (Cate & Lloyd, 1992; Whyte, 1992).

Willard Waller was an early and important scholar in the area of dating and courtship. Waller (1937) referred to the practices of his time as the "rating and dating complex." He found that the goal of dating among college students had shifted from love and mate selection to competition and pleasure. Men desired the most beautiful and popular women for the status that dating these women gave them among their peers, and men pushed for as much sexual interaction as was possible. Women rated their dates by things such as whether or not the men had cars, were athletic, and were popular. This short-term focus separated dating from true courtship, where it is useful to develop good communication skills and find a mate who is mature and ready for family life.

The 1930s and 1940s saw the rise of steady dating as an intermediate step between casual dating and engagement (Whyte, 1992). Rituals such as exchanging class rings and talking frequently on the phone developed as signs of mutual commitment. One result of this seems to be an earlier age of marriage. Young people not going on to college often married shortly after high school, and women in college openly planned to be married by graduation. By 1950, the average age at marriage was 20 years for women and 22 for men—the youngest average of the 20th century (Cate & Lloyd, 1992).

During the contemporary period (since 1960), marriage has continued to be an important rite of passage into adulthood. In spite of the decline in the functions that the family provides for society, marriage continues to be strongly desired by most young Americans. Weddings and honeymoons are often expensive and elaborate (Bulcroft et al., 2000).

The women's movement and improved methods of birth control contributed to more permissive attitudes regarding premarital sexual activity. First, intercourse became common while going steady rather than waiting for engagement. During the 1970s, girls began dating at 14 years of age and began going steady at 16. Dating itself has become much less formal since the 1980s, with young people just "hanging out" together. It has also become acceptable for women to do the asking and to pay for dating activities. During recent years, concerns about sexually transmitted diseases has contributed to a movement back toward more conservative practices in dating. Across time, it appears that most Americans are seriously involved with only one or two others before selecting their eventual lifetime mates. It seems that when one feels ready to marry, that person does so with the next person with whom he or she falls in love (Cate & Lloyd, 1992).

Average age at marriage had increased to 23.6 years for women and to nearly 26.0 for men by 1988 (Surra, 1990). Americans have come to depend on dating activities to provide them with the necessary decision-making information for eventual marriage. However, there is very little evidence that the process contributes to marital success in any significant way (Whyte, 1992).

Dating

In the past, we could say that young people tended to progress through a series of stages that led to marriage: casual dating, steady dating, informal commitment such as "pinning," cohabitation and/or engagement, and marriage. At each stage, fewer people were involved and the commitment was deeper. Modern dating is more fluid and informal, with the adolescents themselves, rather than society at large, in charge of the process.

Smaller communities are more likely to retain some of the formal aspects such as going to the prom and wearing the boyfriend's lettermen's jacket. In high school, the tendency is to date one's friends, so gossip and cliques can play an important role. In college, dating is the process for meeting new people, and it is more relaxed and involves fewer rules.

There are many reasons for dating in addition to mate selection. Dating can simply be for recreation or for the socializing experience of learning how to interact with members of the opposite sex. It can also play a role in one's social status.

Americans are more sexually permissive than they were in the past. The media, fashion, and music all encourage early intimacy in spite of more conservative preferences from parents and other sources. The double standard, which permitted sexual experiences for males but not for females, has been disappearing since the 1960s. Each couple now determines how intimate the man and woman will become (Cox, 2002).

About two thirds of all males and half of all females engage in sexual intercourse by 18 years of age. Females between 14 and 16 years of age are twice as likely to be sexually active today as they were just 15 years ago (Moore et al., 2000, cited in Cox, 2002). Data collected in Los Angeles (Upchurch et al., 1998, cited in Cox, 2002) indicate certain gender and ethnic differences in the timing of first intercourse. The median age for all groups is 16.9 years. The average age is 16.6 years for males and 17.2 for females. The average age is 16.6 years for Caucasians, 15.8 for African Americans, 17.0 for Hispanics, and 18.1 for Asian Americans.

The younger a person is when he or she begins to date, and especially to go steady, the more likely that person is to engage in premarital intercourse. Many young Americans begin dating by 14 years of age, and nearly 90% date before their 17th birthdays. In addition, about three fourths have been in steady relationships by 18 years of age. The earlier a person begins to date, the earlier he or she experiences steady dating, and it is in the latter category that the likelihood of sexual intimacy is high (Thornton, 1990).

Gays and lesbians are socialized in the same ways as are heterosexuals in American society. For example, men are expected to be more dominant and sexually active, whereas women are expected to focus more on nurturance and relationship development. As a result, same-sex couples are similar to cross-sex pairs in their dating approaches and expectations. Like cohabitating cross-sex couples, same-sex couples do tend to be less monogamous than heterosexual married couples. However, AIDS and the aging of the gay male population has resulted in a higher level of support for monogamous relationships (Rutter & Schwartz, 2000).

Studies indicate that 15% to 40% of men and women have been involved in some kind of dating violence. The rates are about the same for both men and women, and the perpetrators are more likely to be friends than strangers (Berkman, 1995; Cox, 2002). A woman's freshman year in college is the most dangerous time for date rape. One large survey (Sweet, 1985) concluded that 12% of college women have been rape victims and that half of the perpetrators were casual dates or romantic acquaintances.

Experience with physical violence varies by age, gender, race, and religion. More than half of those who experience courtship violence do so for the first time between 16 and 18 years of age. In one survey (Makepeace, 1987), approximately 12% of males and nearly 21% of females had experienced courtship violence of some kind. Ethnic and religious rates were as follows: Caucasian, 16.1%; African American, 28.9%; Hispanic, 23.8%; Asian American, 4.8%; Protestant, 14.5%; Catholic, 17.2%; Jewish, 5.9%; and Mormon, 16.6%. Violence rates were tied more closely to church attendance than to denomination. The rate for those who never or rarely attend services was 20.9%, whereas it was only 10.2% for those who attend more than once a week.

Levels of violence are similar for same-sex couples, but men are more likely to reciprocate violence than are women, and lesbians are more likely to leave their relationships than are heterosexual women. Jealousy plays a major role, as it does with cross-sex pairs (Renzetti, 1992).

Dating can be fraught with anxiety due to fear of rejection. As a result, many Americans are willing to present distorted images of themselves to increase the likelihood of success in getting dates. Nearly all Americans want to date people who are physically attractive, and so they attempt to make themselves more attractive so as to better compete (Buss, 1998).

In general, men will exaggerate their sincerity and commitment, as well as their income potential, whereas women will use various kinds of deceptions to enhance their physical appearance. The lying is in the direction of making oneself seem to be more similar to the desired date. Men and women do not differ in their tendency to deceive, and there is a greater likelihood for both groups to dissemble in relation to their physical appearances rather than their personalities (Rowatt, Cunningham, & Druen, 1999).

Another way of attempting to deal with the risks associated with love and dating is the use of technology in presenting oneself. Recent years have witnessed a proliferation of newspaper ads, dating services, and Internet matchmaking. In this way, people can describe themselves and what they are looking for while screening out candidates who do not appeal to them (Bulcroft et al., 2000).

An analysis of newspaper ads concludes that self-descriptions are generally positive. Men tend to stress their occupation, education, and financial status, whereas women tend to highlight their physical appearance. Women also desire men who are taller and older than themselves, whereas men desire just the opposite in potential companions (Cameron, Oskamp, & Sparks, 1977).

Mate Selection

In modern America, there are few arranged marriages. But free mate choice does not mean that a person can marry anyone. All societies have some marital regulations. There are three general rules or pressures that affect a person's ultimate marital decisions. The first is *exogamy*. This means that the individual must not marry someone within his or her own group or family. All cultures have incest taboos, and the United States follows the general Western rules that a person may not marry anyone closer than a second cousin. Some states allow marriages between first cousins in certain circumstances. Marriage to a minor (someone under 18 years of age) without parental consent is also prohibited.

Endogamy refers to the social pressure to marry someone within one's own group. There is a tendency to meet and marry people from the same racial, ethnic, religious, and social backgrounds. This is also called *homogamy*, especially when referring to research that indicates greater marital stability for those who marry individuals similar to themselves. Although it is still important to marry someone who shares one's basic values and role expectations, other aspects of endogamy have declined during recent years.

For instance, the number of interracial marriages has nearly doubled since 1980 and now accounts for about 5% of total marriages (Population Today, 1999, cited in Cox, 2002). Deviations from homogamy often indicate an exchange of economic resources on the part of the male for youth and beauty on the part of the female.

Caucasians may marry black men or women who have higher educational attainment. Endogamy of religion has declined considerably during recent decades for Catholics, Protestants, and Jews (Surra, 1990).

There are about 1.5 million racially mixed marriages in the United States today. Interethnic marriages are also increasing as immigration contributes to a more diverse society. For example, about one sixth of all married Asian Americans and Latinos have spouses from different ethnic groups from their Asian and Latino backgrounds. These couples work to preserve their own traditions while merging into the shared overall identity of being Americans (Clemetson, 2000).

Another factor is *propinquity* or geographic nearness. The closer two people live to each other, the more likely they will meet and perhaps marry. For this reason, parents often send their children to selected universities so that they will interact with others who are homogamous to them in social class, education, religion, and/or other desired traits. There is a human tendency to be friends with those with whom it is convenient to interact.

There is also a tendency for women to marry "up" (hypergamy) and for men to marry "down" (hypogamy). That is, women seek mates who are a little older, better educated, and of equal or higher social status, whereas men prefer companions who are younger, shorter, and of equal or lower social status. This is referred to as the "marriage gradient." Complicating this process is the "marriage squeeze." For everyone to have a mate, there must be an equal sex ratio, but the numbers are seldom even. Although more males than females are born, by the adult years, women outnumber men. This is especially true for African Americans due to lower life expectancy rates and higher incarceration and homicide rates for African American males. This can make it difficult for a woman to find someone to marry at all, much less to marry up (Schwartz & Scott, 1994).

Not only is love by far the most important criterion for marriage, but most Americans seem to be looking for an ideal "soul mate" as well. One large recent survey indicated that 94% of young singles agree that the top priority is to marry one's soul mate. More than 80% of women indicated that it is more important for a husband to be able to communicate his deepest feelings than for him to be a good provider. However, only 42% believed that it is important to marry someone who shares one's religious beliefs (Whitehead & Popenoe, 2001).

The majority of women in college hope to meet their spouses while in school. This is becoming more difficult given that women now outnumber men in college. Perhaps more important, the noncommittal system of just "hooking up" rather than formal dating is making it more difficult for serious relationships to develop (Glenn & Marquardt, 2001).

The United States is an individualistic culture, where persons should be free to make their own decisions based on what is best for them. Romantic love and the idea of the existence of a perfect companion are promoted by the media. Many young Americans believe in the idea of living "happily ever after" (Sastry, 1999). This general mind-set is supported by research that U.S. teens, unlike those in collectivistic cultures, seek partners who are wealthy, attractive, sexy, exciting, and fun (Gibbons, Richter, Wiley, & Stiles, 1996).

Cross-cultural research (Medora, Larson, Hortacsu, & Dave, 2002) indicates that Americans score higher in romanticism than do young people in other countries such as Turkey and India. Romanticism refers to beliefs in an ideal mate and love at first sight and the belief that love can overcome all differences. Women, in particular, are becoming more romantic as time goes on.

Relationship satisfaction is consistently related to communication and self-disclosure. In addition, the particular style of love that individuals manifest is important. Passionate love (eros), friendship (storge), and altruistic love (agape) are positively related to relationship satisfaction, whereas game playing (ludus) is not (Meeks, Hendrick, & Hendrick, 1998).

Cohabitations has become a popular step in the mate selection process. There are more than 4 million unmarried-couple households in the United States today, representing a 400% increase from 1970. More than half of all first marriages are preceded by cohabitation. However, more than 40% of partners living together never marry each other, and of those who do, more than half divorce within 10 years. The divorce rate for those who do not live together first is just 30%. In spite of its high incidence, many studies confirm that cohabitation is negatively related to marital stability (Cox, 2002; Surra, 1990).

Although marriage remains very popular, it is increasingly acceptable to remain single or to postpone marriage to older ages. The stigma of being a bachelor or an "old maid" is disappearing as the media present a positive and exciting view of single life. Many remain single to avoid relationship problems and eventual divorce, especially now that women have sufficient access to economic resources to take care of themselves.

The average age of marriage today is about 25 years for a woman and 27 for men. The proportions of those over 35 years of age who have never married dropped from 88.0% for men and 87.4% for women in 1960 to 68.5% and 71.2%, respectively, in 1999. The percentages are lower for African Americans than for Caucasians (Whitehead & Popenoe, 2001).

Length of courtship, as well as age, has been firmly correlated positively with marital success. Courtships of more than 2 years score consistently high as these couples have had the opportunity to experience and work out conflicts before marrying (Grover, Russell, Schumm, & Paff-Bergen, 1985). Thanks to cohabitation and elaborate wedding plans, modern Americans typically attain the age and length of courtship ideals put forth by family scholars.

Sexually conservative groups, such as Mormons, are exceptions. Age at marriage typically has been about 3 years younger than the national average, and length of courtship has been about half the national average for this religious group. For believers, marriage can be eternal if performed in one of the temples designed for special ordinances. As a result, the focus of mate selection is often on receiving a spiritual confirmation of one's choice. However, Mormons do tend to accept the romantic notions of love described earlier (Ingoldsby, 1992).

Marriage

Once a man and woman decide to marry, they become engaged. There are a number of useful reasons for an official engagement period. The two are now seen as an official couple or "item"—off limits to others. It allows others to know of their intentions and share in their excitement. Having made this formal commitment to each other, the man and woman may now see each other and their relationship in a different light. This can provide for a final, and perhaps more serious, testing of their compatibility.

Marie and Todd's Wedding Reception

There may also be a good deal of preparation that needs to be done for the up-and-coming marriage. The couple will need to begin by setting the date and selecting the location for the wedding. As with other aspects of preparation, family members will need to be consulted because it affects them as well. Usually, female friends and family will throw one or more bridal "showers." Gathering in someone's home, they will play games and give practical gifts as well as intimate ones. The groom's friends may take him out for a final "bachelor party," which tends to be more raucous in movies than they are in real life.

Traditionally, the bride-to-be is given an engagement ring, typically a gold band with one or more diamonds. At the wedding itself, the man and woman may give each other matching wedding bands. All such customs have historical meaning (Ingoldsby & Smith, 1995), most of which has been lost to modern Americans. As a result, couples can pretty much do as they please in their observance of these practices.

There are best men, maids of honor, flower girls, ring bearers, photographers, and caterers to be selected. Usually, the bride's family pays for her gown and the groom's family covers the tuxedo expenses. The groom may also handle the details of the honeymoon. There are literally hundreds of magazines, books, and Web sites that give guidance on all the details of a proper wedding, including who is "responsible" to pay for each part. Today, couples and their parents decide which aspects to follow and which ones to do in their own way. It has become more common for the two families to evenly divide the costs or for the bride and groom to handle most of it themselves.

The wedding itself is bigger and more expensive than it has been during most previous time periods. Close to 90% of couples have formal weddings, continuing with many of the rituals even though some of them (e.g., a white gown to symbolize virginity) have lost much of their meaning. There is a very large industry in the country to aid couples in planning their perfect weddings and honeymoons. The wedding day is seen as one of the very most important days in a person's life and, as a result, can be fairly stressful for those involved. Honeymoons can be extravagant vacations that, although rarely necessary for the initiation of physical intimacy, still have a strong symbolic value (Bulcroft et al., 2000).

Given the range of incomes among American families, it is striking how expensive modern weddings are estimated to be. One survey ("Weddings Cost Most," 2002) claimed that the average cost is about $19,000, ranging from a little more than $17,000 in southeastern and western states to nearly $32,000 in New York City.

Wedding magazines (see, e.g., *Bridal Guide*, 2002; *Elegant Bride*, 2002) are, for the most part, elaborate advertisements for beautiful gowns, jewelry, china, cakes, flowers, and related items. Along with them are a few articles on topics such as how to solve planning problems, budgeting guidance, and sexuality. Most couples will need assistance from some source to remember and plan for all of the many details that can go into a formal wedding. In general, the focus is on the bride.

Whether they are religious or not, most couples prefer to be married in a church by a minister. All that is necessary, however, is a marriage license from the country courthouse and a person authorized by the state to perform the ceremony. Each partner must show that he or she is at least 18 years of age or has parental permission and is not already married. A processing fee is required, and some kind of medical examination may be required as well.

It is not so simple for same-sex couples because only the state of Vermont recognizes any kind of civil union for them. Although religious and political opposition to gay marriages seems to be decreasing, it still remains strong. The large majority of gays and lesbians feel the same need to bond as do heterosexuals, and they prefer being in couple relationships. About 80% indicate that they would legally marry if they could (Rutter & Schwartz, 2000).

Conclusion

Over time, mate selection has moved from the hands of parents and into those of the couples themselves. As the United States has become more individualistic, marriage has come to be seen as the private responsibility of the two who are going to marry each other. Free mate choice prevails, and romantic love has become the essential—and sometimes the only—requirement.

The courtship process of dating and possible cohabitation is generally unsupervised by adults and tends to focus on recreation and pleasure, at least during its early stages. In spite of rising rates of singlehood or delayed age of marriage, being married remains an extremely important goal for most Americans. The wedding day itself is usually the most carefully prepared for and psychologically important day in a person's life, especially for the bride. Marriage is a key rite of passage into adulthood in modern society, and it provides the most important source of companionship in a busy and modern world.

References

Berkman, H. (1995, August 28). Attacks on women usually by intimates. *National Law Journal*, p. A14.

Bridal Guide. (2002, May–June). New York: Warner.

Bulcroft, R., Bulcroft, K., Bradley, K., & Simpson, C. (2000). The management and production of risk in romantic relationships: A postmodern paradox. *Journal of Family History, 25*, 63–92.

Buss, D. (1988). The evolution of human intrasexual competition: Tactics of mate attraction. *Journal of Personality and Social Psychology, 54*, 616–628.

Cameron, C., Oskamp, S., & Sparks, W. (1977, January). Courtship American style: Newspaper ads. *The Family Coordinator*, pp. 27–30.

Cate, R., & Lloyd, S. (1992). *Courtship*. Newbury Park, CA: Sage.

Clemetson, L. (2000, September 18). Love without borders. *Newsweek*, p. 62.

Cox, F. (2002). *Human intimacy: Marriage, the family, and its meaning*. Belmont, CA: Wadsworth.

Elegant Bride. (2002, Summer). New York: Pace Communications.

Gibbons, L., Richter, R., Wiley, D., & Stiles, D. (1996). Adolescents' opposite-sex ideal in four countries. *Journal of Social Psychology, 136*, 531–537.

Glenn, N., & Marquardt, E. (2001). *Hooking up, hanging out, and hoping for Mr. Right: College women on dating and mating today*. New York: Institute for American Values.

Grover, K., Russell, C., Schumm, W., & Paff-Bergen, L. (1985). Mate selection processes and marital satisfaction. *Family Relations, 34*, 383–386.

Ingoldsby, B. (1992). Mormon mate selection. *New Perspectives, 9*, 34–37.

Ingoldsby, B. (2001). The Hutterite family in transition. *Journal of Comparative Family Studies, 32*, 377–392.

Ingoldsby, B. (2002). Bundling. In *International encyclopedia of marriage and family relationships* (2nd ed., pp. 181–182). New York: Macmillan.

Ingoldsby, B., & Smith, S. (1995). *Families in multicultural perspective*. New York: Guilford.

Makepeace, J. (1987). Social factor and victim-offender differences in courtship violence. *Family Relations, 36*, 87–91.

Medora, N., Larson, J., Hortacsu, N., & Dave, P. (2002). Perceived attitudes towards romanticism: A cross-cultural study of American, Asian-Indian, and Turkish young adults. *Journal of Comparative Family Studies, 33*, 155–178.

Meeks, B., Hendrick, S., & Hendrick, C. (1998). Communication, love, and relationship satisfaction. *Journal of Social and Personal Relationships, 15*, 755–773.

Murstein, B. (1974). *Love, sex, and marriage through the ages*. New York: Springer.

Queen, S., Habenstein, R., & Quadagno, J. (1985). *The family in various cultures*. New York: Harper & Row.

Renzetti, C. (1992). *Violent betrayal: Partner abuse in lesbian relationships*. Newbury Park, CA: Sage.

Rowatt, W., Cunningham, M., & Druen, P. (1999). Lying to get a date: The effect of facial physical attractiveness on the willingness to deceive prospective dating partners. *Journal of Social and Personal Relationships, 16*, 209–223.

Rutter, V., & Schwartz, P. (2000). Gender, marriage, and diverse possibilities for cross-sex and same-sex pairs. In D. Demo, K. Allen, & M. Fine (Eds.), *Handbook of family diversity* (pp. 82–104). New York: Oxford University Press.

Sastry, J. (1999). Household structure, satisfaction, and distress in India and the United States: A comparative cultural examination. *Journal of Comparative Family Studies, 30*, 135–152.

Schwartz, M., & Scott, B. (1994). *Marriages and families: Diversity and change*. Englewood Cliffs, NJ: Prentice Hall.

Surra, C. (1990). Research and theory on mate selection and premarital relationships in the 1980s. *Journal of Marriage and the Family, 52*, 844–865.

Sweet, E. (1985, October). Date rape: The story of an epidemic and those who deny it. *Ms./Campus Times*, pp. 56–58, 84–85.

Thornton, A. (1990). The courtship process and adolescent sexuality. *Journal of Family Issues, 11*, 239–273.

Waller, W. (1937). The rating and dating complex. *American Sociological Review, 2*, 737–739.

Weddings cost most in NYC. (2002, May 3). *USA Today*, p. 1.

Whitehead, B., & Popenoe, D. (2001). *The state of our unions: The social health of marriage in America*. New Brunswick, NJ: Rutgers University, National Marriage Project.

Whyte, M. (1992, March–April). Choosing mates–the American way. *Society*, pp. 71–77.

4

The Transition to Marriage

The New Marital System

Chapter Overview

The marriage relationship forms a subsystem within a system of extended family members. This chapter examines the developmental tasks that confront this newly established family subsystem. The tasks of the marital system parallel those that must be executed by the larger family system. As such, newly married couples must deal with the identity transformations that accompany marriage and, in the process, establish marital themes, negotiate marital roles and responsibilities, and establish a congruence of conjugal identities. In addition, marital couples must establish boundary strategies that regulate distances with the extended family, friends, and work. Internal boundary strategies between marital partners also must be established such that a comfortable and satisfying balance of individuality and intimacy can be achieved. In addition, all couples must establish strategies for managing the household and finances. Finally, couples must enact strategies that effectively manage the emotional climate of the marriage. In particular, couples must establish intimacy and support strategies, develop a mutually satisfying sexual script, and evolve strategies for the management of conflict. It should be clear that, from a developmental perspective, the stress associated with the transition to marriage emanates from the wide range of strategies that must be negotiated over a short period of time.

The Transition to Marriage: The New Marital System

In the 1980s an important book, *American Couples* (Blumstein & Schwartz, 1983), was published that explored the experiences of individuals in intimate relationships. The study revealed the existence of a continuum of relationships within the United States. At one end of the continuum were traditional marriages,

Taken from: *Family Interaction: A Multigenerational Developmental Perspective*, Fourth Edition, by Stephen A. Anderson and Ronald M. Sabatelli.

while at the other end were what Blumstein and Schwartz called "experimental forms" of marriage. They labeled their experimental forms "voluntary marriages" (based on love with the commitment to marriage periodically renewed), "trial marriage" (in which a marriage-like relationship is experienced as a prelude to formal marriage), "cohabitators who plan to never marry," and "same-sex couples."

It is fair to conclude that since the 1980s many of these so-called experimental forms of marriage have become more widespread. For example, census data demonstrate that over the past decades cohabitation rates have increased in America while marriage rates have declined. Specifically, the number of unmarried couples living together in the U.S. increased 72 percent between 1990 and 2000 (U.S. Census Bureau, 2005). Over half of all first marriages are now preceded by living together, compared to virtually none fifty years ago (Bumpass & Lu, 2000).

Furthermore, although it is impossible to document whether the number of same-sex households has increased over the past decades, it is clear that there have been remarkable changes within this time period in the sociopolitical context surrounding lesbian and gay families (Laird, 2003). In the 1990s the visibility of gays and lesbians within the society increased in unprecedented ways (Walters, 2001). As a result of this increase in visibility, the rights of domestic partners to employer benefits and the rights of gay and lesbian couples to legally marry have become prominent social and political issues within the last decade.

From a family systems theory and multigenerational perspective, we are not comfortable discussing marriage and marital issues without making it explicitly clear that the issues we address within the text apply to all lifetime partnerships regardless of whether they are legally and culturally sanctioned. For this reason we adopt within this text a postmodern perspective on marriage. This postmodern perspective embraces a generic definition of marriage and assumes that all marriage-like relationships, regardless of their legal status, are similar when it comes to the relationship issues and tasks that they must manage. To our way of thinking, the term **marriage** refers to a specific family subsystem comprising of adults from two different families of origin who have bonded together to form what they intend to be a stable and long-term cohabiting relationship. This generic definition of marriage is employed in this text to enable us to discuss common tasks that must be managed within these intimate ongoing relationships during the transition to marriage—during the time when this newly formed subsystem is integrated into an extended family system.

A Postmodern Perspective on Marriage

Before proceeding with a discussion of the "transition to marriage," we believe that it is important for us to address our reasons for embracing a postmodern perspective on marriage and thereby defining marriage in a generic way. Our inclination to adapt a postmodern perspective on marriage is based in large part on the research that has been done comparing couples residing in these various types of marriage-like relationships. For the most part, this research supports the conclusion that the different types of marriage-like relationships are similar in terms of the system issues and ordinary challenges that they must contend with.

For example, the research of Blumstein and Schwartz (1983) reported the results of over 12,000 questionnaires and more than 300 interviews with gay, lesbian, married heterosexual, and cohabiting heterosexual couples on issues related to money, work, power, and sex. The Blumstein and Schwartz study provided one of the first opportunities to compare different forms of heterosexual and homosexual relationships. They essentially concluded that there were more similarities than differences among all of these relationship types in terms of (1) lifestyle patterns and (2) the patterns of adjustment found within their relationships. This basic conclusion has been supported by the research done since the early 1980s. For example, the longitudinal research done with gay, lesbian, and heterosexual married couples by Kurdek and his associates (Kurdek, 1987, 1988, 1989, 1998; Kurdek & Schmidt, 1986a, 1986b) concluded that gay and lesbian relationships operate on essentially the same principles as heterosexual relationships and that the correlates of relationship quality are similar for heterosexual, gay, and lesbian couples.

Furthermore, the research comparing the patterns of communication and inter-action within same-sex and heterosexual couples supports the existence, once again, of many similarities (Haas & Stafford, 2005). For example, according to Haas and Stafford, couples in heterosexual and same-sex relationships deal with a similar range of issues that create tensions and conflict within their relationships. Couples, in other words, regardless of their sexual orientation, fight about similar issues. In addition, Haas and Stafford report that couples, regardless of their sexual orientation, structure and maintain their relationships in similar ways. For example, they found that the most prevalent "maintenance behaviors" reported across both the heterosexual and same-sex relationships were shared tasks (e.g., paying bills, cooking meals, cleaning, doing laundry, and performing household maintenance). Clearly, couples, regardless of their sexual orientation, feel that behaviors such as these are one way of communicating their commitment to their partners and relationships.

This is not to suggest that there are no differences noted in the research comparing heterosexual and homosexual married partners (Blumstein & Schwartz, 1983; Duffy & Rusbult, 1986; Kurdek & Schmitt, 1986a, 1986b). Compared to married partners, gay partners reported more autonomy, fewer barriers to leaving, and more frequent relationship dissolution. Compared to married partners, lesbian relationships reported more intimacy, more autonomy, more equality, and more frequent relationship dissolution.

Furthermore, the research of Gottman, Levenson, Seanson, Swanson, Tyson, and Yoshimoto (2003) suggests that conflict management processes may differ for heterosexual couples when compared to same-sex couples. Gottman and colleagues found that the "start-up" of conflict within homosexual couples was characterized by greater positivity and acceptance when compared to that of heterosexual couples. Specifically, homosexual partners, during the start-up of a conflict, were less belligerent and less domineering than heterosexual initiators. In addition, Gottman and colleagues found that there was less fear and tension, less sadness, and less whining in homosexual initiators than in heterosexual initiators. Their data also showed that homosexuals throughout conflict situations demonstrated more positive emotions when compared with the heterosexual initiators: more affection, more humor, and more joy and excitement. Gottman and colleagues attribute considerable significance to these findings as the start-up of conflict is highly predictive of relationship stability within heterosexual married couples (Gottman, J., Coan, J., Carrère, S., & Swanson, C., 1998).

Lastly, Haas and Stafford (2005) found that partners within same-sex and heterosexual relationships differed in the degree to which they engaged in open and direct discussions of the current state of their relationship. Haas and Stafford suggest that this finding may be a reflection of same-sex couples lacking a legal bond to hold the relationship together. Unlike heterosexual marriages, emotional commitment is the sole bonding force in same-sex relationships. It appears that to some degree heterosexual married couples may take for granted that they are bound together through legal marriage, whereas gays and lesbians must frequently "take the pulse" of the relationship to assess its status.

Given the available evidence, it is reasonable to conclude that intimate ongoing relationships, regardless of their form, have consistent issues that must be managed to promote the well-being of the relationship. While there are some differences in the patterns and dynamics found within same-sex relationships when compared to heterosexual relationships, it appears to be the case that there are more similarities than differences when it comes to how these relationships are structured and experienced. Furthermore, the differences that are noted have to do with the strategies employed within the relationships to manage conflict or promote cohesion and do not support the conclusion that the relationship issues confronted within these relationships are fundamentally different.

At the same time, it is important for us to point out that our endorsement of a postmodern view of marriage and our generic definition of marriage should not obscure the fact that the form of the marriage still has consequences for how married life is structured and experienced. The sociopolitical context of all of these marriage-like relationships differs. This means that the connections of the couples to the mainstream of the society and the degree of social support available to them will differ, which of course can have an impact on how married life is experienced (Laird, 2003).

Put another way, the different forms of marriage-like relationships that exist in America are more or less culturally endorsed and accepted. For example, the increase in the visibility of homosexual people within the society has been accompanied by a paradox that reveals an underlying ambivalence existing within the country when it comes to the acceptance of homosexuals. That is, while lesbians and gays are depicted as chic and pioneering, they are simultaneously depicted as a major sign of social deterioration and the source of the destruction of the family as we know it (Laird, 2003; Walters, 2001).

Furthermore, even among heterosexual couples there are varying degrees of social support and acceptance experienced by traditional couples when compared to those residing in less conventional types of marriage-like relationships. Couples who have been previously married and divorced operate within a society that seems to blame many of our societal problems on broken homes. Certainly, in the past, and perhaps still today, the support for and social acceptance of mixed race couples differed when compared to the support and acceptance of marriages among couples of similar races.

The point here is that the structure and experience of couples is influenced at any moment in time by a combination of micro- and macrolevel factors (Sabatelli & Ripoll, 2003). There is no doubt that cultural attitudes and the policies and practices found in the political, economic, educational, medical, and religious institutions of society play a role in how married couples experience their lives. Our inclination to adopt a postmodern view of marriage is based in large part on our belief that all married couples experience a similar range of issues and concerns. We nonetheless feel it is important to note how the prevailing attitudes and policies found within the country at any point in time create a different set of "realities" for couples residing in less conventional or legitimate types of marriages as they then deal with the ordinary difficulties that all couples must manage.

The Tasks of the Newly Married Couple

The tasks of the newly formed marital subsystem parallel those that all families must execute. All marital subsystems must establish themes and identities, define their boundaries, maintain a household, and manage the emotional climate within the marriage. Clearly, what makes the beginning of a marriage challenging is that each couple must develop a broad array of rules and strategies for the execution of these tasks.

Establishing an Identity as a Married Couple

When we marry, our personal identity is altered. With marriage comes an acknowledgment that we are ready to assume the roles and responsibilities of adulthood (Rapoport, 1963). This critical identity shift changes how family members and friends relate to us. We are expected to have a "life plan," "have our act together," and be able to plan and organize our lives in a way that enables us to succeed as adult members of society.

Establishing Marital and Family Themes. Moving into the world of adult roles and responsibilities places pressure on newly married couples to develop marital and family themes. These themes reflect the ways in which the couple wishes to represent itself to the outside world. Themes provide the couple with a framework of meaning that serves to guide behavior and orient the couple to extended family, friends, and community. Therefore, the couple's themes become the blueprint for the establishment of their basic values, priorities, and goals.

The choice of family themes is not random but purposeful and goal-directed (Kantor & Lehr, 1975). Themes often reflect the ethnic, religious, and moral convictions of the family. They may also guide the couple's strategies for using its physical and psychological resources. For instance, a couple that wishes to be seen by others as upwardly mobile and achievement-oriented may establish a goal of owning a nice home and possessing quality furnishings as a means of communicating this identity. Couples who adopt a "working-class family" theme, in contrast, may rent a modest apartment when first married, buy used furniture, and set aside money for the future.

Marital and family themes also reflect the manner in which the couple maintains a sense of intergenerational connectedness with the families of origin (Hess & Handel, 1985). By adopting themes that have been central in the family of origin, the couple conveys a willingness to remain identified with and connected to past family experiences. Such themes might be reflected in the perpetuation of cherished holiday customs and traditions or in the reenactment of long-standing shared beliefs such as the "importance of children in families" or the "value of performing public service." Adopting the family's well-established ethnic or religious orientations also maintains intergenerational connectedness. The establishment of such themes not only solidifies the couple's ties to the families of origin but also defines the new couple's identity to family and the community.

Finally, themes also reflect ways in which couples see themselves as unique and different from family and friends (Hess & Handel, 1985). One factor here is the role or personal identity each partner developed within the family of origin. For example, the "rebel" within the family may detest his or her family's emphasis on materialism and adopt a counter-theme of "the simple and rustic life," which is then brought into the marriage. The "rebel" might, on the other hand, reject the "old world" ethnic values of the extended family in favor of a more modern approach to marriage and family life. Such shifts in themes and values can stress the relations between generations.

A major factor that can influence whether couples emphasize "separateness" over "connectedness" in relation to the family of origin is the extent to which each partner experienced their families as functioning successfully. Partners are generally more willing to incorporate major elements of their family's themes into their own marriages when they view their families as having successfully met their own, and other family members' needs. When the family of origin is viewed as inadequate, flawed, or in need of repair, young couples are more likely to disengage from the family and reject its basic themes (Wamboldt & Wolin, 1989). In other words, the legacy each partner has incorporated from the family of origin also influences the themes that are (at least consciously) retained or rejected. Partners whose family legacy included themes of fairness, equity, and trust are more likely to remain intergenerationally connected with the extended family than are those whose family legacy involved themes of deprivation, mistrust, neglect, or exploitation (Wamboldt & Wolin, 1989).

Although some of the themes that are established in a new marriage are passed down from generation to generation, the establishment of these themes within the marriage requires considerable negotiation. Each marital partner seeks to integrate into the marriage the legacies that they bring from their respective families of origin. In some instances, these negotiations result in one legacy taking priority over the other. This occurs, for example, when spouses from different ethnic or religious origins assume the ethnic or religious identity of only one family of origin. In other instances, there is a blending and compromising of themes and identities that result in the emergence of new and novel themes. In still other instances, despite conscious intentions to the contrary, partners may reenact themes that perpetuate unresolved conflicts with the family of origin in the present marriage (Bagarozzi & Anderson, 1989; Napier, 1988).

The challenge confronted by newly married couples, therefore, is not only to establish themes but to integrate the legacies and themes from their respective families of origin. The pressures that couples may experience as they set about this task center around the need to negotiate their marital and family themes in ways that promote harmony both within the marriage and within the extended family system. This is a delicate negotiation, to be sure!

The Negotiation of Marital Roles. Marriage brings with it the acquisition of a new role, that of being a spouse or long-term partner. During the transition to marriage, couples must negotiate how they intend to act in accordance with this new role.

This may seem like a relatively straightforward issue. After all, most heterosexuals have some idea of how husbands and wives are expected to behave. However, there is considerable ambiguity about what is expected of husbands and wives in contemporary society, and certainly even more ambiguity within same-sex relationships about how to organize these role relationships (Blumstein & Schwartz, 1983). This ambiguity amplifies the stress couples experience at the point of marriage.

It is useful at this time to discuss the concepts of roles, conjugal roles, and counter-roles. Simply defined, a **role** is the shared prescriptions for behavior associated with a social position (Heiss, 1981). A **conjugal role** is the prescriptions for behavior associated with the social position of a spouse. Individuals enter marriage with preconceived notions of how they and their partners should act as marital partners. Roles provide predictability and enable the occupants of social positions, and others with whom they interact, to anticipate behavior and maintain order or regularity in their social interactions (Turner, 1970).

Roles can be understood only in relation to complementary or **counter-roles** (LaRossa & Reitzes, 1992). The role of husband, for example, is complemented by the counter-role of wife. Each role carries with it expectations for behavior that superimpose expectations for behavior on the other in the counter-role position. When a man acts in accordance with his beliefs about how he is supposed to behave as a husband, he (1) assumes that his wife will share his expectations; and (2) anticipates that his wife will act in a particular way toward him in return.

To illustrate, when a man believes that husbands should not do housework, implicit in this set of expectations is the expectation that his wife (1) will agree that husbands should not have to do housework; and (2) will accept the responsibility for doing the housework. This expectation, and the behavior that follows from this expectation, does not create conflict in the relationship so long as there is a congruence of expectations and behavior (Burr, Leigh, Day, & Constantine, 1979). In other words, we are likely to be satisfied with our partner's behavior when that behavior is consistent with our own expectations. Conflict, stress, and dissatisfaction ensue, however, when one partner's expectations and behavior are not consistent with the other's expectations and behavior.

Our identities as marital partners are clearly embedded within our own unique conceptualization of how marital roles should be enacted. When expectations are shared, interactions flow smoothly, and we tend to feel satisfied with our partners and our relationship with them. We also tend to feel good about ourselves because the fit between expectations and behaviors confirms our own identities as individuals. In short, the fit between our expectations for our partner and our partner's actual behavior influences how we feel about our partner, our relationship, and ourselves. Thus, a primary task for newly married couples is the development of a relationship reality that makes concrete the expectations that we have for ourselves and our partner in the role of spouse (Berger & Kellner, 1985). Implicit in this process is the need to evolve a clear vision of the prescriptions for behavior associated with these conjugal roles. These transition times are clearly made easier when the norms for roles are clear and shared within the society (Burr et al., 1979; Wiley, 1985). Lack of role clarity and consensus about how roles should be enacted creates the stress of **role conflict,** which brings with it the need for negotiations.

Because a man's and a woman's family of origin and socialization experiences are different, it is likely that husbands and wives will have different views of how conjugal roles should be enacted. The stress experienced by newly married couples may be further amplified because the roles of husbands and wives within contemporary American society are undergoing change. The main point here is that conjugal roles are generally not altogether clear, nor is a consensus between partners guaranteed. For instance, if a woman views her marital role in terms of being a "financial provider" and her husband views her as a "help mate" and "companion," there is bound to be tension.

It is important to note, in addition, how role ambiguity within same-sex relationships contributes to the stress experienced during the transition to marriage. Blumstein and Schwartz (1983) point out that gender prescriptions limit the amount of negotiation necessary when heterosexual couples contend with the organization of conjugal roles. For same-sex married partners, in contrast, greater role ambiguity increases the difficulty of arriving at a consensus regarding the allocation of role responsibilities. More negotiation and bargaining must accompany the initial transition to marriage within same-sex relationships. At the same time, however, Blumstein and Schwartz point out that this ambiguity provides a greater opportunity for innovation and choice than is often found within heterosexual couples.

In summary, at the point of marriage, couples embark on a process of constructing a marital identity that carries with it expectations for how the various role demands of the marriage will be enacted. Role-making and identity-bargaining activities tend to be more stressful when roles are not clear, when expectations are ambiguous, and when the partners' socialization experiences result in them developing different views of what marriage "should" be like.

Evolving a Congruence of Conjugal Identities.

Every system must evolve a consensus about the identities of its members. During early marriage, couples face the task of negotiating a congruence of conjugal identities. **Conjugal identity** represents the unique attributes, traits, and characteristics associated with each individual as a spouse within the marriage. In any relationship, participants become identified as possessing unique attributes, traits, values, and characteristics. The conjugal identities that evolve during marriage influence both the manner in which spouses participate in the marriage and the ease of interaction that develops between spouses.

Arriving at a consensus regarding conjugal identities provides a foundation for the assignment of roles and responsibilities within the marriage. Responsibilities for various tasks are assigned, in part, according to each spouse's personal identity image (Bagarozzi & Anderson, 1989; Hess & Handel, 1985; Kantor & Lehr, 1975). For example, the "responsible spouse" becomes the one who pays the bills, keeps the schedule of appointments, and makes sure that the couple's other responsibilities are met. The "sociable spouse" becomes responsible for maintaining ties to extended family and friends.

Conjugal identities also facilitate the predictability and ease of interaction between marital partners. Knowing a partner's identity allows for assumptions about the values and attitudes the partner may hold or how the partner will act in various situations. We might assume that our "literary" spouse would be interested in going to the theater to see a play or would have no interest whatsoever in going to see the local professional football team play on a Sunday afternoon.

It is important to recognize that these identities are often context dependent. They can apply to an individual when interacting with a spouse but may not apply outside this system. For example, an individual might have established an identity within the marriage that includes being shy, withdrawn, and socially anxious. Yet, these same attributes may not apply to this individual in different contexts, such as at work or with friends.

It also is important to recognize that conjugal identities can constrain an individual's behavior or interests. Being identified as the "responsible spouse," for example, may prohibit one from acting in a carefree manner. Conversely, being identified as the "shy spouse" may limit one's opportunities to attend social gatherings. It is apparent that couples need to negotiate identities that support the full range of each member's interests and abilities, rather than constrain individuals from expressing their full potentials.

Finally, it should be apparent that establishing a congruence between each spouse's conjugal identity is only one element of the larger task of establishing a clearly defined **couple identity.** The couple's identity is further defined by the prevailing marital themes and specific conjugal roles adopted by each spouse. The couple's themes provide a framework of meaning that organizes the couple's basic values and beliefs, and offers guidelines for behavior. Conjugal roles prescribe the specific behaviors associated with the social position of husband or wife.

Defining Marital Boundaries

Marital boundaries must be established as couples make the transition to a newly married system. These boundaries involve the establishment of strategies and rules for (1) regulating distances with others outside the marriage; and (2) regulating patterns of separateness and connectedness within the marriage itself.

Regulating Distances with Family and Friends. Boundaries with both family and friends must be realigned at the point of marriage (McGoldrick, 1999a). Marriage typically carries with it the expectation that our primary loyalty will be to our partner and the marriage. One expression of this loyalty is the manner in which the boundary separating the marital couple from outsiders is established. The external marital boundary regulates the frequency and intensity of each partner's contacts with family and friends. Establishment of this boundary requires development of rules for regulating such factors as how often we visit and call our families, how often we get together for dinner with friends, and how openly we discuss our problems or concerns with parents or friends rather than with the marriage partner. While there is clearly a need for ongoing connections with family and friends following marriage, these connections must be renegotiated such as not to interfere with the primacy of the marital relationship.

The strategies the couple establishes for regulating its external boundaries are influenced by two primary factors. One is the boundary rules that exist in each partner's family of origin, while the other is the manner and extent to which each partner has successfully individuated from his or her family of origin.

The family of origin's boundary rules and, in particular, its tolerance for individuality and intimacy have an effect on how the newly married couple structures its own boundaries. For example, extended families that emphasize personal space and privacy are likely to expect the newly married couple to establish formal, but somewhat distant and private, connections with them following the marriage. Such expectations might include calling parents once a month, talking in general about the weather and the health of family members, or visiting perhaps once or twice a year.

Conversely, the boundary between the extended family and the married couple will differ considerably if one or both partners comes from a family that encourages enmeshment and overinvolvement. Here, the expectations might include eating at parents' homes two or three times a week, talking with parents daily, and spending all holidays, anniversaries, and birthdays with the extended family. Tension may result in this situation if both families of origin compete equally for attention from, and connection to, the newly married couple. In addition, an emphasis on extreme enmeshment or overinvolvement brings with it the risk of the extended family attempting to "run" the marriage. It may become difficult for the newly married pair to find its own identity as a couple while contending with the interference and demands encountered from the families of origin (McGoldrick, 1999a; Rapoport, 1963).

The second factor determining how newly married couples establish their external boundaries is the manner in which each marital partner has individuated from his or her family of origin. Well-individuated spouses can take personal responsibility for their own lives and marriages and also maintain closeness and intimacy with significant others. Such individuals can derive support and other coping resources from available outside relationships, while limiting the impact these significant others have on the overall quality and structure of the marriage.

In the absence of an adequate degree of individuation from the family, the likelihood increases that boundaries with the family of origin will be stressed. Individuals who are fused with their families may allow their continuing loyalty and sense of obligation to the family to interfere with the establishment of a secure and clearly defined marital relationship. Conversely, individuals who reactively cut off from their families may establish a rigid external boundary with the family that deprives the couple of the emotional, informational, and economic support, as well as the access to the intergenerational customs and traditions that could help to ease the transition into a new marriage (Friedman, 1991). In either instance, failure to resolve connections to the family results in the establishment of boundary patterns that interfere with the ability of the newly married couple to operate freely with both a sense of intergenerational continuity and a perception of autonomy and personal authority within the marriage.

The broader point here is that the external boundaries established by the newly married couple must be sufficiently permeable and open to allow for a comfortable interface with others outside the marriage. Newly married couples benefit from being embedded within a network of supportive relationships. At the same time, the boundaries must allow the couple to function as a couple without undue interference from others. All newly formed marriages are likely to experience a certain amount of stress during the establishment of these boundaries. Significant others may be disappointed by the frequency or intensity of contacts with outsiders. We may, in turn, feel guilty about disappointing those outside the marriage. In time, however, patterns generally become established that allow stable and satisfying connections to be made with both families and friends.

Regulating Distances within the New Marriage.   When couples marry, they are not only faced with the task of establishing clear boundaries with extended family and friends but must also negotiate a comfortable and satisfying balance of individuality and intimacy for themselves within the marriage. The successful resolution of this task is aided by each spouse being aware of the emotional needs they bring into the marriage and having clear expectations about how the partner is to meet these emotional needs. The task of establishing clear internal boundaries is further enhanced by an openness toward communicating one's emotional needs to the other and a willingness by both partners to negotiate an equitable balance in meeting each other's needs. Finally, the task of establishing clear internal boundaries requires that each spouse be willing to make (and accept) an honest appraisal of the extent to which the partner may be unable or unwilling to meet some of the other partner's emotional needs. The boundaries established between spouses must also allow each to express his or her individuality and seek needed fulfillment through relationships and activities that do not involve the partner.

Marital boundaries, thus, reflect the tolerance for autonomy and individuality that exists within the marriage. In relationships that are characterized by relatively enmeshed boundaries, there is an emphasis on togetherness and mutuality. Couples expect to share time and activities. For instance, they seldom go out in the evening alone or with friends, preferring, instead, to do things together. They may feel it is important to eat together every day. They will often go to bed at the same time. These boundary patterns should not be viewed as a problem unless the emphasis on togetherness interferes with the abilities of partners to act as individuals within the relationship. Marital partners who are overly enmeshed and involved with one another tend to fuse most of their physical, cognitive, and emotional energies within the relationship. These couples may expect to experience a total oneness with the other by mutually sharing all activities and tasks (Cuber & Harroff, 1972).

Often these overly enmeshed boundary patterns occur when individuals perceive the marriage as a way of meeting needs, such as the need for identity or a sense of belonging, that were unfulfilled within the family of origin (Napier, 1988). As Napier (1988) notes, we may unconsciously bring to marriage "a deep yearning for wholeness, for approval, for all the things we deserved as children and didn't get. . . . We all seem to believe that marriage will change our lives, will make us feel better about ourselves. . . . We dream of a fused, symbiotic union in which we feel nurtured, safe, profoundly valued, and all powerful" (p. 14). Because partners come to depend on the relationship to meet needs that were not met while they were growing up, any violation of the norms of togetherness can be perceived as eroding the foundation of intimacy experienced within the relationship.

At the other end of the continuum are relatively disengaged marital partners who tolerate a great deal of individuality or independent behavior. These couples may spend relatively little time in companionate activities and may maintain a cordial but impassionate connection to one another. Their boundaries permit considerable autonomy of thought, emotion, and behavior. For these couples, the disengagement that has been mutually negotiated emphasizes the primacy of individuality over connectedness. Such boundaries allow partners to pursue their own individual dreams and interests without interference from competing demands for companionship and togetherness (Cuber & Harroff, 1972).

It may seem odd to many that, after marriage, a couple spends little time together. However, it is important to emphasize that there are no right or wrong boundary patterns. What is crucial is that the boundary patterns that are established are mutually acceptable to both partners. Clearly, whether boundaries function in this way depends on whether they fulfill each partner's expectations. When boundary patterns are consistent with each partner's expectations, regardless of the form they take, they will tend to be satisfying. Conversely, when these boundary patterns violate one or both spouses' expectations, conflict ensues (Lewis & Spanier, 1979).

Boundary conflicts that arise during the early marriage period can be minimized to the extent that these issues have been negotiated during the earlier courtship period (Bagarozzi, Bagarozzi, Anderson, & Pollane, 1984). At the same time, it is important to recognize that the boundaries established during the courtship can differ from the boundaries that are established during early marriage. Married couples have different goals for their relationship than do courting couples. It is this shift in goals that characterizes the newly married couple's task of renegotiating its boundary strategies.

During courtship, boundaries are often structured to reinforce the exclusivity and uniqueness of the relationship. There is, therefore, a tendency for most couples to be somewhat overinvolved with one another as each partner invests a considerable part of his or her identity in the relationship. There is a strong tendency to idealize the relationship as well as a high degree of novelty and positive reinforcement in the relationship (Bagarozzi & Anderson, 1989; Jacobson & Margolin, 1979). Couples may spend most, if not all, of their free time with one another. They might not dream of doing something without the partner. Conversely, they may spend their time thinking about and planning their future together.

After marriage, however, the almost exclusive focus on the relationship tends to decline and be replaced with a greater interest in establishing boundaries that also enable each partner to maintain an identity and interests that are separate from the relationship (Napier, 1988). It may, thus, come as quite a shock to us that our partner is interested in going jogging without us, watching TV alone, going to a sporting event with friends instead of us, or going fishing alone on the weekend.

Stress and conflict often accompany this shift in the relationship's internal boundaries as the couple struggles to renegotiate a new, mutually acceptable level of individuality and intimacy. At the point of marriage, couples must work out boundaries that reinforce their identity as a couple and enable each partner to be comfortable with his or her identity as an individual. The particular boundary strategies established by couples can vary greatly, but they are always determined by the expectations that each brings to the relationship.

Managing the Household

The principal tasks associated with managing the household include managing housework and the family finances. While developing strategies for the execution of these tasks may seem straightforward, it is highly likely that couples will have different views about what these strategies should be. Arriving at a consensus about these strategies may require considerable negotiation.

Evolving Housekeeping Strategies. Completing housework is a reality of marriage. How it gets done, however, depends on the specific strategies each couple develops. There are several factors that shape the manner in which couples develop their strategies for completing housework.

One factor is gender socialization. Gender socialization affects many of the role responsibilities that men and women assume within marriage. Housekeeping strategies, as with many other aspects of husbands' and wives' conjugal roles, evolve from each spouse's engendered notions of what husbands and wives should be responsible for in a marriage. For example, traditional gender orientations assume that women should be responsible for cooking, cleaning, and laundry, while husbands should be responsible for yard work, minor indoor and outdoor repairs, painting, and the care of automobiles.

The expectations held by both husbands and wives evolve from a more general view of the roles and responsibilities of males and females within society. For instance, females are often cast in the role of caretaker within the broader society. This can easily account for the kind of housekeeping and caretaking roles and responsibilities that wives assume within the marriage. That is, the expectation for women to assume primary responsibility for housekeeping can be traced to socialization experiences that place a heavy emphasis on caretaking as the principal responsibility of women (Coltrane, 2000).

A second factor influencing the choice of housekeeping strategies is each spouse's unique abilities and areas of expertise. Housekeeping strategies depend on both spouses assessing their own abilities relative to the partner's. Each partner may be expected to assume responsibility for those tasks related to their areas of expertise.

However, being viewed as having a particular area of expertise can also be based on gender role stereotypes and earlier male and female socialization experiences. Most individuals are capable of mastering the knowledge needed to complete housekeeping tasks such as cleaning the bathroom, sorting and washing laundry, or ironing shirts, slacks, and skirts. In spite of this, however, women are often assumed to have more expertise in these areas because of their socialization into the caretaking and housekeeping roles. Consequently, because of this socialization, women typically end up taking responsibility for these tasks, even when employed outside the home. In one study, for instance, wives completed an average of 32 hours of housework per week compared to 10 hours per week by husbands (Blair & Lichter, 1991). Although husbands' participation in household chores has risen dramatically in recent years, the majority of household labor is still done by women. For example, Robinson and Godbey (1999) reported that between 1965 and 1985, husbands' average contributions to routine housework increased from 2 hours per week to 4 hours per week (a 50 percent increase!). However, when this was contrasted with wives who completed an average of 16 hours of housework per week, the differences are clear. Wives still do 4 times more housework per week than husbands.

Finally, management of the household involves the use of family resources (family members' time and energy and the family's finances). This means that issues of power and control also influence the evolution of housekeeping strategies. As a general rule, there is a positive and linear relationship between resources and power, and a negative and linear relationship between dependence and power (Sabatelli & Shehan, 1992). The individual who possesses the greater personal resources within the marriage, and who is the least dependent on the relationship, tends to be the one who has greater power in the relationship. This partner is more likely to delegate responsibility for tasks to others and is less likely to assume responsibility for "low-status" tasks. Some theorists have identified this as another factor that may explain the greater likelihood for wives to assume housekeeping responsibilities. They suggest that the culture's patriarchal system grants greater resources (e.g., higher status and better-paying jobs) to men, who then exert greater power and control in the marital relationship (Baruch, Biener, & Barnett, 1987; Hochschild & Machung, 1989; McGoldrick, 1999b). Men may then feel justified in leaving "low-status" household responsibilities to wives.

All three factors operate within each marital system to account for the strategies that couples use for executing housekeeping responsibilities. The strategies that evolve reflect the power and control dynamics that exist within the relationship. The more powerful spouse is less likely to assume principal responsibility for housekeeping tasks. Earlier gender socialization also contributes to the expectations that men and women bring to their marital relationships. Finally, responsibility for household tasks depends on each spouse's recognized areas of expertise.

The goal here is not to evaluate the adequacy or fairness of these strategies but to account for the factors that influence their development. The adequacy of these strategies is reflected in the satisfaction that spouses experience with respect to how these tasks are executed. Here again, satisfaction depends on whether the chosen strategies are congruent with each spouse's expectations. But when a wife, for example, assumes most of the responsibility for housekeeping tasks and expects to do this, she is likely to be satisfied with the strategy. But when a wife believes that housekeeping responsibilities should be shared equally, dissatisfaction is likely to result if her partner expects her to assume most of the responsibility.

Managing Finances within the New Marital System. Another important task for newly married couples is developing a strategy for managing finances. When couples marry, a great many decisions must be made, such as how checking and saving accounts will be established, who will be responsible for paying bills, and how discretionary income will be spent. Some couples may simply pool their incomes in joint checking and savings accounts, and designate one spouse as responsible for paying bills. They may also establish a rule that any discretionary expenditures must be agreed on by both partners. Other couples may set up separate personal bank accounts. This might provide each spouse with a greater sense of personal control over their own money but would require rules for how household expenses are to be shared. Still other couples might decide that they will alternate paying all the bills every other month or designate separate bills for which each will be responsible. Such arrangements might also include agreed-on rules for each spouse spending their discretionary money without the partner being involved in the decision. Clearly, there are many strategies for managing finances. Establishing these strategies early in marriage becomes important, because it is unlikely that the couple will have negotiated such decisions before they begin living with one another (Bagarozzi et al.,

1984). There is also a great deal of symbolic significance associated with who controls and manages the family's finances. Negotiations around money management can come to reflect themes in the couple's relationship such as "dominance versus submission," "dependence versus independence," or "competence versus incompetence." Therefore, financial management strategies are closely tied to broader issues such as the successful negotiation of power and control, individuation issues, and each spouse's personal sense of competence and self-esteem. Successful strategies are those that leave spouses feeling satisfied that power and control have been equitably distributed and confident that finances are being competently managed. In this regard, it is reasonable to assert that, when couples fight about finances, it is the discomfort with the underlying issues of power and control, individuation, and competence that may be fueling this tension.

In sum, it is apparent that the tasks associated with setting up a household have the potential to stress couples during the transition to marriage. This stress emanates from the new strategies that must be developed to meet the full range of household tasks and responsibilities. Stress is amplified by the differing expectations that partners bring to the relationship (Sabatelli, 1988; Sabatelli & Pearce, 1986). This stress is further amplified since few couples actually discuss their expectations for how these tasks will be executed prior to living together.

Managing the Emotional Climate of the Marriage

When we marry, most of us expect that marriage will provide for our emotional needs and psychological well-being. We may expect marriage to provide us with a safe haven—one in which we can escape from the pressures and demands of life's hectic pace. We may expect that our partner will listen to us, share our concerns, and express the warmth and affection that we need on a day-to-day basis. Therefore, a critical task during early marriage is managing the emotional climate of the marriage. While strategies for managing the emotional climate of the relationship are established during courtship, these strategies will require adjustments when the couple makes the transition from courtship to cohabitation. Living together challenges spouses to balance their individual needs against those of the partner on a daily basis. New strategies will be needed for the expression of emotional support, sexual intimacy, and the management of conflict in a manner that promotes rather than inhibits intimacy.

Expressing Intimacy and Support.　One of the developmental tasks of adolescence and early adulthood is the establishment of support networks that meet our needs for nurturance, support, and a sense of belonging. These needs are often met in our relationships with family and friends. However, when we marry, there is often the expectation that the partner will become the primary source of this type of support.

Although there may be little disagreement that meeting one another's needs for intimacy and support is a vital task of marriage, there is considerable variation in the strategies that couples employ for executing this task. Each of us comes from a family of origin that was likely to have employed somewhat different strategies for expressing intimacy, nurturance, and support. The challenge for the newly married couple is to consolidate these disparate legacies into a shared strategy that leaves both partners feeling supported and cared for.

For example, one spouse may come from a family in which feelings of affection and care were verbally expressed. Another might come from a family in which nurturance was expressed through actions rather than words. In such a family, doing little favors for others, providing for one another's physical needs, or performing household tasks such as cooking or cleaning might have been perceived as expressions of caring and support. When these disparate legacies are united, it is quite possible that each partner's expectations for how intimacy and support should be expressed might be violated by the partner's well-intentioned behavior.

The partner who expects feelings and affection to be openly expressed, for example, may not interpret the partner's well-meaning actions as supportive. Conversely, the partner who expects support to be expressed through actions may wonder why such supportive behaviors are not reciprocated. Intending to nurture and support a partner and having the partner actually feel nurtured and supported are quite different matters. The challenge for the new marital system, assuming that members truly intend to nurture and support one another, is to negotiate a set of shared perceptions and mutually satisfying strategies for the provision of nurturance and support. These negotiations must consider the different family legacies that each spouse brings to the marriage.

It is important, in addition, to consider how gender can affect the nurturance and support strategies established within new marriages. As a general rule, women are more socialized than men to take responsibility for caretaking in intimate relationships. The traditional socialization experiences of men often do not provide them with extensive training in how to attend to the emotional needs of others. These disparate socialization experiences are likely to affect the nurturance and support strategies that become established in marriage, with women assuming more responsibility than men for meeting the emotional needs of the partner.

There is a great deal of ambiguity and uncertainty associated with the transition to marriage (Boss, 1988). This ambiguity is evident in questions regarding how conjugal roles are to be defined and how strategies will be established to meet the wide array of necessary marital tasks. Given this uncertainty, it is likely, at least initially, that each spouse's socialization experiences will influence the emotional caretaking strategies that are established within the marriage.

Disparate caretaking responsibilities may or may not become a problem in marriage. Again, the degree of satisfaction with nurturance and support strategies depends on the degree to which each spouse's experiences are congruent with his or her expectations. It is when expectations change that communication processes become critical to the maintenance of marital stability and satisfaction.

Evolving a Marital Sexual Script. One of the expectations of marriage is that intimacy and support will be expressed through sexual ties. To do so, couples must evolve strategies for meeting the sexual needs of one another. The significance of sexuality lies in its ability to communicate symbolically the exclusiveness of the marital relationship. Sexuality is the means by which the couple establishes a special boundary and a special bond with one another. This important dimension of the marriage relationship becomes one way of communicating intimacy, nurturance, support, closeness, and concern for the partner.

One way to think of this responsibility is to consider how couples evolve a marital **sexual script.** A sexual script can be thought of as a blueprint for sexual activity. The script encompasses the wide range of motives and behaviors that guide how we act in sexual situations (Gagnon, 1977). Sexual motivations have to do with why we have sex. The behavioral aspect of the script addresses the range of sexual activities that are acceptable within the relationship. The script also prescribes where and when it is appropriate to engage in sex. For example, this might include at what times of day, where (in what rooms) in the house, and how frequently sex should occur. Finally, embedded within the script are guidelines for who takes responsibility for initiating sex.

When cohabiting, a mutually pleasing and satisfying sexual script must be negotiated. These negotiations are challenging because there are many potential disagreements around each of the various dimensions of the sexual script that can erode the intimate foundation of sexuality. For example, couples can disagree about the motives for having sex ("You are just interested in sex because you're tense, not because you love me!"); about which activities are appropriate expressions of nurturance and support ("Why won't you please me in the ways I want you to?"); about the frequency of sex; about who should take responsibility for sex; and even about where and when it is appropriate to have sex.

In other words, sexuality becomes one important means of communicating interest in and concern for the marital partner. The sexual scripts that partners establish are negotiated over time and, ideally, in a way that builds, rather than erodes, the foundation of intimacy. It should be clear, however, that evolving a script that fosters intimacy does not simply follow from good intentions. There are many opportunities for couples to misunderstand and disagree about different aspects of the sexual script. In each of these instances, open communication and negotiation are essential to set the script back on course.

Managing Conflict.   Clearly, considerable potential for conflict exists within any close personal relationship. In fact, conflicts in relationships are inevitable (Sprey, 1978; Straus, 1979). **Conflict** can occur whenever one spouse's desires or expectations are incompatible with those of the other. What ensues is a struggle over differences in values, behaviors, powers, or resources in which one partner seeks to achieve his or her goals at the expense of the other (Scanzoni & Polonko, 1980).

In general, any source of stress has the potential to generate conflict. Stress may originate from a source external to the family, such as job pressures or a natural disaster. For example, a fight with a coworker may be brought home and displaced onto the spouse, who may be perceived as a "safer" target for anger. On the other hand, a couple may find that they have very different ideas about how to alter the family budget to recover from the damage caused by a house fire. Stress may also originate from within the family due to each spouse's developmental changes or other internal changes, such as an unexpected illness or disability.

Stress can be thought of as the degree of pressure exerted on the family to alter the strategies it employs to accomplish its basic tasks. It is the alterations in the couple's established strategies that can often produce conflict. Couples generally tend to agree about the basic tasks of marriage. That is, most marital couples agree that establishing a clear couple identity, managing the household, and creating a supportive emotional environment for one another are important. What they often disagree about, however, is the exact manner in which these tasks should be addressed. Conflicts occur when partners disagree about the strategies that should be used to fulfill various system tasks (Kantor & Lehr, 1975).

Couples are constantly confronted by the need to negotiate and renegotiate their strategies for meeting marital tasks. To do this successfully, couples must develop effective strategies for managing conflict. The strategies that evolve are quite variable and are influenced, in part, by the models of conflict management to which each spouse was exposed in the families of origin. Some families yell. Other families go for walks and cool off before discussing conflicts further. Others deny that conflicts exist at all. Each spouse will bring into the marriage predispositions to manage conflict in certain ways based on their own family of origin experiences. These differing predispositions must be reworked into a shared strategy that is acceptable to both partners in the new marital system.

The exact strategies that we employ for the management of conflict are further influenced by the meanings associated with conflict. By meaning, we refer to the overarching interpretation and significance spouses attribute to the presence of conflict within the relationship. Some couples, for example, fear marital conflicts and may seek ways to avoid them (Storaasli & Markman, 1990). Others may readily accept that conflict is inevitable in relationships. Having this view is likely to lead to conflict management strategies that allow for the open discussion of conflicts and the negotiation of mutually agreed on solutions.

In other instances, the presence of conflict can be interpreted as a personal rejection. This can occur when the desires and expectations held for the partner are associated with core elements of his or her personal identity. The greater the personal investment in a particular issue, the more emotional energy is likely to be invested, and the greater the potential for the ensuing conflict to shape feelings about the overall relationship. The emotional response is increased because, on some level, an unwillingness on the part of the partner to comply with a spouse's vision of how tasks should be managed can be experienced as a serious rejection of his or her sense of self.

A disagreement about a husband's unwillingness to clean the bathroom, for example, may be viewed by the wife as something more than a simple disagreement about how a common household task should be managed. She may view his unwillingness to clean the bathroom as expressing a view of her that she finds undesirable. In other words, embedded within this conflict may be the wife's deeper concern about her own identity and about her husband's view of her within the relationship.

When the meaning attributed to conflict lends itself to feelings of personal rejection, couples are more likely to get caught up in opinionated and defensive struggles with one another. These struggles are generally characterized by attempts to influence, convince, or coerce the spouse to adopt the other's point of view. The amount of emotion invested in these struggles reflects the underlying connection between our vision of how tasks should be completed and our vision of ourselves as individuals.

Spouses who experience conflict as personal rejection also may seek to form alliances or coalitions with others outside the marriage. The purpose is to obtain confirmation from others regarding the partner's view of the self as well as to gain outside support for how tasks should be managed. For example, if a husband talks with his parents about his conflict with his wife over his unwillingness to clean the bathroom, he is seeking support for his identity and his view of how men and women should act in marriage.

The broader point here is that all couples must manage conflict. How these conflicts are managed will affect significantly the level of intimacy and support experienced within the relationship. The strategies that spouses evolve for the management of conflict originate in the models they learned in their families of origin. Conflict management strategies are further influenced by the meaning that spouses attribute to the conflict. Conflict in relationships is inevitable. Understanding this and viewing conflict as differing views about which strategies to use to manage marital tasks, rather than as a personal attack upon the other's sense of personal identity, can facilitate the emergence of conflict management strategies that promote rather than inhibit intimacy.

Conclusions

From a developmental perspective, the transition to marriage is complicated by the need for couples to negotiate the many strategies necessary to execute the basic tasks of the new marital system. The demands placed on couples at this point are generally understood as ordinary demands. That is, most couples have the necessary resources and abilities to manage the stresses associated with this transitional period (McCubbin et al., 1980). At the same time, that the demands are ordinary should not undervalue the importance of the issues that must be addressed during this period. The strategies developed for executing system tasks influence how couples feel about their relationship and how they will deal with both the ordinary and extraordinary stresses and strains they will encounter over the life cycle of the family.

In general, adaptation to the demands and challenges of the early marriage stage is facilitated by the couple's ability to negotiate effective strategies. Each partner comes into the marriage having been exposed to a unique set of strategies and models for managing family systems tasks in their own family of origin. The challenge to couples is to merge these different legacies into a system of strategies and rules that foster family stability, the experience of intimacy, and a sense of belonging. Implicit in this process is the need for effective communication and negotiation skills.

Key Terms

Conflict Disagreements over values, behaviors, family strategies, powers, or resources during which one partner seeks to achieve his or her goals at the expense of the other.

Conjugal identity The unique attributes, traits, and characteristics associated with each individual as a spouse within the marriage.

Conjugal role The prescriptions for behavior associated with the social position of a spouse.

Counter-role The complementary expectations for behavior that are superimposed upon the partner as a result of the way an individual performs his or her own role.

Couple identity The framework of meaning couples establish to define themselves in relation to one another as well as to the outside world. This includes (1) each person's conjugal identity; (2) the marital themes that organize the couple's basic values and beliefs, and provide guidelines for behavior; and (3) each partner's conjugal role, which defines the specific behaviors associated with the social position of husband or wife.

Marriage A specific family subsystem comprised of adults from two families of origins who have bonded together to form what they intend to be a stable and long-term cohabiting relationship.

Role The shared prescriptions for behavior associated with a social position.

Role conflict Disagreements between partners about marital roles and responsibilities.

Sexual script A blueprint for sexual activity; the full range of motives and behaviors that guide how we act in sexual situations.

5

The Transition to Parenthood

New Families: Modern Couples as New Pioneers

Philip Cowan and Carolyn Pape Cowan

Mark and Abby met when they went to work for a young, ambitious candidate who was campaigning in a presidential primary. Over the course of an exhilarating summer, they debated endlessly about values and tactics. At summer's end they parted, returned to college, and proceeded to forge their individual academic and work careers. When they met again several years later at a political function, Mark was employed in the public relations department of a large company and Abby was about to graduate from law school. Their argumentative, passionate discussions about the need for political and social change gradually expanded to the more personal, intimate discussions that lovers have.

They began to plan a future together. Mark moved into Abby's apartment. Abby secured a job in a small law firm. Excited about their jobs and their flourishing relationship, they talked about making a long-term commitment and soon decided to marry. After the wedding, although their future plans were based on a strong desire to have children, they were uncertain about when to start a family. Mark raised the issue tentatively, but felt he did not have enough job security to take the big step. Abby was fearful of not being taken seriously if she became a mother too soon after joining her law firm.

Several years passed. Mark was now eager to have children. Abby, struggling with competing desires to have a baby *and* to move ahead in her professional life, was still hesitant. Their conversations about having a baby seemed to go nowhere but were dramatically interrupted when they suddenly discovered that their birth control method had failed: Abby was unmistakably pregnant. Somewhat surprised by their own reactions, Mark and Abby found that they

Reprinted from *All Our Families: New Policies for a New Century*, edited by Mary Ann Mason, Arlene Skolnick, and Stephen D. Sugarman (2007), Oxford University Press.

were relieved to have the timing decision taken out of their hands. Feeling readier than they anticipated, they became increasingly excited as they shared the news with their parents, friends, and coworkers.

Most chapters [in the book from which this reading is taken] focus on high-risk families, a category in which some observers include all families that deviate from the traditional two-parent, nonteenage, father-at-work-mother-at-home "norm." The increasing prevalence of these families has been cited by David Popenoe, David Blankenhorn, and others[1] as strong evidence that American families are currently in a state of decline. In the debate over the state of contemporary family life, the family decline theorists imply that traditional families are faring well. This view ignores clear evidence of the pervasive stresses and vulnerabilities that are affecting most families these days—even those with two mature, relatively advantaged parents.

In the absence of this evidence, it appears as if children and parents in traditional two-parent families do not face the kinds of problems that require the attention of family policymakers. We will show that Abby and Mark's life, along with those of many modern couples forming new families, is less ideal and more subject to distress than family observers and policymakers realize. Using data from our own and others' studies of partners becoming parents, we will illustrate how the normal process of becoming a family *in this culture, at this time* sets in motion a chain of potential stressors that function as risks that stimulate moderate to severe distress for a substantial number of parents. Results of a number of recent longitudinal studies make clear that if the parents' distress is not addressed, the quality of their marriages and their relationships with their children are more likely to be compromised. In turn, conflictful or disengaged family relationships during the family's formative years foreshadow later problems for the children when they reach the preschool and elementary school years. This means that substantial numbers of new two-parent families in the United States do not fit the picture of the ideal family portrayed in the family decline debate.

In what follows we: (1) summarize the changing historical context that makes life for many modern parents more difficult than it used to be; (2) explore the premises underlying the current debate about family decline; (3) describe how conditions associated with the transition to parenthood create risks that increase the probability of individual, marital, and family distress; and (4) discuss the implications of this family strain for American family policy. We argue that systematic information about the early years of family life is critical to social policy debates in two ways: first, to show how existing laws and regulations can be harmful to young families, and second, to provide information about promising interventions with the potential to strengthen family relationships during the early childrearing years.

Historical Context: Changing Families in a Changing World

From the historical perspective of the past two centuries, couples like Mark and Abby are unprecedented. They are a modern, middle-class couple attempting to create a different kind of family than those of their parents and grandparents. Strained economic conditions and the shifting ideology about appropriate roles for mothers and fathers pose new challenges for these new pioneers whose journey will lead them through unfamiliar terrain. With no maps to pinpoint the risks and hardships, contemporary men and women must forge new trails on their own.

Based on our work with couples starting families over the past twenty years, we believe that the process of becoming a family is more difficult now than it used to be. Because of the dearth of systematic study of these issues, it is impossible to locate hard evidence that modern parents face more challenges than parents of the past. Nonetheless, a brief survey of the changing context of family life in North America suggests that the transition to parenthood presents different and more confusing challenges for modern couples creating families than it did for parents in earlier times.

Less Support = More Isolation

While 75 percent of American families lived in rural settings in 1850, 80 percent were living in urban or suburban environments in the year 2000. Increasingly, new families are created far from grandparents, kin, and friends with babies the same age, leaving parents without the support of those who could share their experiences of the ups and downs of parenthood. Most modern parents bring babies home to isolated dwellings where their neighbors are strangers. Many women who stay home to care for their babies find themselves virtually alone in the neighborhood during this major transition, a time when we know that inadequate social support poses a risk to their own and their babies' well-being.[2]

More Choice = More Ambiguity

Compared with the experiences of their parents and grandparents, couples today have more choice about whether and when to bring children into their lives. In addition to the fact that about 4.5 percent of women now voluntarily remain forever childless (up from 2.2 percent in 1980), partners who do become parents are older and have smaller families—only one or two children, compared to the average of three, forty years ago. The reduction in family size tends to make each child seem especially precious, and the decision about whether and when to become parents even more momentous. Modern birth control methods give couples more control over the timing of a pregnancy, in spite of the fact that many methods fail with some regularity, as they did for Mark and Abby. Although the legal and moral issues surrounding abortion are hotly debated, modern couples have a choice about whether to become parents, even after conception begins.

Once the baby is born, there are more choices for modern couples. Will the mother return to work or school, which most were involved in before giving birth, and if so, how soon and for how many hours? Whereas only 18 percent of women with a child under six were employed outside the home in 1960, according to the 2000 census, approximately 55 percent of women with a child *under one* now work at least part time. Will the father take an active role in daily child care, and if so, how much? Although having these new choices is regarded by many as a benefit of modern life, choosing from among alternatives with such far-reaching consequences creates confusion and uncertainty for both men and women—which itself can lead to tension within the couple.

New Expectations for Marriage = New Emotional Burdens

Mark and Abby, like many other modern couples, have different expectations for marriage than their forebears. In earlier decades, couples expected marriage to be a working partnership in which men and women played unequal but clearly defined roles in terms of family and work, especially once they had children. Many modern couples are trying to create more egalitarian relationships in which men and women have more similar and often interchangeable family and work roles.

The dramatic increase of women in the labor force has challenged old definitions of what men and women are expected to do inside and outside the family. As women have taken on a major role of contributing to family income, there has been a shift in *ideology* about fathers' greater participation in housework and child care, although the *realities* of men's and women's division of family labor have lagged behind. Despite the fact that modern fathers are a little more involved in daily family activities than their fathers were, studies in every industrialized country reveal that women continue to carry the major share of the burden of family work and care of the children, even when both partners are employed full time.[3] In a detailed qualitative study, Arlie Hochschild notes that working mothers come home to a "second shift." She describes vividly couples' struggle with contradictions between the values of egalitarianism and traditionalism, and between egalitarian ideology and the constraints of modern family life.

As husbands and wives struggle with these issues, they often become adversaries. At the same time, they expect their partners to be their major suppliers of emotional warmth and support.[4] These demanding expectations for marriage as a haven from the stresses of the larger world come naturally to modern partners, but this comfort zone is difficult to create, given current economic and psychological realities and the absence of helpful models from the past. The difficulty of the task is further compounded by the fact that when contemporary couples feel stressed by trying to work and nurture their children, they feel torn by what they hear from advocates of a "simpler," more traditional version of family life. In sum, we see Abby and Mark as new pioneers because they are creating a new version of family life in an era of greater challenges and fewer supports, increased and confusing choices about work and family arrangements, ambiguities about men's and women's proper roles, and demanding expectations of themselves to be both knowledgeable and nurturing partners and parents.

Political Context: Does Family Change Mean Family Decline?

A number of writers have concluded that the historical family changes we described have weakened the institution of the family. One of the main spokespersons for this point of view, David Popenoe,[5] interprets the trends as documenting a "retreat from the traditional nuclear family in terms of a lifelong, sexually exclusive unit, with a separate-sphere division of labor between husbands and wives." He asserts, "Nuclear units are losing ground to single-parent families, serial and stepfamilies, and unmarried and homosexual couples."[6] The main problem in contemporary family life, he argues, is a shift in which familism as a cultural value has lost ground to other values such as individualism, self-focus, and egalitarianism.[7]

Family decline theorists are especially critical of single-parent families whether created by divorce or out-of-wedlock childbirth.[8] They assume that two-parent families of the past functioned with a central concern for children that led to putting children's needs first. They characterize parents who have children under other arrangements as putting themselves first, and they claim that children are suffering as a result.

The primary index for evaluating the family decline is the well-being of children. Family decline theorists repeatedly cite statistics suggesting that fewer children are being born, and that a higher proportion of them are living with permissive, disengaged, self-focused parents who ignore their physical and emotional needs. Increasing numbers of children show signs of mental illness, behavior problems, and social deviance. The remedy suggested? A social movement and social policies to promote "family values" that emphasize nuclear families with two married, monogamous parents who want to have children and are willing to devote themselves to caring for them. These are the families we have been studying.

Based on the work of following couples starting families over the past twenty years, we suggest that there is a serious problem with the suggested remedy, which ignores the extent of distress and dysfunction in this idealized family form. We will show that in a surprisingly high proportion of couples, the arrival of the first child is accompanied by increased levels of tension, conflict, distress, and divorce, not because the parents are self-centered but because it is inherently difficult in today's world to juggle the economic and emotional needs of all family members, even for couples in relatively "low-risk" circumstances. The need to pay more attention to the underside of the traditional family myth is heightened by the fact that we can now (1) identify in advance those couples most likely to have problems as they make the transition to parenthood, and (2) intervene to reduce the prevalence and intensity of these problems. Our concern with the state of contemporary families leads us to suggest remedies that would involve active support to enable parents to provide nurturance and stability for their children, rather than exhortations that they change their values about family life.

Real Life Context: Normal Risks Associated with Becoming a Family

To illustrate the short-term impact of becoming parents, let us take a brief look at Mark and Abby four days after they bring their daughter, Lizzie, home from the hospital.

> It is 3 A.M. Lizzie is crying lustily. Mark had promised that he would get up and bring the baby to Abby when she woke, but he hasn't stirred. After nudging him several times, Abby gives up and pads across the room to Lizzie's cradle. She carries her daughter to a rocking chair and starts to feed her. Abby's nipples are sore and she hasn't yet been able to relax while nursing. Lizzie soon stops sucking and falls asleep. Abby broods silently, the quiet broken only by the rhythmic squeak of the rocker. She is angry at

Mark for objecting to her suggestion that her parents come to help. She fumes, thinking about his romantic image of the three of them as a cozy family. "Well, Lizzie and I are cozy all right, but where is Mr. Romantic now?" Abby is also preoccupied with worry. She is intrigued and drawn to Lizzie but because she hasn't experienced the "powerful surge of love" that she thinks "all mothers" feel, she worries that something is wrong with her. She is also anxious because she told her boss that she'd be back to work shortly, but she simply doesn't know how she will manage. She considers talking to her best friend, Adrienne, but Adrienne probably wouldn't understand because she doesn't have a child.

Hearing what he interprets as Abby's angry rocking, Mark groggily prepares his defense about why he failed to wake up when the baby did. Rather than engaging in conversation, recalling that Abby "barked" at him when he hadn't remembered to stop at the market and pharmacy on the way home from work, he pretends to be asleep. He becomes preoccupied with thoughts about the pile of work he will face at the office in the morning.

We can see how two well-meaning, thoughtful people have been caught up in changes and reactions that neither has anticipated or feels able to control. Based on our experience with many new parent couples, we imagine that, if asked, Abby and Mark would say that these issues arousing their resentment are minor; in fact, they feel foolish about being so upset about them. Yet studies of new parents suggest that the stage is set for a snowball effect in which these minor discontents can grow into more troubling distress in the next year or two. What are the consequences of this early disenchantment? Will Mark and Abby be able to prevent it from triggering more serious negative outcomes for them or for the baby?

To answer these questions about the millions of couples who become first-time parents each year, we draw on the results of our own longitudinal study of the transition to parenthood and those of several other investigators who also followed men and women from late pregnancy into the early years of life with a first child.[9] The samples in these studies were remarkably similar: the average age of first-time expectant fathers was about thirty years, of expectant mothers approximately one year younger. Most investigators studied urban couples, but a few included rural families. Although the participants' economic level varied from study to study, most fell on the continuum from working class, through lower-middle, to upper-middle class. In 1995 we reviewed more than twenty longitudinal studies of this period of family life; we included two in Germany by Engfer and Schneewind[10] and one in England by Clulow,[11] and found that results in all but two reveal an elevated risk for the marriages of couples becoming parents.[12] A more recent study and review comes to the same conclusion.[13]

We talk about this major normative transition in the life of a couple in terms of risk, conflict, and distress for the relationship because we find that the effects of the transition to parenthood create disequilibrium in each of five major domains of family life: (1) the parents' sense of self; (2) parent-grandparent relationships; (3) the parent-child relationships; (4) relationships with friends and work; and (5) the state of the marriage. We find that "fault lines" in any of these domains before the baby arrives amplify marital tensions during the transition to parenthood. Although it is difficult to determine precisely when the transition to parenthood begins and ends, our findings suggest that it encompasses a period of more than three years, from before conception until at least two years after the first child is born. Since different couples experience the transition in different ways, we rely here not only on Mark and Abby but also on a number of other couples in our study to illustrate what happens in each domain when partners become parents.

Parents' Sense of Self

Henry, aged 32, was doing well in his job at a large computer store. Along with Mei-Lin, his wife of four years, he was looking forward to the birth of his first child. Indeed, the first week or two found Henry lost in a euphoric haze. But as he came out of the clouds and went back to work, Henry began to be distracted by new worries. As his coworkers kept reminding him, he's a father now. He certainly feels like a different person, though he's not quite sure what a new father is supposed to be doing. Rather hesitantly, he confessed his sense of confusion to Mei-Lin, who appeared visibly relieved. "I've been feeling so fragmented," she told him. "It's been difficult to hold on to my sense of *me*. I'm a wife, a daughter, a friend, and a teacher, but the Mother part seems to have taken over my whole being."

Having a child forces a redistribution of the energy directed to various aspects of parents' identity. We asked expectant parents to describe themselves by making a list of the main aspects of themselves, such as son, daughter, friend, worker, and to divide a circle we called *The Pie* into pieces representing how large each aspect of self feels. Men and women filled out *The Pie* again six and eighteen months after their babies were born. As partners became parents, the size of the slice labeled *parent* increased markedly until it occupied almost one-third of the identity of mothers of eighteen-month-olds. Although men's *parent* slice also expanded, their sense of self as father occupied only one-third the "space" of their wives'. For both women and men, the *partner* or *lover* part of their identities got "squeezed" as the *parent* aspect of self expanded.

It is curious that in the early writing about the transition to parenthood, which E. E. LeMasters claimed constituted a crisis for a couple,[14] none of the investigators gathered or cited data on postpartum depression—diagnosed when disabling symptoms of depression occur within the first few months after giving birth. Accurate epidemiological estimates of risk for postpartum depression are difficult to come by. Claims about the incidence in women range from .01 percent for serious postpartum psychosis to 50 percent for the "baby blues." Results of a study by Campbell and her colleagues suggest that approximately 10 percent of new mothers develop serious clinical depressions that interfere with their daily functioning in the postpartum period.[15] There are no epidemiological estimates of the incidence of postpartum depression in new fathers. In our study of 100 couples, one new mother and one new father required medical treatment for disabling postpartum depression. What we know, then, is that many new parents like Henry and Mei-Lin experience a profound change in their view of themselves after they have a baby, and some feel so inadequate and critical of themselves that their predominant mood can be described as depressed.

Relationships with Parents and In-Laws

> Sandra, one of the younger mothers in our study, talked with us about her fear of repeating the pattern from her mother's life. Her mother gave birth at sixteen, and told her children repeatedly that she was too young to raise a family. "Here I am with a beautiful little girl, and I'm worrying about whether I'm really grown up enough to raise her." At the same time, Sandra's husband, Daryl, who was beaten by his stepfather, is having flashbacks about how helpless he felt at those times: "I'm trying to maintain the confidence I felt when Sandra and I decided to start our family, but sometimes I get scared that I'm not going to be able to avoid being the kind of father I grew up with."

Psychoanalytically oriented writers[16] focusing on the transition to parenthood emphasize the potential disequilibration that is stimulated by a reawakening of intrapsychic conflicts from new parents' earlier relationships. There is considerable evidence that having a baby stimulates men's and women's feelings of vulnerability and loss associated with their own childhoods, and that these issues play a role in their emerging sense of self as parents. There is also evidence that negative relationship patterns tend to be repeated across the generations, despite parents' efforts to avoid them;[17] so Sandra and Daryl have good reason to be concerned. However, studies showing that a strong, positive couple relationship can provide a buffer against negative parent-child interactions suggest that the repetition of negative cycles is not inevitable.[18]

We found that the birth of a first child increases the likelihood of contact between the generations, often with unanticipated consequences. Occasionally, renewed contact allows the expectant parents to put years of estrangement behind them if their parents are receptive to renewed contact. More often, increased contact between the generations stimulates old and new conflicts—within each partner, between the partners, and between the generations. To take one example: Abby wants her mother to come once the baby is born but Mark has a picture of beginning family life on their own. Tensions between them around this issue can escalate regardless of which decision they make. If Abby's parents do visit, Mark may have difficulty establishing his place with the baby. Even if Abby's parents come to help, she and Mark may find that the grandparents need looking after too. It may be weeks before Mark and Abby have a private conversation. If the grandparents do not respond or are not invited, painful feelings between the generations are likely to ensue.

The Parent-Child Relationship

Few parents have had adequate experience in looking after children to feel confident immediately about coping with the needs of a first baby.

> Tyson and Martha have been arguing, it seems, for days. Eddie, their six-month-old, has long crying spells every day and into the night. As soon as she hears him, Martha moves to pick him up. When he is home, Tyson objects, reasoning that this just spoils Eddie and doesn't let him learn how to soothe himself. Martha responds that Eddie wouldn't be crying if something weren't wrong, but she worries that Tyson may be right; after all, she's never looked after a six-month-old for more than an evening of

baby-sitting. Although Tyson continues to voice his objections, he worries that if Martha is right, *his* plan may not be the best for his son either.

To make matters more complicated, just as couples develop strategies that seem effective, their baby enters a new developmental phase that calls for new reactions and routines. What makes these new challenges difficult to resolve is that each parent has a set of ideas and expectations about how parents should respond to a child, most based on experience in their families of origin. Meshing both parents' views of how to resolve basic questions about child rearing proves to be a more complex and emotionally draining task than most couples had anticipated.

Work and Friends

Dilemmas about partners' work outside the home are particularly salient during a couple's transition to parenthood.

> Both Hector and Isabel have decided that Isabel should stay home for at least the first year after having the baby. One morning, as Isabel is washing out José's diapers and hoping the phone will ring, she breaks into tears. Life is not as she imagined it. She misses her friends at work. She misses Hector, who is working harder now to provide for his family than he was before José was born. She misses her parents and sisters who live far away in Mexico. She feels strongly that she wants to be with her child full time, and that she should be grateful that Hector's income makes this possible, but she feels so unhappy right now. This feeling adds to her realization that she has always contributed half of their family income, but now she has to ask Hector for household money, which leaves her feeling vulnerable and dependent.
>
> Maria is highly invested in her budding career as an investment counselor, making more money than her husband, Emilio. One morning, as she faces the mountain of unread files on her desk and thinks of Lara at the child care center almost ready to take her first steps, Maria bursts into tears. She feels confident that she and Emilio have found excellent child care for Lara, and reminds herself that research has suggested that when mothers work outside the home, their daughters develop more competence than daughters of mothers who stay home. Nevertheless, she feels bereft, missing milestones that happen only once in a child's life.

We have focused on the women in both families because, given current societal arrangements, the initial impact of the struggle to balance work and family falls more heavily on mothers. If the couple decides that one parent will stay home to be the primary caretaker of the child, it is almost always the mother who does so. As we have noted, in contemporary America, about 50 percent of mothers of very young children remain at home after having a baby and more than half return to work within the first year. Both alternatives have some costs and some benefits. If mothers like Isabel want to be home with their young children, and the family can afford this arrangement, they have the opportunity to participate fully in the early day-to-day life of their children. This usually has benefits for parents and children. Nevertheless, most mothers who stay home face limited opportunities to accomplish work that leads them to feel competent, and staying home deprives them of emotional support that coworkers and friends can provide, the kinds of support that play a significant role in how parents fare in the early postpartum years. This leaves women like Isabel at risk for feeling lonely and isolated from friends and family.[19] By contrast, women like Maria who return to work are able to maintain a network of adults to work with and talk with. They may feel better about themselves and "on track" as far as their work is concerned, but many become preoccupied with worry about their children's well-being, particularly in this age of costly but less than ideal child care. Furthermore, once they get home, they enter a "second shift" in which they do the bulk of the housework and child care.[20]

We do not mean to imply that all the work-family conflicts surrounding the transition to parenthood are experienced by women. Many modern fathers feel torn about how to juggle work and family life, move ahead on the job, and be more involved with their children than their fathers were with them. Rather than receive a reduction in workload, men tend to work longer hours once they become fathers, mainly because they take their role as provider even more seriously now that they have a child.[21] In talking to more than 100 fathers in our ongoing studies, we have become convinced that the common picture of men as resisting the responsibilities and workload involved in family life is seriously in error. We have become painfully aware of the formidable obstacles that bar men from assuming more active roles as fathers and husbands.

First, parents, bosses, and friends often discourage men's active involvement in the care of their children ("How come you're home in the middle of the day?" "Are you really serious about your work here?" "She's got you baby-sitting again, huh?"). Second, the economic realities in which men's pay exceeds women's, make it less viable for men to take family time off. Third, by virtue of the way males and females are socialized, men rarely get practice in looking after children and are given very little support for learning by trial and error with their new babies.

> In the groups that we conducted for expectant and new parents, to which parents brought their babies after they were born, we saw and heard many versions of the following: we are discussing wives' tendency to reach for the baby, on the assumption that their husbands will not respond. Cindi describes an incident last week when little Samantha began to cry. Cindi waited. Her husband, Martin, picked up Samantha gingerly, groped for a bottle, and awkwardly started to feed her. Then, according to Martin, within about sixty seconds, Cindi suggested that Martin give Samantha's head more support and prop the bottle in a different way so that the milk would flow without creating air bubbles. Martin quickly decided to hand the baby back to "the expert" and slipped into the next room "to get some work done."

The challenge to juggle the demands of work, family, and friendship presents different kinds of stressors for men and women, which propels the spouses even farther into separate worlds. When wives stay at home, they wait eagerly for their husbands to return, hoping the men will go "on duty" with the child, especially on difficult days. This leaves tired husbands who need to unwind facing tired wives who long to talk to an adult who will respond intelligibly to them. When both parents work outside the family, they must coordinate schedules, arrange child care, and decide how to manage when their child is ill. Parents' stress from these dilemmas about child care and lack of rest often spill over into the workday—and their work stress, in turn, gets carried back into the family atmosphere.[22]

The Marriage

It should be clearer now why we say that the normal changes associated with becoming a family increase the risk that husbands and wives will experience increased marital dissatisfaction and strain after they become parents. Mark and Abby, and the other couples we have described briefly, have been through changes in their sense of themselves and in their relationships with their parents. They have struggled with uncertainties and disagreements about how to provide the best care for their child. Regardless of whether one parent stays home full or part time or both work full days outside the home, they have limited time and energy to meet conflicting demands from their parents, bosses, friends, child, and each other, and little support from outside the family to guide them on this complex journey into uncharted territory. In almost every published study of the transition conducted over the last four decades, men's and women's marital satisfaction declined. Belsky and Rovine found that from 30 percent to 59 percent of the participants in their Pennsylvania study showed a decline between pregnancy and nine months postpartum, depending on which measure of the marriage they examined.[23] In our study of California parents, 45 percent of the men and 58 percent of the women showed declining satisfaction with marriage between pregnancy and eighteen months postpartum. The scores of approximately 15 percent of the new parents moved from below to above the clinical cutoff that indicates serious marital problems, whereas only 4 percent moved from above to below the cutoff.

Why should this optimistic time of life pose so many challenges for couples? One key issue for couples becoming parents has been treated as a surefire formula for humor in situation comedies—husband-wife battles over the "who does what?" of housework, child care, and decision making. Our own study shows clearly that, regardless of how equally family work is divided before having a baby, or of how equally husbands and wives *expect* to divide the care of the baby, the roles men and women assume tend to be gender-linked, with wives doing more family work than they had done before becoming a parent and substantially more housework and baby care than their husbands do. Furthermore, the greater the discrepancy between women's predicted and actual division of family tasks with their spouses, the more symptoms of depression they report. The more traditional the arrangements—that is, the less husbands are responsible for family work—the greater fathers' *and* mothers' postpartum dissatisfaction with their overall marriage.

Although theories of life stress generally assume that *any* change is stressful, we found no correlation between sheer *amount* of change in the five aspects of family life and parents' difficulties adapting to parenthood. In general, parenthood was followed by increasing discrepancies between husbands' and wives' perceptions of family life and their descriptions of their actual family and work roles. Couples in which the partners showed the greatest increase in those discrepancies—more often those with increasingly traditional role arrangements—described increasing conflict as a couple and greater declines in marital satisfaction.

These findings suggest that whereas family decline theorists are looking at statistics about contemporary families through 1950 lenses, actual families are responding to the realities of life in the twenty-first century. Given historical shifts in men's and women's ideas about family roles and present economic realities, it is not realistic to expect them to simply reverse trends by adopting more traditional values and practices. Contemporary families in which the parents' arrangements are at the more traditional end of the spectrum are *less* satisfied with themselves, with their relationships as couples, and with their role as parents, than those at the more egalitarian end.

Do We Know Which Families Will Be at Risk?

The message for policymakers from research on the transition to parenthood is not only that it is a time of stress and change. We and others have found that there is predictability to couples' patterns of change: this means that it is possible to know whether a couple is at risk for more serious problems before they have a baby and whether their child will be at risk for compromised development. This information is also essential for purposes of designing *preventive* intervention. Couples most at risk for difficulties and troubling outcomes in the early postpartum years are those who were in the greatest individual and marital distress before they became parents. Children most at risk are those whose parents are having the most difficulty maintaining a positive, rewarding relationship as a couple.

The "Baby-Maybe" Decision

Interviews with expectant parents about their process of making the decision to have a baby provide one source of information about continuity of adaptation in the family-making period. By analyzing partners' responses to the question, "How did the two of you come to be having a baby at this time?" we found four fairly distinct types of decision making in our sample of lower-middle- to upper-middle-class couples, none of whom had identified themselves as having serious relationship difficulties during pregnancy: (1) The *Planners*—50 percent of the couples—agreed about whether and when to have a baby. The other 50 percent were roughly evenly divided into three patterns: (2) The *Acceptance of fate couples*—15 percent—had unplanned conceptions but were pleased to learn that they were about to become parents; (3) The *Ambivalent couples*—another 15 percent—continually went back and forth about their readiness to have a baby, even late in pregnancy; and (4) The *Yes-No couples*—the remaining 15 percent—claimed not to be having relationship difficulties but nonetheless had strong disagreements about whether to complete their unplanned pregnancy.

> Alice, thirty-four, became pregnant when she and Andy, twenty-seven, had been living together only four months. She was determined to have a child, regardless of whether Andy stayed in the picture. He did not feel ready to become a father, and though he dearly loved Alice, he was struggling to come to terms with the pregnancy. "It was the hardest thing I ever had to deal with," he said. "I had this idea that I wasn't even going to have to think about being a father until I was over thirty, but here it was, and I had to decide now. I was concerned about my soul. I didn't want, under any circumstances,

to compromise myself, but I knew it would be very hard on Alice if I took action that would result in her being a single parent. It would've meant that I'm the kind of person who turns his back on someone I care about, and that would destroy me as well as her." And so he stayed.[24]

The *Planners* and *Acceptance of fate couples* experienced minimal decline in marital satisfaction, whereas the *Ambivalent couples* tended to have lower satisfaction to begin with and to decline even further between pregnancy and two years later. The greatest risk was for couples who had serious disagreement—more than ambivalence—about having a first baby. In these cases, one partner gave in to the other's wishes in order to remain in the relationship. The startling outcome provides a strong statement about the wisdom of this strategy: all of the *Yes-No couples* like Alice and Andy were divorced by the time their first child entered kindergarten, and the two *Yes-No couples* in which the wife was the reluctant partner reported severe marital distress at every postpartum assessment. This finding suggests that partners' unresolved conflict in making the decision to have a child is mirrored by their inability to cope with conflict to both partners' satisfaction once they become parents. Couples' styles of making this far-reaching decision seem to be a telling indicator of whether their overall relationship is at risk for instability, a finding that contradicts the folk wisdom that having a baby will mend serious marital rifts.

Additional Risk Factors for Couples

Not surprisingly, when couples reported high levels of outside-the-family life stress during pregnancy, they are more likely to be unhappy in their marriages and stressed in their parenting roles during the early years of parenthood. When there are serious problems in the relationships between new parents and their own parents the couples are more likely to experience more postpartum distress.[25] Belsky and colleagues showed that new parents who recalled strained relationships with their own parents were more likely to experience more marital distress in the first year of parenthood.[26] In our study, parents who reported early childhoods clouded by their parents' problem drinking had a more stressful time on every indicator of adjustment in the first two years of parenthood—more conflict, less effective problem solving, less effective parenting styles, and greater parenting stress.[27] Although the transmission of maladaptive patterns across generations is not inevitable, these data suggest that without intervention, troubled relationships in the family of origin constitute a risk factor for relationships in the next generation.

Although it is never possible to make perfect predictions for purposes of creating family policies to help reduce the risks associated with family formation, we have been able to identify expectant parents at risk for later individual, marital, and parenting difficulties based on information they provided during pregnancy. Recall that the participants in the studies we are describing are the two-parent intact families portrayed as ideal in the family decline debate. The problems they face have little to do with their family values. The difficulties appear to stem from the fact that the visible fault lines in couple relationships leave their marriages more vulnerable to the shake-up of the transition-to-parenthood process.

74

Risks for Children

We are concerned about the impact of the transition to parenthood not only because it increases the risk of distress in marriage but also because the parents' early distress can have far-reaching consequences for their children. Longitudinal studies make it clear that parents' early difficulties affect their children's later intellectual and social adjustment. For example, parents' well-being or distress as individuals and as couples during pregnancy predicts the quality of their relationships with their children in the preschool period.[28] In turn, the quality of both parent-child relationships in the preschool years is related to the child's academic and social competence during the early elementary school years.[29] Preschoolers whose mothers and fathers had more responsive, effective parenting styles had higher scores on academic achievement and fewer acting out, aggressive, or withdrawn behavior problems with peers in kindergarten and Grade 1.[30] When we receive teachers' reports, we see that overall, five-year-olds whose parents reported making the most positive adaptations to parenthood were the ones with the most successful adjustments to elementary school.

Alexander and Entwisle[31] suggested that in kindergarten and first grade, children are "launched into achievement trajectories that they follow the rest of their school years." Longitudinal studies of children's academic and social competence[32] support this hypothesis about the importance of students' early adaptation to school: children who are socially rejected by peers in the early elementary grades are more likely to have academic problems or drop out of school, to develop antisocial and delinquent behaviors, and to have difficulty in intimate relationships with partners in late adolescence and early adulthood. Without support or intervention early in a family's development, the children with early academic, emotional, and social problems are at greater risk for later, even more serious problems.

Policy Implications

What social scientists have learned about families during the transition to parenthood is relevant to policy discussions about how families with young children can be strengthened.

We return briefly to the family values debate to examine the policy implications of promoting traditional family arrangements, of altering workplace policies, and of providing preventive interventions to strengthen families during the early childrearing years.

The Potential Consequences of Promoting Traditional Family Arrangements

What are the implications of the argument that families and children would benefit by a return to traditional family arrangements? We are aware that existing data are not adequate to provide a full test of the family values argument, but we believe that some systematic information on this point is better than none. At first glance, it may seem as if studies support the arguments of those proposing that "the family" is in decline.

We have documented the fact that a substantial number of new two-parent families are experiencing problems of adjustment—parents' depression, troubled marriages, intergenerational strain, and stress in juggling the demands of work and family. Nevertheless, there is little in the transition to parenthood research to support the idea that parents' distress is attributable to a decline in their family-oriented *values*. First, the populations studied here are two-parent, married, nonteenage, lower-middle- to upper-middle-class families, who do not represent the "variants" in family form that most writers associate with declining quality of family life.

Second, threaded throughout the writings on family decline is the erroneous assumption that because these changes in the family have been occurring at the same time as increases in negative outcomes for children, the changes are the *cause* of the problems. These claims are not buttressed by systematic data establishing the direction of causal influence. For example, it is well accepted (but still debated) that children's adaptation is poorer in the period after their parents' divorce.[33] Nevertheless, some studies suggest that it is the unresolved conflict between parents prior to and after the divorce, rather than the divorce itself, that accounts for most of the debilitating effects on the children.[34]

Third, we find the attack on family egalitarianism puzzling when the fact is that, despite the increase in egalitarian ideology, modern couples move toward more traditional family role arrangements as they become parents—despite their intention to do otherwise. Our key point here is that traditional family and work roles in families of the last three decades tend to be associated with *more* individual and marital distress for parents. Furthermore, we find that when fathers have little involvement in household and child care tasks, both parents are less responsive and less able to provide the structure necessary for their children to accomplish new and challenging tasks in our project playroom. Finally, when we ask teachers how all of the children in their classrooms are faring at school, it is the children of these parents who are less academically competent and more socially isolated. There is, then, a body of evidence suggesting that a return to strictly traditional family arrangements may not have the positive consequences that the proponents of "family values" claim they will.

Family and Workplace Policy

Current discussions about policies for reducing the tensions experienced by parents of young children tend to be polarized around two alternatives: (1) Encourage more mothers to stay home and thereby reduce their stress in juggling family and work; (2) Make the workplace more flexible and "family friendly" for both parents through parental leave policies, flextime, and child care provided or subsidized by the workplace. There is no body of systematic empirical research that supports the conclusion that when mothers work outside the home, their children or husbands suffer negative consequences.[35] In fact, our own data and others' suggest that (1) children, especially girls, benefit from the model their working mothers provide as productive workers, and (2) mothers of young children who return to work are less depressed than mothers who stay home full time. Thus it is not at all clear that a policy designed to persuade contemporary mothers of young children to stay at home would have the desired effects, particularly given the potential for depression and the loss of one parent's wages in single paycheck families. Unless governments are prepared, as they are in Sweden and Germany, for example, to hold parents' jobs and provide *paid* leave to replace lost wages, a stay-at-home *policy* seems too costly for the family on both economic and psychological grounds.

We believe that the issue should not be framed in terms of policies to support single-worker *or* dual-worker families, but rather in terms of support for the well-being of all family members. This goal could entail financial support for families with very young children so that parents could choose to do full-time or substantial part-time child care themselves *or* to have support to return to work.

What about the alternative of increasing workplace flexibility? Studies of families making the transition to parenthood suggest that this alternative may be especially attractive and helpful when children are young, if it is accompanied by substantial increases in the availability of high-quality child care to reduce the stress of locating adequate care or making do with less than ideal caretakers. Adults and children tend to adapt well when both parents work *if both parents support that alternative.* Therefore, policies that support paid family leave along with flexible work arrangements could enable families to choose arrangements that make most sense for their particular situation.

Preventive Services to Address Family Risk Points

According to our analysis of the risks associated with the formation of new families, many two-parent families are having difficulty coping on their own with the normal challenges of becoming a family. If a priority in our society is to strengthen new families, it seems reasonable to consider offering preventive programs to reduce risks and distress and enhance the potential for healthy and satisfying family relationships, which we know lead to more optimal levels of adjustment in children. What we are advocating is analogous to the concept of Lamaze and other forms of childbirth preparation, which are now commonly sought by many expectant parents. A logical context for these programs would be existing public and private health and mental health delivery systems in which services could be provided for families who wish assistance or are already in difficulty. We recognize that there is skepticism in a substantial segment of the population about psychological services in general, and about services provided for families by government in particular. Nonetheless, the fact is that many modern families are finding parenthood unexpectedly stressful and they typically have no access to assistance. Evidence from intervention trials suggests that when preventive programs help parents move their family relationships in more positive directions, their children have fewer academic, behavioral, and emotional problems in their first years of schooling.[36]

Parent-Focused Interventions. Elsewhere, we reviewed the literature on interventions designed to improve parenting skills and parent-child relationship quality in families at different points on the spectrum from low-risk to high-distress.[37] For parents of children already identified as having serious problems, home visiting programs and preschool and early school interventions, some of which include a broader family focus, have demonstrated positive effects on parents' behavior and self-esteem and on children's academic and social competence, particularly when the intervention staff are health or mental health professionals. However, with the exception of occasional classes, books, or tapes for parents, there are few resources for parents who need to learn more about how to manage small problems before they spiral out of their control.

Couple-Focused Interventions.   Our conceptual model of family transitions and results of studies of partners who become parents suggest that family-based interventions might go beyond enhancing parent-child relationships to strengthen the relationship *between* the parents. We have seen that the couple relationship is vulnerable in its own right around the decision to have a baby and increasingly after the birth of a child. We know of only one pilot program that provided couples an opportunity to explore mixed feelings about the "Baby-Maybe" decision.[38] Surely, services designed to help couples resolve their conflict about whether and when to become a family—especially "Yes-No" couples—might reduce the risks of later marital and family distress, just as genetic counseling helps couples make decisions when they are facing the risk of serious genetic problems.

In our own work, we have been systematically evaluating two preventive interventions for couples who have not been identified as being in a high-risk category. Both projects involved work with small groups of couples who met weekly over many months, in one case expectant couples, in the other, couples whose first child is about to make the transition to elementary school.[39] In both studies, staff couples who are mental health professionals worked with *both parents* in small groups of four or five couples. Ongoing discussion over the months of regular meetings addressed participants' individual, marital, parenting, and three-generational dilemmas and problems. In both cases we found promising results when we compared adjustment in families with and without the intervention.

By two years after the Becoming a Family project intervention, new parents had avoided the typical declines in role satisfaction and the increases in marital disenchantment reported in almost every longitudinal study of new parents. There were no separations or divorces in couples who participated in the intervention for the first three years of parenthood, whereas 15 percent of comparable couples with no intervention had already divorced. The positive impact of this intervention was still apparent five years after it had ended.

In the Schoolchildren and Their Families project intervention, professional staff engaged couples in group discussions of marital, parenting, and three-generational problems and dilemmas during their first child's transition to school. Two years after the intervention ended, fathers and mothers showed fewer symptoms of depression and less conflict in front of their child, and fathers were more effective in helping their children with difficult tasks than comparable parents with no intervention. These positive effects on the parents' lives and relationships had benefits for the children as well: children of parents who worked with the professionals in an ongoing couples group showed greater academic improvement and fewer emotional and behavior problems in the first five years of elementary school than children whose parents had no group intervention.[40]

These results suggest that preventive interventions in which clinically trained staff work with "low-risk" couples have the potential to buffer some of the parents' strain, slow down or stop the spillover of negative and unrewarding patterns from one relationship to another, enhance fathers' responsiveness to their children, and foster the children's ability both to concentrate on their school work and to develop more rewarding relationships with their peers. The findings suggest that *without intervention*, there is increased risk of spillover from parents' distress to the quality of the parent-child relationships. This means that preventive services to help parents cope more effectively with their problems have the potential to enhance their responsiveness to their children *and* to their partners, which, in turn, optimizes their children's chances of making more successful adjustments to school. Such programs have the potential to reduce the long-term negative consequences of children's early school difficulties by setting them on more positive developmental trajectories as they face the challenges of middle childhood.

Conclusion

The transition to parenthood has been made by men and women for centuries. In the past three decades, the notion that this transition poses risks for the well-being of adults and, thus, potentially for their children's development, has been greeted by some with surprise, disbelief, or skepticism. Our goal has been to bring recent social science findings about the processes involved in becoming a family to the attention of social scientists, family policymakers, and parents themselves. We have shown that this often-joyous time is normally accompanied by changes and stressors that increase risks of relationship difficulty and compromise the ability of men and women to create the kinds of families they dream of when they set out on their journey to parenthood. We conclude that there is cause for concern about the health of "the family"—even those considered advantaged by virtue of their material and psychological resources.

Most chapters in this book focus on policies for families in more high-risk situations. We have argued that contemporary couples and their children in two-parent lower- to upper-middle-class families deserve the attention of policymakers as well. We view these couples as new pioneers, because, despite the fact that partners have been having babies for millennia, contemporary parents are journeying into uncharted terrain, which appears to hold unexpected risks to their own and their children's development.

Like writers describing "family decline," we are concerned about the strength and hardiness of two-parent families. Unlike those who advocate that parents adopt more traditional family values, we recommend that policies to address family health and well-being allow for the creation of programs and services for families in diverse family arrangements, with the goal of enhancing the development and well-being of all children. We recognize that with economic resources already stretched very thin, this is not an auspicious time to recommend additional collective funding of family services. Yet research suggests that without intervention, there is a risk that the vulnerabilities and problems of the parents will spill over into the lives of their children, thus increasing the probability of the transmission of the kinds of intergenerational problems that erode the quality of family life and compromise children's chances of optimal development. This will be very costly in the long run.

We left Mark and Abby, and a number of other couples, in a state of animated suspension. Many of them were feeling somewhat irritable and disappointed, though not ready to give up on their dreams of creating nurturing families. These couples provide a challenge—that the information they have offered through their participation in scores of systematic family studies in many locales will be taken seriously, and that their voices will play a role in helping our society decide how to allocate limited economic and social resources for the families that need them.

Endnotes

1. D. Blankenhorn, S. Bayme, and J. B. Elshtain (eds.), *Rebuilding the Nest: A New Commitment to the American Family* (Milwaukee, WI: Family Service America, 1990), 3–26; D. Popenoe, "American Family Decline, 1960–1990," *Journal of Marriage and the Family* 55:527–541, 1993.
2. S. B. Crockenberg, "Infant Irritability, Mother Responsiveness, and Social Support Influences on Security of Infant-Mother Attachment," *Child Development* 52:857–865, 1981; C. Cutrona, "Nonpsychotic Postpartum Depression: A Review of Recent Research," *Clinical Psychology Review* 2:487–503, 1982.
3. A. Hochschild, *The Second Shift: Working Parents and the Revolution at Home* (New York: Viking Penguin, 1989); J. H. Pleck, "Fathers and Infant Care Leave," in E. F. Zigler and M. Frank (eds.), *The Parental Leave Crisis: Toward a National Policy* (New Haven, CT: Yale University Press, 1988).
4. A. Skolnick, *Embattled Paradise: The American Family in an Age of Uncertainty* (New York: Basic Books, 1991).
5. D. Popenoe, *Disturbing the Nest: Family Change and Decline in Modern Societies* (New York: Aldine de Gruyter, 1988); Popenoe, "American Family Decline."
6. Popenoe, "American Family Decline." 41–42. Smaller two-parent families and larger one-parent families are both attributed to the same mechanism: parental self-focus and selfishness.
7. D. Blankenhorn, "American Family Dilemmas," in D. Blankenhorn, S. Bayme, and J. B. Elshtain (eds.), *Rebuilding the Nest. A New Commitment to the American Family* (Milwaukee, WI: Family Service America, 1990), 3–26.
8. Although the proportion of single-parent families is increasing, the concern about departure from the two-parent form may be overstated. Approximately 70 percent of American babies born in the 1990s come home to two parents who are married. If we include couples with long-term commitments who are not legally married, the proportion of modern families that *begins* with two parents is even higher. The prevalence of two-parent families has declined since 1956, when 94 percent of newborns had married parents, but, by far, the predominant family form in the nonteenage population continues to be two parents and a baby.
9. J. Belsky, M. Lang, and M. Rovine, "Stability and Change across the Transition to Parenthood: A Second Study," *Journal of Personality and Social Psychology* 50:517–522, 1985; C. P. Cowan, P. A. Cowan, G. Heming, E. Garrett, W. S. Coysh, H. Curtis-Boles, and A. J. Boles, "Transitions to Parenthood: His, Hers, and Theirs," *Journal of Family Issues* 6:451–481, 1985; M. J. Cox, M. T. Owen, J. M. Lewis, and V. K. Henderson, "Marriage, Adult Adjustment, and Early Parenting," *Child Development* 60:1015–1024, 1989; F. Grossman, L. Eiehler, and S. Winickoff, *Pregnancy, Birth, and Parenthood* (San Francisco: Jossey-Bass, 1980); C. M. Heinicke, S. D. Diskin, D. M. Ramsay-Klee, and D. S. Oates, "Pre- and Postbirth Antecedents of 2-year-old Attention, Capacity for Relationships and Verbal Expressiveness," *Developmental Psychology* 22:777–787, 1986; R. Levy-Shiff, "Individual and Contextual Correlates of Marital Change Across the Transition to Parenthood," *Developmental Psychology* 30:591–601, 1994.

10. A. Engfer, "The Interrelatedness of Marriage and the Mother-Child Relationship," in R. A. Hinde and J. Stevenson-Hinde (eds.), *Relationships within Families: Mutual Influences* (Cambridge UK: Cambridge University Press, 1988), 104–118; K. A. Schneewind, "Konsequenzen der Erstelternschaft" [Consequences of the Transition to Parenthood: An Overview], *Psychologie in Erziehung and Unterricht* 30:161–172, 1983.

11. C. F. Clulow, *To Have and to Hold: Marriage, the First Baby and Preparing Couples for Parenthood* (Aberdeen, Scotland: Aberdeen University Press, 1982).

12. C. P. Cowan and P. A. Cowan, "Interventions to Ease the Transition to Parenthood: Why They Are Needed and What They Can Do," *Family Relations* 44:412–423, 1995.

13. A. F. Shapiro, J. M. Gottman, and S. Carrere, "The Baby and the Marriage. Identifying Factors that Buffer against Decline in Marital Satisfaction after the First Baby Arrives. *Journal of Family Psychology*, 14:59–70, 2000.

14. E. E. LeMasters, "Parenthood as Crisis," *Marriage and Family Living* 19:352–365, 1957.

15. S. B. Campbell, J. F. Cohn, C. Flanagan, S. Popper, and T. Myers, "Course and Correlates of Postpartum Depression during the Transition to Parenthood," *Development and Psychopathology* 4:29–48, 1992.

16. T. Benedek, "Parenthood during the Life Cycle," in E. J. Anthony and T. Benedek (eds.), *Parenthood: Its Psychology and Psychopathology* (Boston: Little, Brown, 1970); J. D. Osofsky and H. J. Osofsky, "Psychological and Developmental Perspectives on Expectant and New Parenthood," in R. D. Parke (ed.), *Review of Child Development Research 7: The Family* (Chicago: University of Chicago Press, 1984), 372–397.

17. A. Caspi and G. H. Elder, Jr. "Emergent Family Patterns: The Intergenerational Construction of Problem Behavior and Relationships," in R. A. Hinde and J. Stevenson-Hinde (eds.), *Relationships Within Families: Mutual Influences* (Oxford: Clarendon Press, 1988), 218–241; M. H. van Ijzendoorn, F. Juffer, M. G. Duyvesteyn, "Breaking the Intergenerational Cycle of Insecure Attachment: A Review of the Effects of Attachment-based Interventions on Maternal Sensitivity and Infant Security," *Journal of Child Psychology & Psychiatry & Allied Disciplines* 36:225–248, 1995.

18. D. A. Cohn, P. A. Cowan, C. P. Cowan, and J. Pearson, "Mothers' and Fathers' Working Models of Childhood Attachment Relationships, Parenting Styles, and Child Behavior," *Development and Psychopathology* 4:417–431, 1992.

19. Crockenberg, "Infant Irritability."

20. Hochschild, *The Second Shift*.

21. C. P. Cowan and P. A. Cowan, *When Partners Become Parents: The Big Life Change for Couples* (Mahwah, NJ: Lawrence Erlbaum, 2000).

22. M. S. Schulz, "Coping with Negative Emotional Arousal: The Daily Spillover of Work Stress into Marital Interactions," Unpublished doctoral dissertation. University of California, Berkeley, 1994; R. Repetti and J. Wood, "Effects of Daily Stress at Work on Mothers' Interactions with Preschoolers," *Journal of Family Psychology*, 11:90–108, 1997.

23. J. Belsky and M. Rovine, "Patterns of Marital Change across the Transition to Parenthood," *Journal of Marriage and the Family* 52:109–123, 1990.

24. We interviewed the couples in the mid-to-late stages of pregnancy. We were not, therefore, privy to the early phases of decision making of these couples, whether wives became pregnant on purpose, or whether husbands were coercive about the baby decision. What we saw in the Yes-No couples, in contrast with the Ambivalent couples, was that the decision to go ahead with the pregnancy, an accomplished fact, was still an unresolved emotional struggle.

25. M. Kline, P. A. Cowan, and C. P. Cowan, "The Origins of Parenting Stress during the Transition to Parenthood: A New Family Model," *Early Education and Development* 2:287–305, 1991.

26. J. Belsky and R. A. Isabella, "Marital and Parent-Child Relationships in Family of Origin and Marital Change Following the Birth of a Baby: A Retrospective Analysis," *Child Development* 56:342–349, 1985; C. P. Cowan, P. A. Cowan, and G. Heming, "Adult Children of Alcoholics: Adaptation during the Transition to Parenthood." Paper presented to the National Council on Family Relations, 1988.

27. Cowan, Cowan, and Heming; "Adult Children of Alcoholics."

28. Belsky, Lang, and Rovine, "Stability and Change across the Transition to Parenthood"; Cowan and Cowan, *When Partners Become Parents*; Cox, Owen, Lewis, and Henderson, "Marriage, Adult Adjustment, and Early Parenting"; Heinicke, Diskin, Ramsay-Klee, and Oates, "Pre- and Postbirth Antecedents of 2-Year-Old Attention, Capacity for Relationships and Verbal Expressiveness."

29. D. Baumrind, "The Development of Instrumental Competence through Socialization," in A. D. Pick (ed.), *Minnesota Symposia on Child Psychology*, vol. 7 (Minneapolis: University of Minnesota Press, 1979); J. H. Block and J. Block, "The Role of Ego-Control and Ego-Resiliency in the Organization of Behavior," in W. A. Collins (ed.), *Minnesota Symposia on Child Psychology*, vol. 13 (Hillsdale, NJ: Erlbaum, 1980).

30. P. A. Cowan, C. P. Cowan, M. Schulz, and G. Heming, "Prebirth to Preschool Family Factors Predicting Children's Adaptation to Kindergarten," in R. Parke and S. Kellam (eds.), *Exploring Family Relationships with Other Social Contexts: Advances in Family Research*, vol. 4 (Hillsdale, NJ: Erlbaum, 1994), 75–114.

31. K. L. Alexander and D. Entwisle, "Achievement in the First 2 Years of School: Patterns and Processes," *Monographs of the Society for Research in Child Development* 53:2, Serial No. 218, 1988.

32. S. Asher and J. D. Coie (eds.), *Peer Rejection in Childhood* (Cambridge: Cambridge University Press, 1990); S. G. Kellam, M. B. Simon, and M. E. Ensminger, "Antecedents in First Grade of Teenage Drug Use and Psychological Well-Being: A Ten-Year Community-wide Prospective Study," in D. Ricks and B. Dohrenwend (eds.), *Origins of Psychopathology: Research and Public Policy* (New York: Cambridge, 1982); N. Lambert, "Adolescent Outcomes for Hyperactive Children: Perspectives on General and Specific Patterns of Childhood Risk for Adolescent Educational, Social, and Mental Health Problems," *American Psychologist* 43:786–799, 1988; E. A. Carlson, L. A. Sroufe et al. "Early Environment Support and Elementary School Adjustment as Predictors of School Adjustment in Middle Adolescence," *Journal of Adolescent Research* 14:72–94, 1999.

33. E. M. Hetherington and J. Kelly, *For Better or for Worse: Divorce Reconsidered* (New York: W. W. Norton, 2002); J. Wallerstein and J. Kelly, *Surviving the Breakup* (New York: Basic Books, 1980).

34. E. M. Cummings and P. T. Davies, *Children and Marital Conflict: The Impact of Family Dispute and Resolution* (New York: Guilford Press, 1994).

35. M. Moorehouse, "Work and Family Dynamics," in P. A. Cowan, D. Field, D. A. Hansen, A. Skolnick, and G. E. Swanson (eds.), *Family, Self, and Society: Toward a New Agenda for Family Research* (Hillsdale, NJ: Erlbaum, 1993).

36. P. A. Cowan and C. P. Cowan, "What an Intervention Design Reveals about How Parents Affect Their Children's Academic Achievement and Behavior Problems," in J. G. Borkowski, S. Ramey, and M. Bristol-Power (eds.), *Parenting and the Child's World: Influences on Intellectual, Academic, and Social-Emotional Development* (Mahwah, NJ: Lawrence Erlbaum, 2002).

37. P. A. Cowan, D. Powell, and C. P. Cowan, "Parenting Interventions: A Family Systems View of Enhancing Children's Development," in I. E. Sigel and K. A. Renninger (eds.), *Handbook of Child Psychology*, 5th ed. vol. 4: *Child Psychology in Practice* (New York: Wiley, 1997).

38. L. Potts, "Considering Parenthood: Group Support for a Critical Life Decision," *American Journal of Orthopsychiatry* 50:629–638, 1980.

39. P. A. Cowan, C. P. Cowan, and T. Heming. "Two Variations of a Preventive Intervention for Couples: Effects on Parents and Children during the Transition to Elementary School," in P. A. Cowan, C. P. Cowan, J. Ablow, V. K. Johnson, and J. Measelle (eds.), *The Family Context of Parenting in Children's Adaptation to Elementary School* (Mahwah, NJ: Lawrence Erlbaum Associates, in press).

40. Ibid.

6

Families with Preschool Children

Caring for Our Young: Child Care in Europe and the United States

Dan Clawson and Naomi Gerstel

When a delegation of American child care experts visited France, they were amazed by the full-day, free *écoles maternelles* that enroll almost 100 percent of French three-, four- and five-year-olds:

> Libraries better stocked than those in many U.S. elementary schools. Three-year-olds serving one another radicchio salad, then using cloth napkins, knives, forks and real glasses of milk to wash down their bread and chicken. Young children asked whether dragons exist [as] a lesson in developing vocabulary and creative thinking.

In the United States, by contrast, working parents struggle to arrange and pay for private care. Publicly-funded child care programs are restricted to the poor. Although most U.S. parents believe (or want to believe) that their children receive quality care, standardized ratings find most of the care mediocre and much of it seriously inadequate.

Looking at child care in comparative perspective offers us an opportunity—almost requires us—to think about our goals and hopes for children, parents, education and levels of social inequality. Any child care program or funding system has social and political assumptions with far-reaching consequences. National systems vary in their emphasis on education; for three- to five-year-olds, some stress child

Reprinted from *All Our Families: New Policies for a New Century*, edited by Mary Ann Mason, Arlene Skolnick, and Stephen D. Sugarman (2007), Oxford University Press.

care as preparation for school, while others take a more playful view of childhood. Systems vary in the extent to which they stress that children's early development depends on interaction with peers or some version of intensive mothering. They also vary in the extent to which they support policies promoting center-based care as opposed to time for parents to stay at home with their very young children. Each of these emphases entails different national assumptions, if only implicit, about children and parents, education, teachers, peers and societies as a whole.

What do we want, why and what are the implications? Rethinking these questions is timely because with changing welfare, employment, and family patterns, more U.S. parents have come to believe they want and need a place for their children in child care centers. Even parents who are not in the labor force want their children to spend time in preschool. In the United States almost half of children less than one year old now spend a good portion of their day in some form of non-parental care. Experts increasingly emphasize the potential benefits of child care. A recent National Academy of Sciences report summarizes the views of experts: "Higher quality care is associated with outcomes that all parents want to see in their children." The word in Congress these days, especially in discussions of welfare reform, is that child care is good—it saves money later on by helping kids through school (which keeps them out of jail), and it helps keep mothers on the job and families together. A generation ago, by contrast, Nixon vetoed a child care bill as a "radical piece of social legislation" designed to deliver children to "communal approaches to child rearing over and against the family-centered approach." While today's vision is clearly different, most attempts to improve U.S. child care are incremental, efforts to get a little more money here or there, with little consideration for what kind of system is being created.

The U.S. and French systems offer sharp contrasts. Although many hold up the French system as a model for children three or older, it is only one alternative. Other European countries provide thought-provoking alternatives, but the U.S.-French contrast is a good place to begin.

France and The United States: Private Versus Public Care

Until their children start school, most U.S. parents struggle to find child care, endure long waiting lists, and frequently change locations. They must weave a complex, often unreliable patchwork in which their children move among relatives, informal settings and formal center care, sometimes all in one day. Among three- to four-year-old children with employed mothers, more than one out of eight are in three or more child care arrangements, and almost half are in two or more arrangements. A very small number of the wealthy hire nannies, often immigrants; more parents place their youngest children with relatives, especially grandmothers, or work alternate shifts so fathers can share child care with mothers (these alternating shifters now include almost one-third of families with infants and toddlers). Many pay kin to provide child care—sometimes not because they prefer it, but because they cannot afford other care, and it is a way to provide jobs and income to struggling family members. For children three and older, however, the fastest-growing setting in the United States is child care centers—almost half of three-year-olds (46 percent) and almost two-thirds of four-year-olds (64 percent) now spend much of their time there.

In France, participation in the *école maternelle* system is voluntary, but a place is guaranteed to every child three to six years old. Almost 100 percent of parents enroll their three-year-olds. Even non-employed parents enroll their children, because they believe it is best for the children. Schools are open from 8:30 A.M. to 4:30 P.M. with an extended lunch break, but care is available at modest cost before and after school and during the lunch break.

Integrated with the school system, French child care is intended primarily as early education. All children, rich and poor, immigrant or not, are part of the same national system, with the same curriculum, staffed by teachers paid good wages by the same national ministry. No major political party or group opposes the system.

When extra assistance is offered, rather than targeting poor children (or families), additional resources are provided to geographic areas. Schools in some zones, mostly in urban areas, receive extra funding to reduce class size, give teachers extra training and a bonus, provide extra materials and employ special teachers. By targeting an entire area, poor children are not singled out (as they are in U.S. free lunch programs).

Staff in the French *écoles maternelles* have master's degrees and are paid teachers' wages; in 1998, U.S. preschool teachers earned an average of $8.32 an hour, and child care workers earned $6.61, not only considerably less than (underpaid) teachers but also less than parking lot attendants. As a consequence employee turnover averages 30 percent a year, with predictably harmful effects on children.

What are the costs of these two very different systems? In almost every community across the United States, a year of child care costs more than a year at a public university—in some cases twice as much. Subsidy systems favor the poor, but subsidies (unlike tax breaks) depend on the level of appropriations. Congress does not appropriate enough money and, therefore, most of the children who qualify for subsidies do not receive them. In 1999, under federal rules 15 million children were eligible to receive benefits, but only 1.8 million actually received them. Middle- and working-class families can receive neither kind of subsidy. An Urban Institute study suggests that some parents place their children in care they consider unsatisfactory because other arrangements are just too expensive. The quality of care thus differs drastically depending on the parents' income, geographic location, diligence in searching out alternatives and luck.

The French system is not cheap. According to French government figures, the cost for a child in Paris was about $5,500 per year in 1999. That is only slightly more than the average U.S. parent paid for the care of a four-year-old in a center ($5,242 in 2000). But in France child care is a social responsibility, and thus free to parents, while in the United States parents pay the cost. Put another way, France spends about 1 percent of its Gross Domestic Product (GDP) on government-funded early education and care programs. If the United States devoted the same share of its GDP to preschools, the government would spend about $100 billion a year. Current U.S. government spending is less than $20 billion a year ($15 billion federal, $4 billion state).

Other European Alternatives

When the American child care community thinks about European models, the French model is often what they have in mind. With its emphasis on education, the French system has an obvious appeal to U.S. politicians, educators and child care advocates. Politicians' central concern in the United States appears to be raising children's test scores; in popular and academic literature, this standard is often cited as the major indicator of program success. But such an educational model is by no means the only alternative. Indeed, the U.S. focus on the French system may itself be a telling indicator of U.S. experts' values as well as their assessments of political realities. Many advocates insist that a substantial expansion of the U.S. system will be possible only if the system is presented as improving children's education. These advocates are no longer willing to use the term "child care," insisting on "early education" instead. The French model fits these priorities: it begins quasi-school about three years earlier than in the United States. Although the French obviously assist employed parents and children's center activities are said to be fun, the system is primarily touted and understood as educational—intended to treat children as pupils, to prepare them to do better in school.

The 11 European nations included in a recent Organization for Economic Cooperation and Development study (while quite different from one another) all have significantly better child care and paid leave than the United States. Each also differs significantly from France. Offering alternatives, these models challenge us to think even more broadly about childhood, parenting and the kind of society we value.

Non-School Model: Denmark

From birth to age six most Danish children go to child care, but most find that care in non-school settings. Overseen by the Ministry of Social Affairs (rather than the Ministry of Education), the Danish system stresses "relatively unstructured curricula" that give children time to "hang out." Lead staff are pedagogues, not teachers. Although pedagogues have college degrees and are paid teachers' wages, their role is "equally important but different" from that of the school-based teacher. "Listening to children" is one of the government's five principles, and centers emphasize "looking at everything from the child's perspective."

The Danish model differs from the French system in two additional ways that clarify its non-school character. First, in the Danish system, pedagogues care for very young children (from birth to age three as well as older children ages three to six). The French preschool (*école maternelle*) model applies only to children three and older. Before that, children of working parents can attend *crèches*. *Crèche* staff, however, have only high school educations and are paid substantially less than the (master's degree-trained) *écoles maternelles* teachers. Second, while the *écoles maternelles* are available to all children, the Danish system (like the French *crèches*) is only available to children with working parents because it is intended to aid working parents, not to educate children.

The Danish system is decentralized, with each individual center required to have a management board with a parent majority. But the system receives most of its money from public funding, and parents contribute only about one-fifth of total costs.

Given its non-school emphasis, age integration, and the importance it assigns to local autonomy, the Danish system might be appealing to U.S. parents, especially some people of color. To be sure, many U.S. parents—across race and class—are ambivalent about child care for their youngest children. Especially given the growing emphasis on testing, they believe that preschool might give them an edge, but they also want their children to have fun and play—to have, in short, what most Americans still consider a childhood. Some research suggests that Latina mothers are especially likely to feel that center-based care, with its emphasis on academic learning, does not provide the warmth and moral guidance they seek. They are, therefore, less likely to select center-based care than either white or African-American parents, relying instead on kin or family child care providers whom they know and trust. U.S. experts' emphasis on the French model may speak not only to political realities but also to the particular class and even more clearly race preferences framing those realities.

Mothers or Peers

The United States, if only implicitly, operates on a mother-substitute model of child care. Because of a widespread assumption in the United States that all women naturally have maternal feelings and capacities, child care staff, who are almost all women (about 98 percent), are not required to have special training (and do not need to be well paid). Even for regulated providers, 41 out of 50 states require no pre-service training beyond orientation. Consequently, in the United States the child-staff ratio is one of the most prominent measures used to assess quality and is central to most state licensing systems. The assumption, based on the mother-substitute model, is that emotional support can be given and learning can take place only with such low ratios.

Considering the high quality and ample funding of many European systems, it comes as a surprise that most have much higher child-staff ratios than the United States. In the French *écoles maternelles*, for example, there is one teacher and one half-time aide for every 25 children. In Italy, in a center with one adult for every eight children (ages one to three years) the early childhood workers see no need for additional adults and think the existing ratios are appropriate. Leading researchers Sheila Kamerman and Alfred Kahn report that in Denmark, "what is particularly impressive is that children are pretty much on their own in playing with their peers. An adult is present all the time but does not lead or play with the children." In a similar vein, a cross-national study of academic literature found substantial focus on adult-child ratios in the United States, but very little literature on the topic in German-, French- or Spanish-language publications. Why not? These systems have a different view of children and learning. Outside the United States systems often center around the peer group. In Denmark the role of staff is to work "alongside children, rather than [to be] experts or leaders who teach children." Similarly, the first director of the early childhood services in Reggio, Italy, argues that children learn through conflict and that placing children in groups facilitates learning through "attractive," "advantageous," and "constructive" conflict "because among children there are not strong relationships of authority and dependence." In a non-European example, Joseph Tobin, David Wu, and Dana Davidson argue that in Japan the aim is ratios that "keep teachers from being too mother-like in their interactions with students . . . Large class sizes and large ratios have become increasingly important strategies for promoting the Japanese values of groupism and selflessness." Such practices contrast with the individualistic focus in U.S. child care.

Family Leaves and Work Time

When we ask how to care for children, especially those younger than three, one answer is for parents to stay home. Policy that promotes such leaves is what one would expect from a society such as the United States, which emphasizes a mothering model of child care. It is, however, European countries that provide extensive paid family leave, usually universal, with not only job protection but also substantial income replacement. In Sweden, for example, parents receive a full year and a half of paid parental leave (with 12 months at 80 percent of prior earnings) for each child. Because so many parents (mostly mothers) use family leave, fewer than 200 children under one year old in the entire country are in public care. Generous programs are common throughout Europe (although the length, flexibility and level of payment they provide vary).

The United States provides far less in the way of family leaves. Since its passage in 1993, the Family and Medical Leave Act (FMLA) has guaranteed a 12-week job-protected leave to workers of covered employers. Most employers (95 percent) and many workers (45 percent), however, are not covered. And all federally mandated leaves are unpaid.

The unpaid leaves provided by the FMLA, like the private system of child care, accentuate the inequality between those who can afford them and those who can't. Although the FMLA was touted as a "gender neutral" piece of legislation, men (especially white men) are unlikely to take leaves; it is overwhelmingly women (especially those who are married) who take them. As a result, such women pay a wage penalty when they interrupt their careers. To address such inequities, Sweden and Norway have introduced a "use it or lose it" policy. For each child, parents may divide up to a year of paid leave (say nine months for the mother, three for the father), *except* that the mother may not use more than eleven months total. One month is reserved for the father; if he does not use the leave, the family loses the month.

Finally, although not usually discussed as child care policy in the United States, policy makers in many European countries now emphasize that the number of hours parents work clearly shapes the ways young children are cared for and by whom. Workers in the United States, on average, put in 300 hours more per year than workers in France (and 400 more than those in Sweden).

Conclusion

The child care system in the United States is a fragmentary patchwork, both at the level of the individual child and at the level of the overall system. Recent research suggests that the quality of care for young children is poor or fair in well over half of child care

---

2002–2003 Fee Schedule

(Prices effective until July 1, 2003)

Application Fee　　　　　　　$50.00
(nonrefundable/annual fee)
Materials Fee　　　　　　　$30.00 Full-time Enrollment
(nonrefundable)　　　　　　$20.00 Part-time Enrollment
Tuition Deposit* *amount equal to one month's tuition*
(due in two installments)
a. Space Guarantee Fee**　　$150.00
　　(due upon acceptance to the school)
b. Balance due two months prior to starting date.
**See enrollment contract for refund conditions.

Full-time	$859.00/month

Morning Preschool (9:00 a.m.–1.00 p.m.)
three mornings	$321.00/month
four mornings	$397.00/month
five mornings	$462.00/month

Afternoon Preschool (1:00 p.m.–5.00 p.m.)
three afternoons	$285.00/month
four afternoons	$350.00/month
five afternoons	$404.00/month

Kindergarten Program (11:25 a.m.–5.00 p.m.)
three days	$339.00/month
four days	$416.00/month
five days	$486.00/month

—Extended Care (hour before 9:00 a.m. and the hour after
5.00 p.m.)　　　　　　　$5.25/hour
—Unscheduled Drop-in　　　$6.25/hour

Participating Parents (P.P.) & Board Members receive tuition
credit. P.P. credit is $25.00 per day of participation. Board
credits vary with position.

Tuition and fees for the U.S. preschool illustrated here, a
non-profit, parent-run cooperative that costs almost $1,000 per
month.

settings. This low quality of care, in concert with a model of intensive mothering,
means that many anxious mothers privately hunt for high-quality substitutes while trying to ensure they are not being really replaced. System administrators need to patch
together a variety of funding streams, each with its own regulations and paperwork.
Because the current system was fashioned primarily for the affluent at one end and
those being pushed off welfare at the other, it poorly serves most of the working class
and much of the middle class.

Most efforts at reform are equally piecemeal, seeking a little extra money here or there in ways that reinforce the existing fragmentation. Although increasing numbers of advocates are pushing for a better system of child care in the United States, they rarely step back to think about the characteristics of the system as a whole. If they did, what lessons could be learned from Europe?

The features that are common to our peer nations in Europe would presumably be a part of a new U.S. system. The programs would be publicly funded and universal, available to all, either at no cost or at a modest cost with subsidies for low-income participants. The staff would be paid about the same as public school teachers. The core programs would cover at least as many hours as the school day, and "wrap-around" care would be available before and after this time. Participation in the programs would be voluntary, but the programs would be of such a high quality that a majority of children would enroll. Because the quality of the programs would be high, parents would feel much less ambivalence about their children's participation, and the system would enjoy strong public support. In addition to child care centers, parents would be universally offered a significant period of paid parental leave. Of course, this system is expensive. But as the National Academy of Science Report makes clear, not caring for our children is in the long term, and probably even in the short term, even more expensive.

Centers in all nations emphasize education, peer group dynamics, and emotional support to some extent. But the balance varies. The varieties of European experience pose a set of issues to be considered if and when reform of the U.S. system is on the agenda:

- To what degree should organized care approximate school and at what age, and to what extent is the purpose of such systems primarily educational?

- To what extent should we focus on adult-child interactions that sustain or substitute for mother care as opposed to fostering child-child interactions and the development of peer groups?

- To what extent should policies promote parental time with children versus high-quality organized care, and what are the implications for gender equity of either choice?

These are fundamental questions because they address issues of social equality and force us to rethink deep-seated images of children and parents.

Recommended Resources

Cooper, Candy J. *Ready to Learn: The French System of Early Education and Care Offers Lessons for the United States.* New York: French American Foundation, 1999.

Gornick, Janet, and Marcia Meyers. "Support for Working Families: What the United States Can Learn from Europe." *The American Prospect* (January 1–15, 2001): 3–7.

Helburn, Suzanne W., and Barbara R. Bergmann. *America's Childcare Problem: The Way Out.* New York: Palgrave/St. Martin's, 2002.

Kamerman, Sheila B., and Alfred J. Kahn. *Starting Right: How America Neglects Its Youngest Children and What We Can Do About It.* New York: Oxford University Press, 1995.

Moss, Peter. "Workforce Issues in Early Childhood Education and Care Staff." Paper prepared for consultative meeting on International Developments in Early Childhood Education and Care, The Institute for Child and Family Policy, Columbia University, May 11–12, 2000.

Organization for Economic Co-operation and Development. *Starting Strong—Early Education and Care: Report on an OECD Thematic Review*. Online. www.oecd.org.

Shonkoff, Jack P., and Deborah Phillips, eds. *From Neurons to Neighborhoods: The Science of Early Childhood Development*. Washington, DC: National Academy of Sciences, 2000.

7

Balancing Work and Family

There's No Place Like Work

Arlie Russell Hochschild

It's 7:40 a.m. when Cassie Bell, 4, arrives at the Spotted Deer Child-Care Center, her hair half-combed, a blanket in one hand, a fudge bar in the other. "I'm late," her mother, Gwen, a sturdy young woman whose short-cropped hair frames a pleasant face, explains to the child-care worker in charge. "Cassie wanted the fudge bar so bad, I gave it to her," she adds apologetically.

"*Pleeese*, can't you take me with you?" Cassie pleads.

"You know I can't take you to work," Gwen replies in a tone that suggests that she has been expecting this request. Cassie's shoulders droop. But she has struck a hard bargain—the morning fudge bar—aware of her mother's anxiety about the long day that lies ahead at the center. As Gwen explains later, she continually feels that she owes Cassie more time than she gives her—she has a "time debt."

Arriving at her office just before 8, Gwen finds on her desk a cup of coffee in her personal mug, milk no sugar (exactly as she likes it), prepared by a co-worker who managed to get in ahead of her. As the assistant to the head of public relations at a company I will call Amerco, Gwen has to handle responses to any reports that may appear about the company in the press—a challenging job, but one that gives her satisfaction. As she prepares for her first meeting of the day, she misses her daughter, but she also feels relief; there's a lot to get done at Amerco.

Over three years, I interviewed 130 respondents for a book. They spoke freely and allowed me to follow them through "typical" days, on the understanding that I would protect their anonymity. I have changed the names of the company and of those I interviewed, and altered certain identifying details. Their words appear here as they were spoken. —A. R. H.

Gwen used to work a straight eight-hour day. But over the last three years, her workday has gradually stretched to eight and a half or nine hours, not counting the E-mail messages and faxes she answers from home. She complains about her hours to her co-workers and listens to their complaints—but she loves her job. Gwen picks up Cassie at 5:45 and gives her a long, affectionate hug.

At home, Gwen's husband, John, a computer programmer, plays with their daughter while Gwen prepares dinner. To protect the dinner "hour"—8:00–8:30—Gwen checks that the phone machine is on, hears the phone ring during dinner but resists the urge to answer. After Cassie's bath, Gwen and Cassie have "quality time," or "Q.T.," as John affectionately calls it. Half an hour later, at 9:30, Gwen tucks Cassie into bed.

There are, in a sense, two Bell households: the rushed family they actually are and the relaxed family they imagine they might be if only they had time. Gwen and John complain that they are in a time bind. What they say they want seems so modest—time to throw a ball, to read to Cassie, to witness the small dramas of her development, not to speak of having a little fun and romance themselves. Yet even these modest wishes seem strangely out of reach. Before going to bed, Gwen has to E-mail messages to her colleagues in preparation for the next day's meeting; John goes to bed early, exhausted—he's out the door by 7 every morning.

Nationwide, many working parents are in the same boat. More mothers of small children than ever now work outside the home. In 1993, 56 percent of women with children between 6 and 17 worked outside the home full time year round; 43 percent of women with children 6 and under did the same. Meanwhile, fathers of small children are not cutting back hours of work to help out at home. If anything, they have increased their hours at work. According to a 1993 national survey conducted by the Families and Work Institute in New York, American men average 48.8 hours of work a week, and women 41.7 hours, including overtime and commuting. All in all, more women are on the economic train, and for many—men and women alike—that train is going faster.

But Amerco has "family friendly" policies. If your division head and supervisor agree, you can work part time, share a job with another worker, work some hours at home, take parental leave or use "flex time." But hardly anyone uses these policies. In seven years, only two Amerco fathers have taken formal parental leave. Fewer than 1 percent have taken advantage of the opportunity to work part time. Of all such policies, only flex time—which rearranges but does not shorten work time—has had a significant number of takers (perhaps a third of working parents at Amerco).

Forgoing family-friendly policies is not exclusive to Amerco workers. A 1991 study of 188 companies conducted by the Families and Work Institute found that while a majority offered part-time shifts, fewer than 5 percent of employees made use of them. Thirty-five percent offered "flex place"—work from home—and fewer than 3 percent of their employees took advantage of it. And an earlier Bureau of Labor Statistics survey asked workers whether they preferred a shorter workweek, a longer one or their present schedule. About 62 percent preferred their present schedule; 28 percent would have preferred longer hours. Fewer than 10 percent said they wanted a cut in hours.

Still, I found it hard to believe that people didn't protest their long hours at work. So I contacted Bright Horizons, a company that runs 136 company-based child-care centers associated with corporations, hospitals and Federal agencies in 25 states. Bright Horizons allowed me to add questions to a questionnaire they sent out to 3,000 parents whose children attended the centers. The respondents, mainly middle-class parents in their early 30's, largely confirmed the picture I'd found at Amerco. A third of fathers and a fifth of mothers described themselves as "workaholic," and 1 out of 3 said their partners were.

To be sure, some parents have tried to shorten their hours. Twenty-one percent of the nation's women voluntarily work part time, as do 7 percent of men. A number of others make under-the-table arrangements that don't show up on surveys. But while working parents say they need more time at home, the main story of their lives does not center on a struggle to get it. Why? Given the hours parents are working these days, why aren't they taking advantage of an opportunity to reduce their time at work?

The most widely held explanation is that working parents cannot afford to work shorter hours. Certainly this is true for many. But if money is the whole explanation, why would it be that at places like Amerco, the best-paid employees—upper-level managers and professionals—were the least interested in part-time work or job sharing, while clerical workers who earned less were more interested?

Similarly, if money were the answer, we would expect poorer new mothers to return to work more quickly after giving birth than rich mothers. But among working women nationwide, well-to-do new mothers are not much more likely to stay home after 13 weeks with a new baby than low-income new mothers. When asked what they look for in a job, only a third of respondents in a recent study said salary came first. Money is important, but by itself, money does not explain why many people don't want to cut back hours at work.

A second explanation goes that workers don't dare ask for time off because they are afraid it would make them vulnerable to layoffs. With recent downsizings at many large corporations, and with well-paying, secure jobs being replaced by lower-paying, insecure ones, it occurred to me that perhaps employees are "working scared." But when I asked Amerco employees whether they worked long hours for fear of getting on a layoff list, virtually everyone said no. Even among a particularly vulnerable group—factory workers who were laid off in the downturn of the early 1980's and were later rehired—most did not cite fear for their jobs as the only, or main, reason they worked overtime. For unionized workers, layoffs are assigned by seniority, and for nonunionized workers, layoffs are usually related to the profitability of the division a person works in, not to an individual work schedule.

Were workers uninformed about the company's family friendly policies? No. Some even mentioned that they were proud to work for a company that offered such enlightened policies. Were rigid middle managers standing in the way of work-ers using these policies? Sometimes. But when I compared Amerco employees who worked for flexible managers with those who worked for rigid managers, I found that the flexible managers reported only a few more applicants than the rigid ones. The evidence, however counterintuitive, pointed to a paradox: workers at the company I studied weren't protesting the time bind. They were accommodating to it.

Why? I did not anticipate the conclusion I found myself coming to: namely, that work has become a form of "home" and home has become "work." The worlds of home and work have not begun to blur, as the conventional wisdom goes, but to reverse places. We are used to thinking that home is where most people feel the most appreciated, the most truly "themselves," the most secure, the most relaxed. We are used to thinking that work is where most people feel like "just a number" or "a cog in a machine." It is where they have to be "on," have to "act," where they are least secure and most harried.

But new management techniques so pervasive in corporate life have helped transform the workplace into a more appreciative, personal sort of social world. Meanwhile, at home the divorce rate has risen, and the emotional demands have become more baffling and complex. In addition to teething, tantrums and the normal developments of growing children, the needs of elderly parents are creating more tasks for the modern family—as are the blending, unblending, reblending of new stepparents, stepchildren, exes and former in-laws.

This idea began to dawn on me during one of my first interviews with an Amerco worker. Linda Avery, a friendly, 38-year-old mother, is a shift supervisor at an Amerco plant. When I meet her in the factory's coffee-break room over a couple of Cokes, she is wearing blue jeans and a pink jersey, her hair pulled back in a long, blond ponytail. Linda's husband, Bill, is a technician in the same plant. By working different shifts, they manage to share the care of their 2-year-old son and Linda's 16-year-old daughter from a previous marriage. "Bill works the 7 a.m. to 3 p.m. shift while I watch the baby," she explains. "Then I work the 3 p.m. to 11 p.m. shift and he watches the baby. My daughter works at Walgreen's after school."

Linda is working overtime, and so I begin by asking whether Amerco required the overtime, or whether she volunteered for it. "Oh, I put in for it," she replies. I ask her whether, if finances and company policy permitted, she'd be interested in cutting back on the overtime. She takes off her safety glasses, rubs her face and, without answering my question, explains: "I get home, and the minute I turn the key, my daughter is right there. Granted, she needs somebody to talk to about her day. . . . The baby is still up. He should have been in bed two hours ago, and that upsets me. The dishes are piled in the sink. My daughter comes right up to the door and complains about anything her stepfather said or did, and she wants to talk about her job. My husband is in the other room hollering to my daughter, 'Tracy, I don't ever get any time to talk to your mother, because you're always monopolizing her time before I even get a chance!' They all come at me at once."

Linda's description of the urgency of demands and the unarbitrated quarrels that await her homecoming contrast with her account of arriving at her job as a shift supervisor: "I usually come to work early, just to get away from the house. When I arrive, people are there waiting. We sit, we talk, we joke. I let them know what's going on, who has to be where, what changes I've made for the shift that day. We sit and chitchat for 5 or 10 minutes. There's laughing, joking, fun.

For Linda, home has come to feel like work and work has come to feel a bit like home. Indeed, she feels she can get relief from the "work" of being at home only by going to the "home" of work. Why has her life at home come to seem like this? Linda explains it this way: "My husband's a great help watching our baby. But as far as doing housework or even taking the baby when I'm at home, no. He figures he works five days a week; he's not going to come home and clean. But he doesn't stop to think that I work seven days a week. Why should I have to come home and do the housework without help from anybody else? My husband and I have been through this over and over again. Even if he would just pick up from the kitchen table and stack the dishes for me, that would make a big difference. He does nothing. On his weekends off, he goes fishing. If I want any time off, I have to get a sitter. He'll help out if I'm not here, but the minute I am, all the work at home is mine."

With a light laugh, she continues: "So I take a lot of overtime. The more I get out of the house, the better I am. It's a terrible thing to say, but that's the way I feel."

When Bill feels the need for time off, to relax, to have fun, to feel free, he climbs in his truck and takes his free time without his family. Largely in response, Linda grabs what she also calls "free time"—at work. Neither Linda nor Bill Avery wants more time together at home, not as things are arranged now.

How do Linda and Bill Avery fit into the broader picture of American family and work life? Current research suggests that however hectic their lives, women who do paid work feel less depressed, think better of themselves and are more satisfied than women who stay at home. One study reported that women who work outside the home feel more valued at home than housewives do. Meanwhile, work is where many women feel like "good mothers." As Linda reflects: "I'm a good mom at home, but I'm a better mom at work. At home, I get into fights with Tracy. I want her to apply to a junior college, but she's not interested. At work, I think I'm better at seeing the other person's point of view."

Many workers feel more confident they could "get the job done" at work than at home. One study found that only 59 percent of workers feel their "performance" in the family is "good or unusually good," while 86 percent rank their performance on the job this way.

Forces at work and at home are simultaneously reinforcing this "reversal." The lure of work has been enhanced in recent years by the rise of company cultural engineering—in particular, the shift from Frederick Taylor's principles of scientific management to the Total Quality principles originally set out by W. Edwards Deming. Under the influence of a Taylorist world view, the manager's job was to coerce the worker's mind and body, not to appeal to the worker's heart. The Taylorized worker was de-skilled, replaceable and cheap, and as a consequence felt bored, demeaned and unappreciated.

Using modern participative management techniques, many companies now train workers to make their own work decisions, and then set before their newly "empowered" employees moral as well as financial incentives. At Amerco, the Total Quality worker is invited to feel recognized for job accomplishments. Amerco regularly strengthens the familylike ties of co-workers by holding "recognition ceremonies" honoring particular workers or self-managed production teams. Amerco employees speak of "belonging to the Amerco family," and proudly wear their "Total Quality" pins or "High Performance Team" T-shirts, symbols of their loyalty to the company and of its loyalty to them.

The company occasionally decorates a section of the factory and serves refreshments. The production teams, too, have regular get-togethers. In a New Age recasting of an old business slogan—"The Customer Is Always Right"—Amerco proposes that its workers "Value the Internal Customer." This means: Be as polite and considerate to co-workers inside the company as you would be to customers outside it. How many recognition ceremonies for competent performance are being offered at home? Who is valuing the internal customer there?

Amerco also tries to take on the role of a helpful relative with regard to employee problems at work and at home. The education-andtraining division offers employees free courses (on company time) in "Dealing With Anger," "How to Give and Accept Criticism," "How to Cope With Difficult People."

At home, of course, people seldom receive anything like this much help on issues basic to family life. There, no courses are being offered on "Dealing With Your Child's Disappointment in You" or "How to Treat Your Spouse Like an Internal Customer."

If Total Quality calls for "re-skilling" the worker in an "enriched" job environment, technological developments have long been de-skilling parents at home. Over the centuries, store-bought goods have replaced homespun cloth, homemade soap and homebaked foods. Day care for children, retirement homes for the elderly, even psychotherapy are, in a way, commercial substitutes for jobs that a mother once did at home. Even family-generated entertainment has, to some extent, been replaced by television, video games and the VCR. I sometimes watched Amerco families sitting together after their dinners, mute but cozy, watching sitcoms in which television mothers, fathers and children related in an animated way to one another while the viewing family engaged in relational loafing.

The one "skill" still required of family members is the hardest one of all—the emotional work of forging, deepening or repairing family relationships. It takes time to develop this skill, and even then things can go awry. Family ties are complicated. People get hurt. Yet as broken homes become more common—and as the sense of belonging to a geographical community grows less and less secure in an age of mobility—the corporate world has created a sense of "neighborhood," of "feminine culture," of family at work. Life at work can be insecure; the company can fire workers. But workers aren't so secure at home, either. Many employees have been working for Amerco for 20 years but are on their second or third marriages or relationships. The shifting balance between these two "divorce rates" may be the most powerful reason why tired parents flee a world of unresolved quarrels and unwashed laundry for the orderliness, harmony and managed cheer of work. People are getting their "pink slips" at home.

Amerco workers have not only turned their offices into "home" and their homes into workplaces; many have also begun to "Taylorize" time at home, where families are succumbing to a cult of efficiency previously associated mainly with the office and factory. Meanwhile, work time, with its ever longer hours, has become more hospitable to sociability—periods of talking with friends on E-mail, patching up quarrels, gossiping. Within the long workday of many Amerco employees are great hidden pockets of inefficiency while, in the far smaller number of waking weekday hours at home, they are, despite themselves, forced to act increasingly time-conscious and efficient.

The Averys respond to their time bind at home by trying to value and protect "quality time." A concept unknown to their parents and grandparents, "quality time" has become a powerful symbol of the struggle against the growing pressures at home. It reflects the extent to which modern parents feel the flow of time to be running against them. The premise behind "quality time" is that the time we devote to relationships can somehow be separated from ordinary time. Relationships go on during quantity time, of course, but then we are only passively, not actively, whole-heartedly, specializing in our emotional ties. We aren't "on." Quality time at home becomes like an office appointment. You don't want to be caught "goofing off around the water cooler" when you are "at work."

Quality time holds out the hope that scheduling intense periods of togetherness can compensate for an overall loss of time in such a way that a relationship will suffer no loss of quality. But this is just another way of transferring the cult of efficiency from office to home. We must now get our relationships in good repair in less time. Instead of nine hours a day with a child, we declare ourselves capable of getting "the same result" with one intensely focused hour.

Parents now more commonly speak of time as if it is a threatened form of personal capital they have no choice but to manage and invest. What's new here is the spread into the home of a financial manager's attitude toward time. Working parents at Amerco owe what they think of as time debts at home. This is because they are, in a sense, inadvertently "Taylorizing" the house—speeding up the pace of home life as Taylor once tried to "scientifically" speed up the pace of factory life.

Advertisers of products aimed at women have recognized that this new reality provides an opportunity to sell products, and have turned the very pressure that threatens to explode the home into a positive attribute. Take, for example, an ad promoting Instant Quaker Oatmeal: it shows a smiling mother ready for the office in her square-shouldered suit, hugging her happy son. A caption reads: "Nicky is a very picky eater. With Instant Quaker Oatmeal, I can give him a terrific hot breakfast in just 90 seconds. And I don't have to spend any time coaxing him to eat it!" Here, the modern mother seems to have absorbed the lessons of Frederick Taylor as she presses for efficiency at home because she is in a hurry to get to work.

Part of modern parenthood seems to include coping with the resistance of real children who are not so eager to get their cereal so fast. Some parents try desperately not to appease their children with special gifts or smooth-talking promises about the future. But when time is scarce, even the best parents find themselves passing a system-wide familial speed-up along to the most vulnerable workers on the line. Parents are then obliged to try to control the damage done by a reversal of worlds. They monitor mealtime, homework time, bedtime, trying to cut out "wasted" time.

In response, children often protest the pace, the deadlines, the grand irrationality of "efficient" family life. Children dawdle. They refuse to leave places when it's time to leave. They insist on leaving places when it's not time to leave. Surely, this is part of the usual stop-and-go of childhood itself, but perhaps, too, it is the plea of children for more family time, and more control over what time there is. This only adds to the feeling that life at home has become hard work.

Instead of trying to arrange shorter or more flexible work schedules, Amerco parents often avoid confronting the reality of the time bind. Some minimize their ideas about how much care a child, a partner or they themselves "really need." They make do with less time, less attention, less understanding and less support at home than they once imagined possible. They *emotionally downsize* life. In essence, they deny the needs of family members, and they themselves become emotional ascetics. If they once "needed" time with each other, they are now increasingly "fine" without it.

Another way that working parents try to evade the time bind is to buy themselves out of it—an approach that puts women in particular at the heart of a contradiction. Like men, women absorb the work-family speed-up far more than they resist it; but unlike men, they still shoulder most of the workload at home. And women still represent in people's minds the heart and soul of family life. They're the ones—especially women of the urban middle and upper-middle classes—who feel most acutely the need to save time, who are the most tempted by the new "time saving" goods and services—and who wind up feeling the most guilty about it. For example, Playgroup Connections, a Washington-area business started by a former executive recruiter, matches playmates to one another. One mother hired the service to find her child a French-speaking playmate.

In several cities, children home alone can call a number for "Grandma, Please!" and reach an adult who has the time to talk with them, sing to them or help them with their homework. An ad for Kindercare Learning Centers, a for-profit child-care chain, pitches its appeal this way: "You want your child to be active, tolerant, smart, loved, emotionally stable, self-aware, artistic and get a two-hour nap. Anything else?" It goes on to note that Kindercare accepts children 6 weeks to 12 years old and provides a number to call for the Kindercare nearest you. Another typical service organizes children's birthday parties, making out invitations ("sure hope you can come") and providing party favors, entertainment, a decorated cake and balloons. Creative Memories is a service that puts ancestral photos into family albums for you.

An overwhelming majority of the working mothers I spoke with recoiled from the idea of buying themselves out of parental duties. A bought birthday party was "too impersonal," a 90-second breakfast "too fast." Yet a surprising amount of lunchtime conversation between female friends at Amerco was devoted to expressing complex, conflicting feelings about the lure of trading time for one service or another. The temptation to order flash-frozen dinners or to call a local number for a homework helper did not come up because such services had not yet appeared at Spotted Deer Child-Care Center. But many women dwelled on the question of how to decide where a mother's job began and ended, especially with regard to baby sitters and television. One mother said to another in the break-room of an Amerco plant: "Damon doesn't settle down until 10 at night, so he hates me to wake him up in the morning and I hate to do it. He's cranky. He pulls the covers up. I put on cartoons. That way, I can dress him and he doesn't object. I don't like to use TV that way. It's like a drug. But I do it."

The other mother countered. "Well, Todd is up before we are, so that's not a problem. It's after dinner, when I feel like watching a little television, that I feel guilty, because he gets too much TV at the sitter's."

As task after task falls into the realm of timesaving goods and services, questions arise about the moral meanings attached to doing or not doing such tasks. Is it being a good mother to bake a child's birthday cake (alone or together with one's partner)? Or can we gratefully save time by ordering it, and be good mothers by planning the party? Can we save more time by hiring a planning service, and be good mothers simply by watching our children have a good time? "Wouldn't that be nice!" one Amerco mother exclaimed. As the idea of the "good mother" retreats before the pressures of work and the expansion of motherly services, mothers are in fact continually reinventing themselves.

The final way working parents tried to evade the time bind was to develop what I call "potential selves." The potential selves that I discovered in my Amerco interviews were fantasy creations of time-poor parents who dreamed of living as time millionaires.

One man, a gifted 55-year-old engineer in research and development at Amerco, told how he had dreamed of taking his daughters on a camping trip in the Sierra Mountains: "I bought all the gear three years ago when they were 5 and 7, the tent, the sleeping bags, the air mattresses, the backpacks, the ponchos. I got a map of the area. I even got the freeze-dried food. Since then the kids and I have talked about it a lot, and gone over what we're going to do. They've been on me to do it for a long time. I feel bad about it. I keep putting it off, but we'll do it, I just don't know when."

Banished to garages and attics of many Amerco workers were expensive electric saws, cameras, skis and musical instruments, all bought with wages it took time to earn. These items were to their owners what Cassie's fudge bar was to her—a substitute for time, a talisman, a reminder of the potential self.

Obviously, not everyone, not even a majority of Americans, is making a home out of work and a workplace out of home. But in the working world, it is a growing reality, and one we need to face. Increasing numbers of women are discovering a great male secret—that work can be an escape from the pressures of home, pressures that the changing nature of work itself are only intensifying. Neither men nor women are going to take up "family friendly" policies, whether corporate or governmental, as long as the current realities of work and home remain as they are. For a substantial number of time-bound parents, the stripped-down home and the neighborhood devoid of community are simply losing out to the pull of the workplace.

There are several broader, historical causes of this reversal of realms. The last 30 years have witnessed the rapid rise of women in the workplace. At the same time, job mobility has taken families farther from relatives who might lend a hand, and made it harder to make close friends of neighbors who could help out. Moreover, as women have acquired more education and have joined men at work, they have absorbed the views of an older, male-oriented work world, its views of a "real career," far more than men have taken up their share of the work at home. One reason women have changed more than men is that the world of "male" work seems more honorable and valuable than the "female" world of home and children.

So where do we go from here? There is surely no going back to the mythical 1950's family that confined women to the home. Most women don't wish to return to a full-time role at home—and couldn't afford it even if they did. But equally troubling is a workaholic culture that strands both men and women outside the home.

For a while now, scholars on work-family issues have pointed to Sweden, Norway and Denmark as better models of work-family balance. Today, for example, almost all Swedish fathers take two paid weeks off from work at the birth of their children, and about half of fathers and most mothers take additional "parental leave" during the child's first or second year. Research shows that men who take family leave when their children are very young are more likely to be involved with their children as they grow older. When I mentioned this Swedish record of paternity leave to a focus group of American male managers, one of them replied, "Right, we've already heard about Sweden." To this executive, paternity leave was a good idea not for the U.S. today, but for some "potential society" in another place and time.

Meanwhile, children are paying the price. In her book "When the Bough Breaks: The Cost of Neglecting Our Children," the economist Sylvia Hewlett claims that "compared with the previous generation, young people today are more likely to "underperform at school; commit suicide; need psychiatric help; suffer a severe eating disorder; bear a child out of wedlock; take drugs, be the victim of a violent crime." But we needn't dwell on sledgehammer problems like heroin or suicide to realize that children like those at Spotted Deer need more of our time. If other advanced nations with two-job families can give children the time they need, why can't we?

8

Families with School-Age Children

Unequal Childhoods: Class, Race, and Family Life

Annette Lareau

There are many studies that tell us of the detrimental effects of poverty on children's lives, but it is less clear what the mechanisms are for the transmission of class advantage across generations.

I suggest that social class has an important impact on the cultural logic of childrearing (see Lareau 2003 for details). Middle-class parents, both white *and* black, appear to follow a cultural logic of childrearing that I call "concerted cultivation." They enroll their children in numerous age-specific organized activities that come to dominate family life and create enormous labor, particularly for mothers. Parents see these activities as transmitting important life skills to children. Middle-class parents also stress language use and the development of reasoning. Talking plays a crucial role in the disciplinary strategies of middle-class parents. This "cultivation" approach results in a frenetic pace for parents, creates a cult of individualism within the family, and emphasizes children's performance.

Among white and black working-class and poor families, childrearing strategies emphasize the "accomplishment of natural growth." These parents believe that as long as they provide love, food, and safety, their children will grow and thrive. They do not focus on developing the special talents of their individual children. Working-class and poor children have more free time and deeper and richer ties within their extended families than the middle-class children.

Reprinted from *Inequality Reader*, edited by David Grusky (2006), Perseus Books Group.

Some participate in organized activities, but they do so for different reasons than their middle-class counterparts. Working-class and poor parents issue many more directives to their children and, in some households, place more emphasis on physical discipline than do middle-class parents.

The pattern of concerted cultivation, with its stress on individual repertoires of activities, reasoning, and questioning, encourages an *emerging sense of entitlement* in children. Of course, not all parents and children are equally assertive, but the pattern of questioning and intervening among the white and black middle-class parents in the study contrasts sharply with the definitions of how to be helpful and effective observed among the white and black working-class and poor families. The pattern of the accomplishment of natural growth, with its emphasis on child-initiated play, autonomy from adults, and directives, encourages an *emerging sense of constraint* (Table 1). Members of these families, adults as well as children, tend to be deferential and outwardly accepting (with sporadic moments of resistance) in their interactions with professionals such as doctors and educators. At the same time, however, compared to their middle-class counterparts, the white and black working-class and poor families are more distrustful of professionals in institutions. These are differences with long-term consequences. In a historical moment where the dominant society privileges active, informed, assertive clients of health and educational services, the various strategies employed by children and parents are not equally valuable. In sum, differences in family life lie not only in the advantages parents are able to obtain for their children, but also in the skills being transmitted to children for negotiating their own life paths.

Table 1

Argument of Unequal Childhoods: Class Differences in Childrearing

| | Childrearing Approach | |
	Concerted Cultivation	Accomplishment of Natural Growth
Key elements	Parent actively fosters and assesses child's talents, opinions, and skills	Parent cares for child and allows child to grow
Organization of daily life	*multiple child leisure activities are orchestrated by adults	*child "hangs out" particularly with kin
Language use	*reasoning/directives *child contestation of adult statements *extended negotiations between parents and child	*directives *rare for child to question or challenge adults *general acceptance by child of directives
Interventions in institutions	*criticisms and interventions on behalf of child *training of child to take on this role	*dependence on institutions *sense of powerlessness and frustrations *conflict between childrearing practices at home and at school
Consequences	Emerging sense of entitlement on the part of the child	Emerging sense of constraint on the part of the child

Methodology

Study Participants

The study is based on interviews and observations of children eight to ten years of age and their families. A team of graduate research assistants and I collected the data. The first phase involved observations in third-grade public school classrooms, mainly in a metropolitan area in the Northeast. The schools serve neighborhoods in a white suburban area and two urban locales—one a white working-class neighborhood and the other a nearby poor black neighborhood. About one-half of the children are white and about one-half are black. One child is interracial. The research assistants and I carried out individual interviews (averaging two hours each) with all of the mothers and most of the fathers (or guardians) of 88 children, for a total of 137 interviews. We also observed children as they took part in organized activities in the communities surrounding the schools. The most intensive part of the research, however, involved home observations of 12 children and their families. Nine of the 12 families came from the classrooms I observed, but the boy and girl from the two black middle-class families and the boy from the poor white family came from other sites. Most observations and interviews took place between 1993 and 1995, but interviews were done as early as 1990 and as late as 1997. This chapter focuses primarily on the findings from the observations of these 12 families since the key themes discussed here surfaced during this part of the fieldwork. I do include some information from the larger study to provide a context for understanding the family observations. All names are pseudonyms.

Intensive Family Observations

The research assistants and I took turns visiting the participating families daily, for a total of about 20 visits in each home, often in the space of one month. The observations were not limited to the home. Fieldworkers followed children and parents as they took part in school activities, church services and events, organized play, kin visits, and medical appointments. Most field observations lasted about three hours; sometimes, depending on the event (e.g., an out-of-town funeral, a special extended family event, or a long shopping trip), they lasted much longer. In most cases, there was one overnight visit. We often carried tape recorders with us and used the audiotapes for reference in writing up field notes. Families were paid $350, usually at the end of the visits, for their participation.

A Note on Class

My purpose in undertaking the field observations was to develop an *intensive*, realistic portrait of family life. Although I deliberately focused on only 12 families, I wanted to compare children across gender and race lines. Adopting the fine-grained differentiation of categories characteristic of current neo-Marxist and neo-Weberian empirical studies was not tenable. My choice of class categories was further limited by the school populations at the sites I had selected. Very few of the students were children of employers or of self-employed workers. I decided to concentrate exclusively on those whose parents were employees. Various criteria have been proposed to differentiate within this heterogeneous group, but authority in the workplace and "credential barriers" are the two most commonly used. I assigned the families in the study to a working-class or middle-class category based on discussions with each of the employed adults. They provided extensive information about the work they did, the nature of the organization that employed them, and their educational credentials. I added a third category: families not involved in the labor market (a population traditionally excluded from social class groupings) because in the first school I studied, a substantial number of children were from households supported by public assistance. To ignore them would have restricted the scope of the study arbitrarily. The final sub-sample contained 4 middle-class, 4 working-class, and 4 poor families.

Children's Time Use

In our interviews and observations of white and black middle-class children, it was striking how busy they were with organized activities. Indeed, one of the hallmarks of middle-class children's daily lives is a set of adult-run organized activities. Many children have three and four activities per week. In some families, every few days activities conflict, particularly when one season is ending and one is beginning. For example in the white middle-class family of the Tallingers, Garrett is on multiple soccer teams—the "A" traveling team of the private Forest soccer club and the Intercounty soccer team—he also has swim lessons, saxophone lessons at school, private piano lessons at home, and baseball and basketball. These organized activities provided a framework for children's lives; other activities were sandwiched between them.

These activities create labor for parents. Indeed, the impact of children's activities takes its toll on parents' patience as well as their time. For example, on a June afternoon at the beginning of summer vacation, in a white-middle-class family, Mr. Tallinger comes home from work to take Garrett to his soccer game. Garrett is not ready to go, and his lackadaisical approach to getting ready irks his father:

> Don says, "Get your soccer stuff—you're going to a soccer game!" Garrett comes into the den with white short leggings on underneath a long green soccer shirt; he's number 16. He sits on an armchair catty-corner from the television and languidly watches the World Cup game. He slowly, abstractedly, pulls on shin guards, then long socks. His eyes are riveted to the TV screen. Don comes in: "Go get your other stuff." Garrett says he can't find his shorts. Don: "Did you look in your drawer?" Garrett nods. . . . He gets up to look for his shorts, comes back into the den a few minutes later. I ask, "Any luck yet?" Garrett shakes his head. Don is rustling around elsewhere in the house. Don comes in, says to Garrett, "Well, Garrett, aren't you wearing shoes?" (Don leaves and returns a short time later): "Garrett, we HAVE to go! Move! We're late!" He says this shortly, abruptly. He comes back in a minute and drops Garrett's shiny green shorts on his lap without a word.

This pressured search for a pair of shiny green soccer shorts is a typical event in the Tallinger household. Also typical is the solution—a parent ultimately finds the missing object, while continuing to prod the child to hurry. The fact that today's frenzied schedule will be matched or exceeded by the next day's is also par:

> Don: (describing their day on Saturday) Tomorrow is really nuts. We have a soccer game, then a baseball game, then another soccer game.

This steady schedule of activity—that none of the middle-class parents reported having when they were a similar age—was not universal. Indeed, while we searched for a middle-class child who did not have a single organized activity we could not find one, but in working-class and poor homes, organized activities were much less common and there were many children who did not have any. Many children "hung out." Television and video games are a major source of entertainment but outdoor play can trump either of these. No advanced planning, no telephone calls, no consultations between mothers, no drop-offs or pickups—no particular effort at all—is required to launch an activity. For instance, one afternoon, in a black working-class family, Shannon (in 7th grade) and Tyrec (in 4th grade) walk out their front door to the curb of the small, narrow street their house faces. Shannon begins playing a game with a ball; she soon has company:

> (Two boys from the neighborhood walk up.) Shannon is throwing the small ball against the side of the row house. Tyrec joins in the game with her. As they throw the ball against the wall, they say things they must do with the ball. It went something like this: Johnny Crow wanted to know.... (bounces ball against the wall), touch your knee (bounce), touch your toe (bounce), touch the ground (bounce), under the knee (bounce), turn around (bounce). Shannon and Tyrec played about four rounds.

Unexpected events produce hilarity:

> At one point Shannon accidentally threw the ball and it bounced off of Tyrec's head. All the kids laughed; then Tyrec, who had the ball, went chasing after Shannon. It was a close, fun moment—lots of laughter, eye contact, giggling, chasing.

Soon a different game evolves. Tyrec is on restriction. He is supposed to remain inside the house all day. So, when he thinks he has taught a glimpse of his mom returning home from work, he dashes inside. He reappears as soon as he realizes that it was a false alarm. The neighborhood children begin an informal game of baiting him:

> The kids keep teasing Tyrec that his mom's coming—which sends him scurrying just inside the door, peering out of the screen door. This game is enacted about six times. Tyrec also chases Shannon around the street, trying to get the ball from her. A few times Shannon tells Tyrec that he'd better "get inside"; he ignores her. Then, at 6:50 [P.M.] Ken (a friend of Tyrec's) says, "There's your mom!" Tyrec scoots inside, then, says, "Oh, man. You were serious this time."

Informal, impromptu outdoor play is common in Tyrec's neighborhood. A group of boys approximately his age, regularly numbering four or five but sometimes reaching as many as ten, play ball games together on the street, walk to the store to get treats, watch television at each other's homes, and generally hang out together.

Language Use

In addition to differences by social class in time use, we also observed differences in language use in the home. As others have noted (Bernstein, 1971; Heath, 1983) middle-class parents used more reasoning in their speech with children while working-class and poor parents used more directives. For example, in observations of the African American home of Alex Williams, whose father was a trial lawyer and mother was a high level corporate executive, we found that the Williamses and other middle-class parents use language frequently, pleasurably, and instrumentally. Their children do likewise. For example, one January evening, Alexander is stumped by a homework assignment to write five riddles. He sits at the dinner table in the kitchen with his mother and a fieldworker. Mr. Williams is at the sink, washing the dinner dishes. He has his back to the group at the dinner table. Without turning around, he says to Alex, "Why don't you go upstairs to the third floor and get one those books and see if there is a riddle in there?"

> Alex [says] smiling, "Yeah. That's a good idea! I'll go upstairs and copy one from out of the book." Terry turns around with a dish in hand, "That was a joke—not a valid suggestion. That is not an option." He smiled as he turned back around to the sink. Christina says, looking at Alex: "There is a word for that you know, plagiarism." Terry says (not turning around), "Someone can sue you for plagiarizing. Did you know that?" Alex: "That's only if it is copyrighted." They all begin talking at once.

Here we see Alex cheerfully (though gently) goading his father by pretending to misunderstand the verbal instruction to consult a book for help. Mr. Williams dutifully rises to the bait. Ms. Williams reshapes this movement of lightheartedness by introducing a new word into Alexander's vocabulary. Mr. Williams goes one step further by connecting the new word to a legal consequence. Alex upstages them both. He demonstrates that he is already familiar with the general idea of plagiarism and that he understands the concept of copyright, as well.

In marked contrast to working-class and poor parents, however, even when the Williamses issue directives, they often include explanations for their orders. Here, Ms. Williams is reminding her son to pay attention to his teacher:

> I want you to play close attention to Mrs. Scott when you are developing your film. Those chemicals are very dangerous. Don't play around in the classroom. You could get that stuff in someone's eye. And if you swallow it, you could die.

Alex chooses to ignore the directive in favor of instructing his misinformed mother:

> Alex corrects her, "Mrs. Scott told us that we wouldn't die if we swallowed it. But we would get very sick and would have to get our stomach pumped." Christina does not follow the argument any further. She simply reiterates that he should be careful.

Possibly because the issue is safety, Ms. Williams does not encourage Alex to elaborate here, as she would be likely to do if the topic were less charged. Instead, she restates her directive and thus underscores her expectation that Alex will do as she asks.

Although Mr. and Ms. Williams disagreed on elements of how training in race relations should be implemented, they both recognized that their racial and ethnic identity profoundly shaped their and their son's everyday experiences. They were well aware of the potential for Alexander to be exposed to racial injustice, and they went to great lengths to try to protect their son from racial insults and other forms of discrimination. Nevertheless, race did not appear to shape the dominant cultural logic of childrearing in Alexander's family or in other families in the study. All of the middle-class families engaged in extensive reasoning with their children, asking questions, probing assertions, and listening to answers. Similar patterns appeared in interviews and observations with other African American middle-class families.

A different pattern appeared in working-class and poor homes where there was simply less verbal speech than we observed in middle-class homes. There was also less speech between parents and children, a finding noted by other observational studies (Hart and Risley, 1995). Moreover, interspersed with intermittent talk are adult-issued directives. Children are told to do certain things (e.g., shower, take out the garbage) and not to do others (e.g., curse, talk back). In an African American home of a family living on public assistance in public housing, Ms. McAllister uses one-word directives to coordinate the use of the single bathroom. There are almost always at least four children in the apartment and often seven, plus Ms. McAllister and other adults. Ms. McAllister sends the children to wash up by pointing to a child, saying, "Bathroom," and handing him or her a washcloth. Wordlessly, the designated child gets up and goes to the bathroom to take a shower.

Children usually do what adults ask of them. We did not observe whining or protests, even when adults assign time-consuming tasks, such as the hour-long process of hair-braiding Lori McAllister is told to do for the four-year-old daughter of Aunt Dara's friend Charmaine:

> Someone tells Lori, "Go do [Tyneshia's] hair for camp." Without saying anything, Lori gets up and goes inside and takes the little girl with her. They head for the couch near the television; Lori sits on the couch and the girl sits on the floor. [Tyneshia] sits quietly for about an hour, with her head tilted, while Lori carefully does a multitude of braids.

Lori's silent obedience is typical. Generally, children perform requests without comment. For example, at dinner one night, after Harold McAllister complains he doesn't like spinach, his mother directs him to finish it anyway:

> Mom yells (loudly) at him to eat: "EAT! FINISH THE SPINACH!" (No response. Harold is at the table, dawdling.) Guion and Runako and Alexis finish eating and leave. I finish with Harold; he eats his spinach. He leaves all his yams.

The verbal world of Harold McAllister and other poor and working-class children offers some important advantages as well as costs. Compared to middle-class children we observed, Harold is more respectful towards adults in his family. In this setting, there are clear boundaries between adults and children. Adults feel comfortable issuing directives to children, which children comply with immediately. Some of the directives that adults issue center on obligations of children to others in the family ("don't beat on Guion" or "go do [her] hair for camp"). One consequence of this is that Harold, despite occasional tiffs, is much nicer to his sister (and his cousins) than the siblings we observed in middle-class homes. The use of directives and the pattern of silent compliance are not universal in Harold's life. In his interactions with peers, for example on the basketball "court," Harold's verbal displays are distinctively different than inside the household, with elaborated and embellished discourse. Nevertheless, there is a striking difference in linguistic interaction between adults and children in poor and working-class families when compared to that observed in the home of Alexander Williams. Ms. McAllister has the benefit of being able to issue directives without having to justify their decisions at every moment. This can make childrearing somewhat less tiring.

Another advantage is that Harold has more autonomy than middle-class children in making important decisions in daily life. As a child, he controls his leisure schedule. His basketball games are impromptu and allow him to develop important skills and talents. He is resourceful. He appears less exhausted than ten-year-old Alexander. In addition, he has important social competencies, including his deftness in negotiating the "code of the street."[1] His mother has stressed these skills in her upbringing, as she impresses upon her children the importance of "not paying no mind" to others, including drunks and drug dealers who hang out in the neighborhoods which Harold and Alexis negotiate.

Still, in the world of schools, health care facilities, and other institutional settings, these valuable skills do not translate into the same advantages as the reasoning skills emphasized in the home of Alexander Williams and other middle-class children. Compared to Alexander Williams, Harold does not gain the development of a large vocabulary, an increase of his knowledge of science and politics, a set of tools to customize situations outside the home to maximize his advantage, and instruction in how to defend his argument with evidence. His knowledge of words, which might appear, for example, on future SAT tests, is not continually stressed at home.

In these areas, the lack of advantage is *not* connected to the intrinsic value of the McAllister family life or the use of directives at home. Indeed, one can argue raising children who are polite and respectful children and do not whine, needle, or badger their parents is a highly laudable childrearing goal. Deep and abiding ties with kinship groups are also, one might further argue, important. Rather, it is the specific ways that institutions function that ends up conveying advantages to middle-class children. In their standards, these institutions also permit, and even demand, active parent involvement. In this way as well, middle-class children often gain an advantage.

Intervention in Institutions

Children do not live their lives inside of the home. Instead, they are legally required to go to school, they go to the doctor, and many are involved in church and other adult-organized activities. In children's institutional lives, we found differences by social class in how mothers monitored children's institutional experiences. While in working-class and poor families children are granted autonomy to make their own way in organizations, in the middle-class homes, most aspects of the children's lives are subject to their mother's *ongoing* scrutiny.

For example in an African American middle-class home, where both parents are college graduates and Ms. Marshall is a computer worker and her husband a civil servant, their two daughters have a hectic schedule of organized activities including gymnastics for Stacey and basketball for Fern. When Ms. Marshall becomes aware of a problem, she moves quickly, drawing on her work and professional skills and experiences. She displays tremendous assertiveness, doggedness, and, in some cases, effectiveness in pressing institutions to recognize her daughters' individualized needs. Stacey's mother's proactive stance reflects her belief that she has a duty to intervene in situations where she perceives that her daughter's needs are not being met. This perceived responsibility applies across all areas of her children's lives. She is no more (or less) diligent with regard to Stacey and Fern's leisure activities than she is with regard to their experiences in school or church or the doctor's office. This is clear in the way she handles Stacey's transition from her township gymnastics classes to the private classes at an elite private gymnastic program at Wright's.

Ms. Marshall describes Stacey's first session at the club as rocky:

> The girls were not warm. And these were little . . . eight and nine year old kids. You know, they weren't welcoming her the first night. It was kinda like eyeing each other, to see, you know, "Can you do this? Can you do that?"

More importantly, Ms. Marshall reported that the instructor is brusque, critical and not friendly toward Stacey. Ms. Marshall cannot hear what was being said, but she could see the interactions through a window. A key problem is that because her previous instructor had not used the professional jargon for gymnastic moves, Stacey does not know these terms. When the class ends and she walks out, she is visibly upset. Her mother's reaction is a common one among middle-class parents: She does not remind her daughter that in life one has to adjust, that she will need to work even harder, or that there is nothing to be done. Instead, Ms. Marshall focuses on Tina, the instructor, as the source of the problem:

> We sat in the car for a minute and I said, "Look, Stac," I said. She said, "I-I," and she started crying. I said, "You wait here." The instructor had come to the door, Tina. So I went to her and I said, "Look." I said, "Is there a problem?" She said, "Aww . . . she'll be fine. She just needs to work on certain things." Blah-blah-blah. And I said, "She's really upset. She said you-you-you [were] pretty much correcting just about everything." And [Tina] said, "Well, she's got—she's gotta learn the terminology."

Ms. Marshall acknowledges that Stacey isn't familiar with specialized and technical gymnastics terms. Nonetheless, she continues to defend her daughter:

> I do remember, I said to her, I said, "Look, maybe it's not all the student." You know, I just left it like that. That, you know, sometimes teaching, learning and teaching, is a two-way proposition as far as I'm concerned. And sometimes teachers have to learn how to, you know, meet the needs of the kid. Her style, her immediate style was not accommodating to—to Stacey.

Here Ms. Marshall is asserting the legitimacy of an individualized approach to instruction. She frames her opening remark as a question ("Is there a problem?"). Her purpose, however, is to alert the instructor to the negative impact she has had on Stacey ("She's really upset."). Although her criticism is indirect ("Maybe it's not all the student . . ."), Ms. Marshall makes it clear that she expects her daughter to be treated differently in the future. In this case, Stacey does not hear what her mother says, but she knows that her wishes and feelings are being transmitted to the instructor in a way that she could not do herself.

Although parents were equally concerned about their children's happiness, in working-class and poor homes we observed different patterns of oversight for children's institutional activities. For example in the white working-class home of Wendy Driver. Wendy's mother does not nurture her daughter's language development like Alexander Williams' mother does her son's. She does not attempt to draw Wendy out or follow up on new information when Wendy introduces the term mortal sin while the family is sitting around watching television. But, just like Ms. Williams, Ms. Driver cares very much about her child and just like middle-class parents she wants to help her daughter succeed. Ms. Driver keeps a close and careful eye on her Wendy's schooling. She knows that Wendy is having problems in school. Ms. Driver immediately signs and returns each form Wendy brings home from school and reminds her to turn the papers in to her teacher.

Wendy is "being tested" as part of an ongoing effort to determine why she has difficulties with spelling, reading, and related language-based activities. Her mother welcomes these official efforts but she did not request them. Unlike the middle-class mothers we observed, who asked teachers for detailed information about every aspect of their children's classroom performance and relentlessly pursued information and assessments outside of school as well, Ms. Driver seems content with only a vague notion of her daughter's learning disabilities. This attitude contrasts starkly with that of Stacey Marshall's mother, for example. In discussing Stacey's classroom experiences with fieldworkers, Ms. Marshall routinely described her daughter's academic strengths and weaknesses in detail. Ms. Driver never mentions that Wendy is doing grade-level work in math but is reading at a level a full three years below her grade. Her description is vague:

> She's having problems. . . . They had a special teacher come in and see if they could find out what the problem is. She has a reading problem, but they haven't put their finger on it yet, so she's been through all kinds of special teachers and testing and everything. She goes to Special Ed, I think it's two classes a day . . . I'm not one hundred percent sure—for her reading. It's very difficult for her to read what's on paper. But then—she can remember things. But not everything. It's like she has a puzzle up there. And we've tried, well, they've tried a lot of things. They just haven't put their finger on it yet.

Wendy's teachers uniformly praise her mother as "supportive" and describe her as "very loving," but they are disappointed in Ms. Driver's failure to take a more active, interventionist role in Wendy's education, especially given the formidable nature of her daughter's learning problems. From Ms. Driver's perspective, however, being actively supportive means doing whatever the teachers tell her to do.

Whatever they would suggest, I would do. They suggested she go to the eye doctor, so I did that. And they checked her and said there was nothing wrong there.

Similarly, she monitors Wendy's homework and supports her efforts to read:

We listen to her read. We help her with her homework. So she has more attention here in a smaller household than it was when I lived with my parents. So, we're trying to help her out more, which I think is helping. And with the two [special education] classes a day at the school, instead of one like last year, she's learning a lot from that. So, we're just hoping it takes time and that she'll just snap out of it.

But Ms. Driver clearly does not have an *independent* understanding of the nature or degree of Wendy's limitations, perhaps because she is unfamiliar with the kind of terms the educators use to describe her daughter's needs (e.g., a limited "sight vocabulary," underdeveloped "language arts skills"). Perhaps, too, her confidence in the school staff makes it easier for her to leave "the details" to them: "Ms. Morton, she's great. She's worked with us for different testing and stuff." Ms. Driver depends on the school staff's expertise to assess the situation and then share the information with her:

I think they just want to keep it in the school till now. And when they get to a point where they can't figure out what it is, and then I guess they'll send me somewhere else. . . .

Her mother is not alarmed, because "the school" has told her not to worry about Wendy's grades:

Her report card—as long as it's not spelling and reading—spelling and reading are like F's. And they keep telling me not to worry, because she's in the Special Ed class. But besides that, she does good. I have no behavior problems with her at all.

Ms. Driver wants the best possible outcome for her daughter and she does not know how to achieve that goal without relying heavily on Wendy's teachers:

I wouldn't even know where to start going. On the radio there was something for children having problems reading and this and that, call. And I suggested it to a couple different people, and they were like, wait a second, it's only to get you there and you'll end up paying an arm and a leg. So I said to my mom, "No, I'm going to wait until the first report card and go up and talk to them up there."

Thus, in looking for the source of Ms. Driver's deference toward educators, the answers don't seem to lie in her having either a shy personality or underdeveloped mothering skills. To understand why Wendy's mother is accepting where Stacey Marshall's mother would be aggressive, it is more useful to focus on social class position, both in terms of how class shapes worldviews and how class affects economic and educational resources. Ms. Driver understands her role in her daughter's education as involving a different set of responsibilities from those perceived by middle-class mothers. She responds to contacts from the school—such as invitations to the two annual parent-teacher conferences—but she does not initiate them. She views Wendy's school life as a separate realm, and one in which she, as a parent, is only an infrequent visitor. Ms. Driver expects that the teachers will teach and her daughter will learn and that, under normal circumstances, neither requires any additional help from her as a parent. If problems arise, she presumes that Wendy will tell her; or, if the issue is serious, the school will contact her. But what Ms. Driver fails to understand, is that the educators expect her to take on a pattern of "concerted cultivation" where she actively monitors and intervenes in her child's schooling. The teachers asked for a complicated mixture of deference and engagement from parents; they were disappointed when they did not get it.

Conclusions

I have stressed how social class dynamics are woven into the texture and rhythm of children and parents' daily lives. Class position influences critical aspects of family life: time use, language use, and kin ties. Working-class and middle-class mothers may express beliefs that reflect a similar notion of "intensive mothering," but their behavior is quite different. For that reason, I have described sets of paired beliefs and actions as a "cultural logic" of childrearing. When children and parents move outside the home into the world of social institutions, they find that these cultural practices are not given equal value. There are signs that middle-class children benefit, in ways that are invisible to them and to their parents, from the degree of similarity between the cultural repertoires in the home and those standards adopted by institutions.

Note

1. Elijah Anderson, *Code of the Street*, New York: W. W. Norton (1999).

Bibliography

Anderson, Elijah. 1999. *Code of the Street*. New York, NY: W. W. Norton.

Bernstein, Basil. 1971. *Class, Codes, and Control: Theoretical Studies Towards a Sociology of Language*. New York, NY: Schocken.

Hart, Betty and Todd R. Risley. 1995. *Meaningful Differences in the Everyday Experiences of Young American Children*. New Haven: Yale University Press.

Heath, Shirley Brice. 1983. *Ways with Words: Language, Life, and Work in Communities and Classrooms*. Cambridge: Cambridge University Press.

Lareau, Annette. 2003. *Unequal Childhoods: Class, Race, and Family Life*. Berkeley, CA: University of California Press.

9

Families with Teenagers

Transformation of the Family System During Adolescence

Nydia Garcia Preto

The adaptations in family structure and organization that are required to handle the tasks of adolescence are so basic that the family itself is transformed from a unit that protects and nurtures young children to one that is a preparation center for the adolescent's entrance into the world of adult responsibilities and commitments. This family metamorphosis involves profound shifts in relationship patterns across the generations, and while it may be signaled initially by the adolescent's physical maturity, it often parallels and coincides with changes in parents as they enter midlife and with major transformations faced by grandparents facing old age. There are significant differences in the ways families adapt to these changes depending on the meaning that the family gives to adolescence as a life stage and to adolescent roles and behaviors. Cultural factors and socioeconomic forces greatly affect how families define this stage of development.

As the twenty-first century approaches, families in the United States are more than ever challenged by the risks of living in an increasingly endangered environment and in a society in which, largely for economic reasons, parents choose or are forced to work longer and longer hours, limiting the time they can spend at home with their children. Diminished connections to extended family and community have left parents struggling alone and more dependent on external systems for teaching children and for setting limits on them. At the same time, teenagers are turning more and more to their peers for emotional support and to the pop culture promoted by the media for values and ideas about life. As a result, the family's function as an emotional support system is threatened.

Taken from: *The Expanded Family Life Cycle: Individual, Family, and Social Perspectives*, Third Edition, edited by Betty Carter and Monica McGoldrick.

The threat is greater for families that are economically disadvantaged and living in poor urban and rural neighborhoods.

This chapter focuses on the overall transformation that families experience as they try to master the tasks of adolescence, keeping in mind that perceptions about adolescent roles and behaviors vary depending on the socioeconomic and cultural context. Most families, after a certain degree of confusion and disruption, are able to change the rules and limits and reorganize themselves to allow adolescents more autonomy and independence. However, certain universal problems are associated with this transition that can result in the development of symptoms in the adolescent or in other family members. Clinical cases will illustrate some of the blocks that families experience during this phase, as well as factors that may contribute to family disorganization or symptomatic behavior and therapeutic interventions that may be effective with these families.

The Sociocultural Context

The experiences that we have during adolescence in our families, community, and society greatly affect the way in which we teach and guide adolescents later in life. Our cultural values, attitudes about gender, and beliefs about life and death are central factors influencing the formation of their identities. However, the culture in which we live has a tremendous impact on that process.

In the United States, patriarchal values and racism shape relationship patterns between men and women. Men have more political and economic power than women. Whites have more privilege than people of color do. Sexism and racism are sources of social oppression that affect all men and women in this culture and that marginalize and abuse women, people of color, and homosexuals. The media promote and reinforce these values on a daily basis. Adolescents, particularly, are vulnerable to media exploitation. Their values and beliefs about life, their views about gender relationships, the way they dress, talk, and walk are all greatly influenced by what they see on TV and in films and by the music they hear.

The music they listen to, especially, reflects the attitudes of the peer group with which they identify. In most schools and communities in the United States, adolescents, like adults, segregate along racial, cultural, and class lines. Their identity as female, male, lesbian, gay, White, Black, Asian, Latino, rich, poor, smart, or learning disabled is partly shaped by how the media portray those roles. Yet many adolescents cannot identify with the images promoted by the media, nor do they have access to the products being sold. They feel marginalized by society and invisible, and some don't even experience the process of adolescence because they go from childhood directly into adulthood.

In White, middle-class mainstream America, turning 13 "normally" means becoming a legitimate teenager, an adolescent, and symbolizes growth toward physical and emotional maturity, responsibility, and independence. But turning 13 doesn't necessarily have the same meaning for poor African Americans or for Latino and Asian immigrants who are marginalized in this society and have little access to economic resources. Adolescence, for many in these groups, means assuming adult responsibilities as soon as possible. Many have children at age 14, quit school, and go to work as soon as they can be hired. Others stay home to take care of brothers, sisters, or parents who are unable to take care of themselves (Burton, Obeidallah, & Allison, 1996). Some cultures may encourage adolescents to fulfill adult responsibilities, such as caretaking duties, or to contribute financially to the home, yet still expect them to remain obedient to and respectful of parents. Becoming independent, living on one's own, such an important goal in the United States, may not have the same value in other cultures, in which interdependence is preferred (McGoldrick, Giordano, & Pearce, 1996).

Developing a Gender Identity

By age 2, children are able to distinguish girls from boys, and by age 4, they begin to identify tasks according to gender. As they develop physically, emotionally, spiritually, and intellectually, distinct differences between boys and girls can be observed. Maccoby (1990) summarizes research findings that show differences in patterns of interaction between boys and girls. For instance, boys tend to be more rough in their play than girls and are more inclined toward dominance. They are also less likely to be influenced by girls, who tend to adopt a style of making polite suggestions. Although this may seem to reinforce the idea that "boys will be boys, and girls will be girls," it is becoming more and more clear that some of our beliefs about gender differences are constructed by culture and society (Mann, 1996). For instance, in *Manhood in America*, Kimmel (1996) writes that "manhood is not the manifestation of an inner essence; it's socially constructed. Manhood does not bubble up to consciousness from our biological constitution; it is created in our culture" (p. 5). In a similar way, girls in this society learn that to become good women, they must be "willing to take care of, or to take on the cares of others, a willingness often to sacrifice oneself for others in the hope that if one cared for others one would be loved and cared for by them" (Gilligan, Lyons, & Hanmer, 1990, p. 8).

Growing up in this context, girls and boys learn that there are different sets of expectations for males and females. It has also been observed that "gender segregation is a widespread phenomenon found in all the cultural settings in which children are in social groups large enough to permit choice" (Maccoby, 1990, p. 414). As they grow, there is an increased emphasis on the separation of genders. The evolution of separate spheres for males and females in this country can be traced back to the mid-1800s (Kimmel, 1996). To become "real men" in the new land, boys had to gain independence from the family as soon as possible. Girls, on the other hand, lost their independence once they matured and married. Being in control was essential for men to compete and be successful, and the presence of women in the workplace threatened that goal. Women became increasingly bound to the home, and their worth was largely measured by their ability to raise children and by their domestic talents. These patterns are intrinsic in patriarchal societies and are not unique to the United States. By observing the adults in their lives and through exposure to television and the media, children learn that men have more power and privilege than women do. Unless children live with adults whose behavior challenges these beliefs, by adolescence they have incorporated into their identities the stereotypes about gender that our culture promotes (Mann, 1996).

Girls growing up in the United States today are perhaps more oppressed than in earlier decades (Pipher, 1994). Even though the women's movement has opened certain doors for females, girls

> *are coming of age in a more dangerous, sexualized and media-saturated culture. They face incredible pressures to be beautiful and sophisticated, which in junior high means using chemicals and being sexual. As they navigate in a more dangerous world, girls are less protected. America today limits girls' development, truncates their wholeness and leaves them traumatized. (Pipher, 1994, p. 12).*

Boys face a different dilemma. As Kimmel (1996) puts it,

> *they are growing up in a society where the structural foundations of traditional manhood, such as economic independence, geographic mobility, and domestic dominance, have all been eroding. Patterns of self control, exclusion of others, and escape from the home, which in the past had helped males become successful bread winners and providers, are no longer effective (p. 298).*

Yet, rather than looking at how changes in the social structure in this country have affected men and women, a major part of the blame for men's dissatisfactions and limitations continues to be placed on women. For instance, the belief that to find themselves and become true men, boys need to separate from their mothers and bond with their fathers and other men (Bly, 1990; Keen, 1991) perpetuates the problem. Rather than learning to be accountable and responsible to others and to fight against injustice based on difference, they fight for power by excluding and dominating the weaker. And as Gilligan et al., (1990) tell us, "for girls to remain responsive to themselves, they must resist the conventions of feminine goodness; to remain responsive to others, they must resist the values placed on self-sufficiency and independence in North American culture" (p. 10) They must make a commitment to resist and to ask questions about what relationship means to themselves, to others, and to the world.

For African American adolescents, forming an identity goes beyond values and beliefs about gender, since they have to first cope with "society's definition of them as, first and foremost, black" (Hardy, 1996, p. 55). Forming a positive identity as a Black male or Black female in a racist society in which being Black is demeaned poses a dilemma for adolescents. Learning to repudiate society's negative stereotypes and to include their Blackness as positively valued and desired is necessary for Black adolescents to form a positive identity. This is also true for other adolescents of color, such as Latinos and Asians. Living among Whites and facing daily situations based on skin color that are hurtful, humiliating, and devaluing at school and in the street is never an easy experience. The darker the skin, the more difficult it is. Being Black and female means having two strikes against you (Ward, 1990). For Black males, the risk of being killed in the street, incarcerated, or assumed to be involved in criminal activities is much higher than it is for Whites. African American males, especially, have a much lower life expectancy than African American women or Whites of either sex (Hines & Boyd-Franklin, 1996). "Concerns for their children's futures may reactivate parents' sense of powerlessness and rage about racism, sometimes resulting in self-defeating behavior" (Hines & Boyd-Franklin, 1996, p. 76). It is important for parents to help their children cope with the anger and frustration by reconnecting with strategies and stories that have given them strength and sharing them with their children (Hardy, 1996; Hines & Boyd-Franklin, 1996).

These questions are critical, and because during adolescence children acquire the ability to think abstractly, having an adult discussion with them would be possible. Yet the two major forces of adolescence (Wolf, 1991), the onset of sexuality and the mandate that commands adolescents to turn away from parents and childhood, could make such a conversation between parents and children very strained, though perhaps possible with either extended family members or in therapy. These forces are similar for boys and girls. However, there are very distinct differences in the way boys and girls experience the physical, emotional, and sexual changes that adolescence triggers in them and in the way parents tend to react to these changes. Following is a closer look at how boys and girls experience those changes.

Physical Changes

The differences between males and females during this stage of development are clearly visible when it comes to physical changes. Generally, girls tend to grow faster than boys. The experience of having their bodies grow so rapidly elicits reactions of confusion both in them and in their parents. Our little kids begin to turn into adult-looking people. Their features change as their faces become more elongated, and their legs and arms dangle from a trunk that is too small to carry them, especially during early adolescence. Parents are constantly buying new clothes and shoes with mixed feelings of excitement and sadness as they try to keep up with the growth spurts.

The physical growth makes adolescents eat more and sleep longer. Following the growth spurt, their chests expand, their trunks lengthen, and their voices deepen; additionally, shoulders develop in boys and hips in girls. They also seem to have spurts of physical energy, followed by periods of lethargy. This change leads to conflicts between parents and adolescents in most families. Parents become nags in the eyes of their children, and children become inconsiderate, lazy, and disobedient in the eyes of parents.

Outside the home, adolescents have to deal with the pressures of fitting into a peer group. These pressures are, for the most part, gender specific and result from social and cultural expectations based on patriarchal values. For example, although the emphasis on physical attractiveness is strong for both boys and girls, the pressure to be beautiful is enormous for girls. For boys, being physically strong and athletic has more importance. And although being slight in weight and short in stature may cause boys to feel insecurities, girls who don't fit the social ideal of beauty seem to be at greater risk. One reason is that in our culture being beautiful also has negative connotations, as demonstrated by the jokes and caricatures about the "dumb blonde," creating a dilemma for girls. Another is that physical attractiveness means being thin. At an age when their bodies are changing and getting softer and fuller, girls may begin to see themselves as fat.

For many girls, dieting becomes a way to control weight. Bulimia, anorexia, and compulsive eating are conditions that are rarely found in males. Out-of-control eating is often associated with out-of-control emotions. Some studies report that on any given day, half the teenage girls in the United States are dieting, one in five young women has an eating disorder, and 8 million women of all ages have eating disorders (Pipher, 1994). Although clinicians tend to see eating disorders as behavioral manifestations of complex family dysfunction, many see the media as contributing to the problem by setting dangerous standards of beauty and thinness to which girls aspire (Mann, 1996). Some of these standards for thinness are very close to the standards for anorexia (Mann, 1996). An important point here is that although the detection of eating disorders in African Americans and Latinos seems to be increasing, the group that seems to be more affected by this problem continues to be White middle-and upper-class girls.

Sexual Changes

The development of secondary sexual changes ends the growth spurt but not all growth. For girls, this is usually marked by menarche, and for boys by the experience of ejaculations. Most girls reach menarche by age 12 (Males, 1996) and some as early as 9 (Pipher, 1994). Boys tend to reach puberty a year later than girls, usually by age 14 (Males, 1996). Both experience sexual feelings coming to the surface, which is unavoidable because of the biological changes their bodies undergo, and they also feel somewhat awkward and self conscious about their sexually maturing bodies. The implications for girls, however, are different than those for boys. Girls are emotionally unprepared for the sexual harassment they encounter because of these changes (Pipher, 1994).

The reality is that in today's world, girls are at risk, not only for sexual harassment but also for rape and sexual abuse. For instance, the National Women's Study of 4,000 women in 1992 found that one in eight women, a projected 12.1 million in the U.S. population, had been raped. Of the victims, 62 percent were raped before age 18 and 29 percent before age 11. "The survey found that rape in America is a tragedy of youth, with the majority of rape cases occurring during childhood and adolescence" (Pipher, 1994, p. 219). A study by the Alan Guttmacher Institute (1994) asked junior high school girls what they meant by having sex. For 40 percent of girls under age 15 who had had sex, their only experience with sex had been a rape, and the men involved in these rapes were substantially older. This alone is a good reason for parents to feel more protective of daughters and anxious about giving them the same freedom as boys.

The psychological results of rape and sexual abuse of children and adolescents are often depression, eating disorders, suicide, and other emotional disturbances. A major factor in drug and alcohol abuse for both males and females is a history of sexual abuse and rape. The 1992 Rape in America Study (National Victim Center, 1992) found that the age at which a girl's first rape occurred was younger than the age at which she first became intoxicated on alcohol or used drugs. Serious drinking problems were 12 times higher, and serious drug abuse problems 25 times higher in rape victims than in nonvictims. There is also a higher possibility for rape victims to become pregnant than for girls who have not been abused (The Arizona Family Planning Council, 1995). Studies of urban adolescents of color (Smith, 1997) concur with research that points to the interlinking of risk factors in the lives of adolescents, as well as the interlinking of problem behaviors (Ooms, 1995). Sexual abuse, rape, and substance use are clearly linked, as well as the risk for early pregnancy. Teenage boys in the study were more likely to have sex earlier, therefore increasing their exposure to disease. Girls who initiated sex earlier were more likely to become pregnant earlier.

Generally, girls and boys are having sex earlier than in previous generations, and although they are taught at most schools about sexually transmitted diseases, pregnancy, and AIDS, they tend to not use condoms or other forms of protection (Wolf, 1991; Pipher, 1994). Especially for girls, social sanctions against sex have dropped sharply. Behaviors that in the past would have branded a girl a slut among her friends are now more accepted (Wolf, 1991). However, boys are still given more leeway when it comes to sexual behavior. We still live in a society in which "boys, because they are males, have to be aggressive, and they have to use this aggression to prove themselves, not only athletically, intellectually, but sexually as well" (Silverstein & Rashbaum, 1994, p. 120).

For gay and lesbian youths, adolescence is a time when they are more likely to label and understand their sexual orientation. Because of the greater visibility of homosexuals in today's society, there are more possibilities for adolescents to be exposed to role models and to a gay and lesbian culture (Savin-Williams, 1996). The prejudice that adolescents in this situation face is still overwhelming. Coming out to their parents is probably the event that provokes the most anxiety and fear for them, especially for minority adolescents who depend on the family as the primary support system for dealing with the discrimination they experience outside (Savin-Williams, 1996; Morales, 1996).

Generally, gay and lesbian adolescents are more likely to disclose to mothers, fearing more the reaction from fathers. In fact, Herdt and Boxer (1993) found that one in ten youths who disclosed being homosexual to their fathers was expelled from the home. Sometimes, the reaction at home is dangerous and violent. Hunter (1990) found that the majority of violent physical attacks experienced by 500 primarily Black or Latino minority youths occurred in the family and were gay-related. Yet, most adolescents in this situation want their parents to know, and even though initially the relationship usually deteriorates, it tends to improve thereafter (Savin-Williams, 1996).

However, for many, like Horace, a 16-year-old White male of German ancestry, the situation at school and home can lead to suicidal behavior. In therapy, he talked about the loneliness and fear that he experienced.

> My attraction to men is not something I chose. I tried for the longest time to push it out of my mind, and do all the things that boys are supposed to do, but I can't change myself. Sometimes I get scared, especially when I hear about all the gay men who are dying of AIDS. I feel bad for my parents. They love me, but don't understand why this is happening, and are ashamed of me. They also fear for my life. No one else knows in the family, and I hate pretending in front of my grandparents. At school I'm constantly on the look out, worried that they'll find me out and lynch me. I'd be better off dead. I don't see another way out.

Most gay and lesbian adolescents remain closeted, particularly in high school. When there is outside recognition that leads to intense harassment from peers and lack of support at home, emotional problems are likely to emerge. In these cases, there is a high risk of suicide. Some studies have found that 20 to 40 percent of gay and lesbian adolescents have made suicide attempts, half of them have made multiple attempts, and they are two or three times more likely to actually commit suicide than heterosexual youths (Savin-Williams, 1996). However, Shaffer, D.; Fisher, P.; Hicks, R. H.; Parides, M.; & Gould, M. (1995) conducted a psychological autopsy study of 120 of 170 consecutive suicides under age 20 and 147 community, age, sex, and ethnic matched controls living in the greater New York City area that found no evidence that the risk factors for suicide among gays were any different from those among straight teenagers. The data in that study shows that although the experience of establishing a gay orientation may be painful, it does not lead disproportionately to suicide.

Emotional Changes

The emotional immaturity that boys and girls experience during early adolescence is manifested by changeable and intense moods. This instability of feelings leads to unpredictable behavior. Emotional reactions are not always proportionate to the precipitating event, causing confusion for parents and other adults as they try to reason with adolescents (Pipher, 1994). While maturing emotionally, adolescents feel the need to move toward independence, and to do that, they feel compelled to turn away from their childish ways. Implicit in this task is the need to transform the relationship with their parents. As with sexual feelings, it is a process that cannot be avoided. This is complicated, however, because along with wanting to venture out and become independent, there is also a part of them that pulls toward wanting parents to take care of them. They do not want to break the emotional bond they have with their parents. Instead, they want a different balance in the relationship that allows for validation of their changing selves (Apter, 1990). "They want the nurturance without the fuss" (Wolf, 1991). Away from home, they can begin to act mature and responsible, but at home they want to be left alone with no demands and no expectations.

While both girls and boys may go through a similar emotional experience, their patterns for expressing emotion and relating to mothers and to fathers are different. For instance, boys tend to be more withdrawn, going into themselves, and, as in the case of my son, sometimes become clams. Girls don't necessarily stop talking or withdraw; instead, they fight. What I have observed in my clinical practice, and at home with my son and daughter, is that girls are more likely to let parents know what they feel by yelling, while boys are more avoidant and tend to deal with situations by leaving the scene. For boys, engaging in fights with parents may lead to aggressive behavior such as punching holes in walls or breaking furniture, while girls are more likely to scream, cry, and proclaim their hate. These patterns seem to fit cultural and social expectations for gender-specific behavior. For example, boys are usually given more freedom than girls to leave the house, while girls have more permission to express a wider range of emotions (Pipher, 1994). Boys, as Silverstein and Rashbaum (1994) state, learn only to express anger. A similarity between boys and girls, however, seems to be that the more dependent they feel on their parents, the more turbulent this process will be (Silverstein and Rashbaum, 1994; Pipher, 1994; Wolf, 1991).

Another difference between boys and girls is in their pattern of establishing friendships. Girls tend to talk to each other on the phone for longer periods of time and to care more about what one thinks of the other. They spend more energy dealing with relationships and change friendships with greater frequency than boys do.

Boys tend to hold on longer to the same friends and to build relationships around activities and sports. However, regardless of these differences, boys and girls are similar in that they are more interested in their friends than in adults. They want to fit in with their peers and, depending on how secure they feel, are easily influenced by group pressures.

Changes in the Family Structure

The adolescent's demands for greater independence tend to precipitate structural shifts and renegotiation of roles in families involving at least three generations of relatives. It is not uncommon for parents and grandparents to redefine their relationships during this period, as well as for spouses to renegotiate their marriage, and siblings to question their position in the family. Because these demands are so strong, they also serve as catalysts for reactivating unresolved conflicts between parents and grandparents or between the parents themselves and to set triangles in motion. For instance, efforts to resolve conflicts between adolescents and parents often repeat earlier patterns of relating in parents' families of origin. Parents who have made a conscious effort to raise their children differently by avoiding the same "mistakes" their parents made often have a particularly rude awakening. When their children reach adolescence, they are often surprised to observe similarities in personality between children and parents. Parents in this situation may react with extreme confusion, anger, or resentment or may themselves get in touch with similar needs and, in turn, make the same requests of their own parents or of each other.

Families during this period are also responding and adjusting to the new demands of other family members, who themselves are entering new stages of the life cycle. For example, most parents with adolescents in the mainstream U.S. culture are in middle age. Their focus is on such major midlife issues as reevaluating their marriage and careers. The marriage emerging from the heavy caretaking responsibilities of young children may be threatened as parents review personal satisfaction in the light of the militant idealism of their adolescent children. For many women, this may actually be the first opportunity to work outside the home without the restrictions they faced when the children were young. However, because of the economic situation in this country, there is an increasing need for both parents to work to meet the expenses of raising children and maintaining a home. Especially for working-class families, fathers may have a particularly hard time. Finding that they have reached their limits of earning and advancement or facing layoffs as their place of work no longer needs them makes them feel very insecure.

The normal stress and tension posed to the family by an adolescent are exacerbated when the parents experience acute dissatisfaction and feel compelled to make changes in themselves. At the same time, the grandparents face retirement and possible moves, illness, and death. These stressful events call for a renegotiation of relationships, and parents may be called upon to be caretakers of their own parents or to assist them in integrating the losses of old age. What often forms is a field of conflicting demands, in which the stress seems to be transmitted both up and down the generations. For example, if there is conflict between parents and grandparents, it may have a negative effect on the marital relationship that filters down into the relationship between the parents and the adolescent. Or the conflict may travel in the opposite direction. A conflict between the parents and adolescent may affect the marital relationship, which ultimately affects the relationship between the parents and grandparents.

These patterns may differ depending on factors such as race, class, and ethnicity. For instance, Burton et al. (1996) conducted a study of poor inner-city African American teens and found that in many of the families, there was a narrow age difference between the generations, which tended to blur developmental boundaries and roles of family members. The blurring of intergenerational boundaries in these age-condensed families affected the authority that parents had over children as well as the adolescents' perceptions of appropriate behavior. Consider, for example, a family where the

> *child generation included both a young mother (age fifteen) and her child (age one), a young-adult generation, which is comprised of a twenty-nine-year-old grandmother, and a middle-age generation, which includes a forty-three-year-old great-grandmother.*
>
> *The adolescent mother, as a function of giving birth, is launched into the young-adult role status; however, she remains legally and developmentally a member of the child generation. Similarly, the young-adult female has moved to status of grandmother, a stage typically embodied by middle-aged or older women. Further, the middle-aged woman has been propelled to the status of great-grandmother, a role usually occupied by women in their later years."* (Burton et al., 1996, p. 406).

The example illustrates the point that as a result of the closeness in generations, chronological and developmental challenges often become inconsistent with generational roles. The result may be that parents and children behave more like siblings, making it difficult for parents to discipline their children. Families may also have difficulty identifying adolescence as a specific life stage.

There are remarkable differences in the rituals that ethnic groups use to handle adolescence. For instance, Anglo Americans (McGill & Pearce, 1996) do not struggle to keep their children at home, as do Italians, Jews, and Latinos. Historically they have promoted early separation of adolescents and the development of an individualistic, self-defined, adult identity. As McGill and Pearce (1996) observe, "if contemporary parents try to promote independence by withdrawing physical, financial, or emotional support too soon, the Anglo American adolescent will probably feel abandoned. The result may be a kind of false adulthood with premature identity foreclosure" (p. 456).

Renegotiating rules and limits is key during this stage of development for most families. "You can't treat me like a baby anymore" may be said in the middle of a "childish tantrum," but the message must be heard and taken seriously. Parents must be ready to let go and yet stay connected to guide, and be protective when necessary. This is much easier said than done. It is true that, adolescents are not babies or little children, but neither are they adults. Even when they fulfill adult roles during early adolescence, such as having children themselves or taking care of ill parents, they are not emotionally mature until later in the process. The family must be strong and able to make its boundaries more flexible. This is usually easier with each successive child but is particularly difficult when parents are unable to support each other, are isolated, and lack the support of extended family or community.

Therapeutic Interventions

The Carnegie Council on Adolescent Development (1995), a ten-year national study of adolescence, reported that rates of teen drug and alcohol use, unprotected sexual activity, violent victimization, delinquency, eating disorders, and depression are now sufficiently widespread that nearly half of American adolescents are at high or moderate risk of seriously damaging their life chances. This is true of adolescents across all demographic lines. This finding coincides with the types of problems that are presented in therapy. Parents seeking help for their troubled adolescent in the United States at this point in time are likely to be overworked, overcommitted, tired, and poor and to have little outside support (Pipher, 1994). Many are single parents, mothers in most cases (Sandmaier, 1996). They tend to feel inadequate, see their families as dysfunctional, and expect their children to rebel and to distance themselves emotionally. Viewing these families as dysfunctional is also a widespread tendency among mental health professionals that limits our ability to intervene from a perspective that considers the context in which they live and the effect that culture has on them.

Helping parents to maintain an emotional bond with adolescents in a culture that says that parents are supposed to pull away when a child reaches adolescence is a challenge for most therapists. Yet we all need encouragement to hang in there, listen differently, confront our own limits, and take the necessary measures to earn our child's trust (Sandmaier, 1996). Recent studies find that teenagers who feel close to their families were the least likely to engage in any of the risky behaviors that were studied, which included smoking marijuana or cigarettes, drinking, and having sex, and that high expectations from parents for their teenagers' school performance were nearly as important (Gilbert, 1997). In my clinical practice, I am constantly trying to maintain a balance that respects the parents' responsibility to protect adolescents yet encourages the adolescents' need for independence. At home, I struggle to do the same with my 18-year-old son, and 14-year-old daughter and feel the range of emotions most parents feel when children pull away, keep secrets, and tell us "you don't understand."

Renegotiating Relationships between Parents and Adolescents

What also happens as parents and adolescents try to redefine relationships is that parents often experience a resurfacing of emotions related to unresolved issues with their own parents. In therapy, paying attention to the triangles that operated in the parents' families of origin and coaching them to do so some work with their own parents can be very helpful in furthering their ability to listen and feel less reactive to their children's behavior. Such was the case with Clara and her mother:

> Clara, 15, lived with her 39-year-old mother, Mrs. Callahan, her 12-year-old sister, Sonia, and her mother's paternal aunt. Her parents had been divorced since she was ten. Her mother was Puerto Rican, and her father was Irish. He was remarried to an Asian woman. Mrs. Callahan had remained unmarried. She was a professional woman who kept herself isolated from peers and focused her energy on being a good mother. Clara,

who had always been very close to her mother, had begun to pull away, stay out late, and show interest in boys. Mrs. Callahan, afraid of the dangers in the street and worried that Clara would become pregnant, restricted her outings. The more Clara challenged the limits, the stricter her mother became. Clara threatened to run away and kill herself. After she spoke to a teacher at school, the referral for therapy was made.

Mrs. Callahan was angry with Clara and unwilling to listen to her daughter's criticisms. She felt rejected by her daughter, for whom she had sacrificed so much. Clara felt bad about hurting her mother but was angry at what she thought was her mother's unfairness. Supporting Mrs. C.'s intention to protect her daughter by validating the dangers that girls are exposed to in this society made it easier for her to listen to Clara's position. Inviting Clara's great-aunt, who lived with them, to the sessions clarified how Clara's adolescence had activated a triangle similar to one that had operated in the previous generation. The triangle, triggered by discipline issues, involved Clara, Mrs. C., and the great-aunt. Clara thought her great-aunt was too old-fashioned and resented her attempts to discipline. Both would complain to Mrs. C., who would try to mediate by explaining cultural differences but was confused about which values to keep and would end up feeling powerless. The aunt would react by moving in to support Mrs. C., and Clara would distance herself, feeling rejected by both.

During her adolescence, Mrs. C. had been involved in a triangle with her mother and this aunt, who was her father's youngest sister. The aunt would try to mediate between Mrs. C. and her mother when they had arguments but would usually end up defending her niece. The mother would then get angry and distance herself from Mrs. C., who in turn would feel rejected. I was able to help shift the triangle by telling them that Clara needed support from both of them but primarily from her mother. I suggested that Clara was as confused as they by the different ways in which the two cultures dealt with adolescence.

Asking them to identify which Puerto Rican values were creating the greatest conflict at home led them to thinking about a compromise. They agreed that dating was the greatest source of conflict, since in Puerto Rico, this practice has very different rules and connotations. Dating does not start until much later, and it is usually in the company of family or friends. I pointed out that for Clara to live in this culture and feel comfortable with her peers, they needed to adapt to some of the values of this culture. As a compromise, they agreed to let Clara go on double dates, but only with people they knew, and to negotiate a curfew with Clara's input.

To make additional changes in the relationship between Clara and her mother, work had to be done with Mrs. Callahan and her mother, who lived in Puerto Rico. Coaching Mrs. C. to share some of her conflicts with her mother through letters and on a visit to Puerto Rico and to ask her advice about disciplining Clara was a way to lessen the emotional distance between them. Mrs. C. became more accepting of her mother's limitations and began to appreciate the attention she gave. This helped her to listen more attentively to her daughter.

Another factor that this case elucidates is the considerable impact that the lack of extended family or other supports has on how families manage adolescence. Some ethnic groups, such as Puerto Ricans, rely heavily on extended family members to help with the discipline of adolescents and the clarification of boundaries. It is common for Puerto Rican parents to send a rebellious adolescent to live with an uncle or godparent who can be more objective about setting limits. This move also provides time for parents and adolescents to obtain enough emotional distance from each other to regain control and reestablish a more balanced relationship. Relying solely on the nuclear family to provide control, support, and guidance for adolescents can overload the circuits and escalate conflicts.

For instance, my home is considered a safe haven for my 17-year-old nephew, my dead brother's son, who lives with his mother. The two of them have a very close relationship, but sometimes they have extremely intense conflict. My nephew was 11 when his father died, and through the years, he has assumed an adult role at times when his mother felt overwhelmed and hopeless. At 17, he challenges her limits, feeling that since she expects him to act as an adult at times, he should be entitled to adult privileges. Not long ago, when I called my sister-in-law to say hello, they were in the middle of a fight. She was desperate, and he had left the house to avoid her screams. He returned while I was on the phone, and I suggested that he come for a visit.

He did, and we talked about the problems at home and about how he misses his father. My husband and I told stories about my brother and how much he had loved the boy. It was easier for him to hear from us that he was not entitled to adult privileges yet and that challenging his mother's limits by screaming and making threats was not helpful or appropriate. I was also able to talk with my sister-in-law after she calmed down about how difficult it is to raise adolescent sons, and how much I respect her for doing it alone without another adult at home. It was good for me to spend time with him. It was good for her to have a break from him and to know that he could talk and reason.

Strengthening the Parental Bond

Whether parents are living together or apart, it is critical for them to agree on rules for adolescents. Adolescents tend to do better in families in which they are encouraged to participate in decision making but parents have rational control and ultimately decide what is appropriate (Henry & Peterson, 1995). Parents who are in control and high in acceptance have adolescents who are independent, socially responsible, and confident (Pipher, 1994). It is also important for parents to resist the impulse to focus entirely on the adolescent's problems and to pay attention to themselves and their own relationship (Carter & Peters, 1996). When parents disagree and one becomes involved in alliances with the children against the other, the problems presented by adolescents escalate. The case of 17-year-old Tom Murphy illustrates some of the shifts that may occur during adolescence when the child is in a triangle with parents who are in a struggle:

> Tom no longer wanted to be an engineer, as his parents were planning for him, but had become interested in lighting and theater. However, his parents, disapproved of his interest and were constantly urging him to go to college. Afraid to cause arguments, he avoided conversations with his parents and refused to go places with them, especially with his mother, to whom he had been a constant companion. At school, he gave up, failing to do assignments that were required for graduation and dropping courses he did not want. His behavior alarmed the teachers enough to ask the psychologist to see him. When his parents were told, they reacted with fear and anger, confused by his behavior, which they experienced as a rejection of their values and efforts to give him a good future.

In therapy, it became clear that Tom was caught in a classic triangle, trying to please his parents and feeling responsible for their arguments. But pleasing one parent meant disappointing the other. Marital problems and arguments in this family had gone on for years. Mrs. Murphy was very dissatisfied with the marital relationship and claimed that Tom, their only child, was the only reason she stayed in it. Mr. Murphy was resentful and tried to minimize the problems, claiming that she and Tom were against him. Mr. Murphy was also involved in a midlife reevaluation of his own work life, which meant coming to terms with disappointments and letting go of unfulfilled dreams. Overwhelmed by conflicts in their marriage and their own midlife struggles, Mr. and Mrs. Murphy had been unable to be objective and supportive of Tom's moves toward independence. Instead they experienced his behavior as Tom's collusive alliance with one parent against the other. His move toward independence represented a threat to the system, especially to the parent's relationship.

The initial focus in therapy was to help the family make decisions about handling the present problem. Mr. and Mrs. Murphy were asked to take a break from making plans for Tom's future, to back off and let him take responsibility for negotiating at school. Instead, they were to make a plan clarifying their expectations of Tom if he did not go to college. Working on this task strengthened their bond as parents and helped Tom to gain confidence about his own choices. As they reviewed their own adolescence and patterns of relationships in their families of origin, they became more objective about each other and were able to make connections between the past and present. Asking them to talk about their plans for the future as a couple enabled them to focus on their relationship and begin to face their problems directly. Tom began to make more responsible decisions about his future.

Building Community

"It takes a village to raise a child" may sound trite, but it is a concept that has deep meaning for any parent who experiences the loneliness and shame of raising adolescents who are troubled. I sit in my office with parents and adolescents and feel their pain as they tell me their stories, sharing their fear as they worry about their children's futures. I worry about my children and pray that the world will heal itself. I don't want them exposed to racism, sexism, violence, and apathy, and yet they are. I see their smiles and know that they have dreams and feel hopeful. I want to extend my heart and give them hope, confidence, strength, and love. In my practice of therapy these have become my most powerful tools.

There is no reason for blame; it accomplishes nothing. It does not heal adolescents or parents. Making connections with other families, other adults, other adolescents and opening our minds and hearts to others who are also struggling are healing. What I can do in my office is limited. I can help them look beyond themselves, at the pressures that affect their lives—our lives. We are in it together. Their children are also mine. I can help parents think about protecting their children, yet be aware of the limits that bound us. I can encourage mothers to defy society by not buying into the belief that boys need to separate from mothers to become "real men." I have become much softer with my son, letting him know that I love him and think that he is a sensitive, caring, and funny young man. I encourage fathers to look inside and outside and get in touch with how sexism limits and isolates them. I try to keep the real self in my daughter alive and look for it in every adolescent girl I meet. Sometimes, it is difficult to look beyond the pain I see in their eyes as they tell me stories of sexual abuse, violence, addictions, and self-mutilation and to consider what there is that is positive in their lives to help them feel strong. I have learned from them that sometimes their only salvation lies in their spiritual beliefs or in their connections to others.

> Tanya, a 14-year-old African American who came in to therapy after reporting at school that her mother's boyfriend had tried to rape her found support and strength in her church. Her mother was angry with her for reporting the boyfriend and blamed Tanya for seducing him. Tanya felt rejected and hurt but knew that she was not responsible for his behavior. She wanted her mother to believe her but had given up hope. In the church, she had found other adults who believed her and encouraged her to ask God's help to forgive her mother. I worked with her mother to help her see her daughter as a 14-year-old girl who did the right thing by reporting an adult man who abused her. I wanted her to feel angry at him and protective of her daughter; instead, she was angry about losing him. I encouraged her to go to church with Tanya, hoping that she would hear God's message and make connections with the adults who supported her daughter. She was not ready, and I had to accept it. Tanya had learned through her faith that there is strength in forgiving, and I was reminded of my limitations and felt grateful to the 14-year-old who was teaching me a lesson.

Establishing support networks with other professionals and working with other systems that may be part of the community in which adolescents live, such as schools, churches, and legal authorities, are crucial. Connecting parents with teachers at schools and with other parents is an essential type of intervention that works toward strengthening natural support systems and lessening the isolation that families experience in our present-day communities (Pipher, 1994; Taffel, 1996) Interventions that take into account the sociopolitical context in which we live and its effect on families and adolescents are critical.

References

Alan Guttmacher Institute. (1994). *Sex and America's teenagers.* New York: AGI.

Angelini, P. J. (1995, 17 November). *The relationship of childhood sexual victimization to teenage pregnancy and STDs.* Phoenix, AZ: Arizona Planning Council.

Apter, T. (1990). *Altered loves.* New York: Fawcett Columbine.

Bly, R. (1990). *Iron John.* Reading, MA: Addison-Wesley.

Burton, L., Obeidallah, D. A., & Allison, K. (1996). Ethnographic insights on social context and adolescent development among inner-city African-American teens. In R. Jessor, A. Colby, & R. Shweder (Eds.), *Essays on ethnography and human development.* Chicago: University of Chicago Press.

Carnegie Council on Adolescent Development. (1995). *Great transitions: Preparing adolescents for a new century.* New York: Carnegie Corporation.

Carter, B., & Peters, J. K. (1996). *Love, honor, and negotiate: Making your marriage work.* New York: Pocket Books.

Gilbert, S. (1997, September 10). Youth study elevates family's role. *New York Times.*

Gilligan, C., Lyons, N. P., & Hanmer, T. (1990). *Making connections.* Cambridge, MA: Harvard University Press.

Hardy, K. (1996, May/June), Breathing room. *The Family Networker,* 53–59.

Henry, S., & Peterson, G. W. (1995). Adolescent social competence, parental qualities, and parental satisfaction. *American Journal of Orthopsychiatry, 65* (2) 249–262.

Herdt, G. L., & Boxer, A. M. (1993). *Children of horizons: How gay and lesbian teens are leading a new way out of the closet.* Boston: Beacon Press.

Hines, P., & Boyd-Franklin, N. (1996). African American families. In M. McGoldrick, J. Giordano, & J. K. Pearce (Eds.), *Ethnicity and family therapy.* (pp. 66–84). New York: The Guilford Press.

Hunter, J. (1990). Violence against lesbian and gay male youths. *Journal of Interpersonal Violence, 5,* 295–300.

Keen, S. (1991). *Fire in the belly: On being a man.* New York: Bantam.

Kimmel, M. (1996). *Manhood in America: A cultural history.* New York: The Free Press.

Maccoby, E. (1990). Gender and relationships: A developmental account. *American Psychologist, 45,* (4), 513–520.

Males, M. A. (1996). *The Scapegoat generation: America's war on adolescents.* Monroe, ME: Common Courage Press.

Mann, J. (1996). *The difference: Discovering the hidden ways we silence girls–Finding alternatives that can give them a voice.* New York: Warner Books.

McGill, D., & Pearce, J. (1996). American families with English ancestors from the colonial era: Anglo Americans. In McGoldrick, M., Giordano, J., & Pearce, J. K. (Eds.), *Ethnicity and Family Therapy.* (pp. 451–466) New York: The Guilford Press.

McGoldrick, M., Giordano, J., & Pearce, J. K. (Eds.). (1996). *Ethnicity and family therapy.* New York: The Guilford Press.

Morales, E. (1996). Gender roles among Latino gay and bisexual men: Implications for family and couple relationships. In J. Laird & R. -J. Green (Eds.), *Gays and lesbians in couples and families.* (pp. 272–297) San Francisco: Jossey-Bass.

National Victim Center. (1992). *Rape in America.* Washington DC: Author.

Ooms, T. (1995). Strategies to reduce non-marital childbearing. In K. A. Moore (Ed.), *Report to Congress on out-of-wedlock childbearing* (pp. 241–265). Hyattsville, MD: U.S. Department of Health and Human Services.

Pipher, M. (1994). *Reviving Ophelia.* New York: Ballantine Books.

Sandmaier, M. (1996 May/June.). More than love. *The Family Networker,* 21–33.

Savin-Williams, R. C. (1996). Self-labeling and disclosure among gay, lesbian, and bisexual youths. In J. Laurd & R. -J. Green (Eds.), *Lesbians and gays in couples and families,* (pp. 153–182), San Francisco: Jossey-Bass.

Shaffer, D., Fisher, P., Hicks, R. H., Raudes, M., & Gould, M. (1995). Suicide and life threatening behavior. *American Association of Suicidology, 25* (Supplement) pp. 64–71.

Silverstein, O., & Rashbaum, B. (1994). *The courage to raise good men.* New York: Penguin Books.

Smith, C. A. (1997). Factors associated with early sexual activity among urban adolescents. *Social Work, 42*(4) 334–346.

Taffel, R. (1996 May/June). The second family. *The Family Networker,* 36–45.

Ward, J. V. (1990). Racial identity formation and transformation. In C. Gilligan, N. P. Lyons, & T. Hammer (Eds.), *Making connections.* (pp. 215–232). Cambridge, MA: Harvard University Press.

Wolf, A. E. (1991). *Get out of my life but first could you drive me and Cheryl to the mall?* New York: The Noonday Press.

10

Families Launching Young Adults; Middle-Aged Parents

The Launching Phase of the Life Cycle

Lynn Blacker

Overview

Myths of Midlife

"Launching children," "empty nest," "midlife crisis"—These phrases conjure up the widely held image of midlife and beyond as the end of meaningful life, a period of decline, depression, and death. Women are pictured as being worse off than men, their primary role of child-rearing completed. They are thought to be rattling around their empty homes or frantically attempting to make a life for themselves. Men are viewed more optimistically, since they have a longstanding career as their primary focus and source of self-esteem. They are disconnected from their unfulfilled wives, but if they want, they can always have one last fling. Given these divergent paths, marriages are assumed to be at their low point of satisfaction. In the 1960s, this constellation of negative images was named the "empty nest syndrome" (Shapiro, 1996).

This is a dramatic scenario and might make a good film script, but it does not match reality. First, midlifers who have launched their children report more enjoyment of life and more happiness in their marriages than do people the same age who have children at home (White & Edwards, 1993). A study of 3,000 adults found that empty nesters were actually less depressed than adults living with children or those who never had children (Shapiro, 1996). Second, women anticipate and welcome the departure of their children from the home (Mitchell & Helson, 1990) and cope even better than men do with this stage of the life cycle

Taken from: *The Expanded Family Life Cycle: Individual, Family, and Social Perspectives,* Third Edition, edited by Betty Carter and Monica McGoldrick.

(Bergquist, Greenberg, & Klaum, 1993). Women say that they have a better quality of life at midlife than at any other time (Mitchell & Helson, 1990). Third, men go through a period of reassessment at midlife, and most of them experience an increase in their capacity for relationship skills and an interest in connecting with family members (Levinson, 1978). The concept of the launching stage as a period of depressed women, distant, workaholic men, and the nadir of marital happiness has been refuted in study after study, so that by now the term "empty nest syndrome" has been minimized to the point of irrelevance (Dowling, 1996; Shapiro, 1996).

How do we explain these counterintuitive results of studies of parents whose children have left the home? The launching phase must be understood in terms of the life stage in which it occurs: midlife. Although the terms "launching" and "midlife" overlap, they are not synonymous. Launching is just one of many life cycle tasks that must be accomplished during the midlife years. Like launching children, the other midlife tasks involve a significant realignment of family roles. These other tasks of midlife include becoming a couple again; developing adult relationships with adult children; accepting new family members through marriage and birth; and resolving issues with, providing care for, and finally burying their parents. Once again, the popular view of midlife is characterized by negative stereotypes and misconceptions. Rather than worrying about declining health and diminished energy and feeling generally demoralized about the idea of impending mortality, most midlifers are in excellent health, feel young and vigorous and are excited by the many choices they have before them (Bergquist et al., 1993).

Middle Age: A New Life Cycle Stage

Like "empty nest syndrome," "middle age" is a relatively new term. It is the most recently identified phase of the life cycle, having first been described in 1978 by Levinson (Dowling, 1996). The newness of the construct reflects the fact that we are living longer; therefore, life cycle tasks have a new normative timetable. In 1900, when people died by age 49 (Pogrebin, 1996), life cycle tasks were compressed. Launching and marrying off children, burying parents, becoming grandparents and becoming widows commonly occurred concurrently in one decade. But now, this phase may last 20 years or more and is currently the longest phase in the life cycle. Midlife is commonly defined as spanning the ages of roughly 45 to 65, encompassing the period from launching the first child to retirement. Because of better health and increasing longevity, it may get expanded even more in the future. Of course, a significant number of men and women are beginning new families at midlife rather than launching them.

The Graying of America and the Midlife Stage

The "graying of America" is one of the most significant new features of contemporary society. Not only are we living longer, but also the large cohort of post–World War II baby boomers is now entering middle age. Their faces are everywhere, from television advertisements to the President of the United States. They have higher expectations of their own productivity and expect more of their middle years than previous midlifers. Intact midlife households have the highest mean income of any age group

(McCullough & Rutenberg, 1989), and services are popping up continually to address this huge market, which has not yet even peaked. The impact of the aging of America is related to and compounded by other significant phenomena of the latter part of twentieth century: the reduced size of families, more women in the workforce, higher divorce rates than in the past, more elderly surviving parents, and more middle-aged single women (McCullough & Rutenberg, 1989).

Taken together, this means that families, having fewer children, will finish the launching task at an earlier age than past generations and will experience a longer postlaunch period until retirement. This provides many midlife women with an opportunity to expand their part-time work or even begin careers outside the home for the first time and provides men with a new opportunity for reassessment. The high midlife divorce rates mean that for many people, especially women, being in the workforce will be a necessity. Finally, during this elongated postlaunch period, their parents are also living longer, so midlifers, especially daughters, will be involved in their care. All in all, as midlifers gradually make the transition through this lengthy period, they will be making significant reassessments of their roles in their families, their marriages, their work lives, their support systems, and their life expectations to adapt to the dramatic changes they experience over this twenty- to twenty-five-year period.

Awareness of Mortality

Before the identification of midlife as a life stage, it was thought that human development stabilized in early adulthood. Then, Erik Erikson in the 1960s and Daniel Levinson in the 1970s developed frameworks that describe life cycle stages and accompanying developmental tasks that occur throughout life. Both of these theorists suggest that the developmental tasks of midlife must include an attentiveness to developing meaning and purpose in one's life, which Erikson calls "generativity" (Julian, McKenry, & McKelvey, 1992). Therefore, it is not coincidental that the concept of reassessment permeates the family tasks of the midlife/launching stage. A key impetus for this reassessment is the realization that time is running out. As Bernice Neugarten (1968) notes, individuals at midlife begin to measure their position in the life cycle in terms of time left to live rather than time since birth. With this new perspective, priorities change. People may choose to no longer put aspirations and dreams on hold. The loss of some hopes and plans may also need to be mourned. However, as will be seen throughout this chapter, people tend to experience midlife not as an end, but as a time of great potential.

The Impact of Class and Culture

Although many people consider the stage of mid-life to be the prime of life (Gallagher, 1993; Mitchell & Helson, 1990), this rosy picture applies mainly to the middle and upper socioeconomic classes. For the less economically secure, the outlook is very different. The lower socioeconomic classes can anticipate decreasing job opportunities, especially with the massive downsizings and closings of industrial sites in the last decade and the increasingly technological work environment. Furthermore, working-class and poor women typically anticipate being both homemakers and employees throughout their adult lives, working in jobs that may not be particularly fulfilling (Bergquist et al., 1993). Working-class men, who often depend on physical strength for their jobs, may be considered middle aged in their thirties, and with their poor access to health care, they may not expect to live beyond retirement. This is particularly true of African American men, who have high mortality rates due to heart disease. For these men and women, having little economic autonomy, the midlife tasks of reevaluating the life course and developing new plans and dreams are not realistic. In fact, it has been suggested that the very idea of a midlife crisis is a cultural construct that is relevant only to the middle and upper classes (Gallagher, 1993).

Cultural and ethnic identification is another consideration in understanding the way families approach the tasks of the midlife stage. For example, in Anglo American or Polish families, children are expected to establish their independence with less parental assistance or involvement than is seen in Italian or Brazilian families. Dutch families tend to have greater acceptance of adult children continuing to reside in the home than German families do. Greek families may have a greater adherence to the traditional value of women not seeking employment out of the home than Jewish families do. Poor African American families, which place a high value on interconnectedness between family members, may never actually have an "empty nest," as elderly family members are likely to be active members of their expanding households and family systems (McGoldrick, Giordano, & Pearce, 1996). These intergenerationally transmitted influences contribute to the family's ease or difficulty in moving through this phase.

Gender Issues: Men and Women at Midlife

Baby Boomer Values

Although every generation must go through approximately the same life cycle transitions and accomplish the same tasks, each cohort brings its own unique historical experience. Those who are now entering midlife are baby boomers. This is the generation born just after World War II and raised in the 1950s and 1960s with traditional values and gender role expectations, namely, to be heterosexual, find a spouse, marry early, and, if female, stay home. Male entitlement strongly permeated their socialization. Then, in 1963, Betty Friedan published *The Feminine Mystique*, and the baby boomers, then in their midteens, were introduced to the sexual revolution. They became the generation that transitioned between postwar traditional values and the changing social climate that followed. Many baby boomers, especially the women, responded to the new prescription for social change. For the first time in great numbers, women attended college, entered the full-time workforce, and got divorced in great numbers. Although they attempted to create more egalitarian marriages, they still struggled with two conflicting sets of values, and even the most "liberated" couples tended to revert to traditional marriages after their children were born. Nonetheless, the values of individual entitlement, self-fulfillment, and gender equality oriented this group to the massive social changes of the last quarter century, and these values continue to be relevant as they face the challenges and demands of midlife.

However, some baby boomers entered adulthood with traditional values still intact. For them, the tasks of midlife collide with these values, and the dissonance of role expectations or the stress of having partially changed values creates another layer of adjustment as women and men redefine their roles at midlife with each other, within the family, and in society (Carter & Peters, 1996).

Middle-Aged Women: Postmenopausal Zest

According to the popular depiction in the mass media, the physical changes associated with menopause are unbearably uncomfortable, and the loss of fertility is thought to trigger a preoccupation with mortality that may lead to depression. Actually, although women do experience changes and may feel a sense of discomfort and/or loss, the most commonly expressed feeling about the cessation of menstruation is relief (Shapiro, 1996). Current research indicates that most women anticipate and welcome the arrival of menopause and find the transition uneventful (Mitchell & Helson, 1990). Ninety percent of menopausal women report no significant changes in anger, anxiety, depression, or self-consciousness related to menopause (Gallagher, 1993). In fact, fewer menopausal women are depressed than women with young children (Apter, 1995). Nonetheless, 75 percent of menopausal women do notice some physical changes related to menopausal hormonal shifts, such as hot flashes, vaginal dryness, weight gain, increased vulnerability to osteoporosis, and changes in cognitive processing (Leiblum, 1990; Warga, 1997). These women may find hormone replacement therapy helpful. While hormone replacement therapy is now the focus of considerable media coverage, women are advised to consult their physicians to assess the risk factors of using or not using the treatment.

Contrary to the negative stereotype of menopause as a time of constriction, many women actually experience it as a catalyst for change and growth. Women describe themselves as feeling more assertive, confident, energetic, and sexually freer. Margaret Mead dubbed this phenomenon "postmenopausal zest," which she defined as "that creativity and energy released when we no longer need to care for children" (Apter, 1995, p. 201). Menopause is not credited with physically causing postmenopausal zest; instead, it creates the conditions for women to experience freedom and the opportunity for change.

The Male Midlife Crisis

Unlike women, whose postlaunch wake-up call leads to an energized zest for life, men's experience of mortality is a lengthy, internal process. By age 40, men begin to experience a gradual series of physical changes that do not really bring them much below their maximal level of functioning; however, these changes are significant enough to notice, such as baldness, paunchiness, and wrinkles. Levinson (1978) theorizes that every man must grieve and accept the symbolic death of the youthful hero in himself and then work through a process of reevaluation and reassessment, which Levinson views as a normative task for all men in their forties. However, according to the popular conceptualization of the midlife crisis, this process of reassessment is traumatic. The stereotype suggests that men, feeling that they have squandered their dreams and have nothing to live for, suddenly quit their jobs, dash out of their marriages, and begin a spending spree on high-ticket items to bolster their self-esteem. Again, research indicates that the overwhelming majority of men accomplish the developmental tasks of reevaluation and regrouping through a long, introspective process rather than an acute acting-out crisis. Although they will be making adjustments in their relationships and in their worklives, relatively few men experience the process as catastrophic (Gallagher, 1993).

Men and Women Out of Sync

It is clear that the actual experience of men and women as they pass through midlife turns several stereotypes on their heads. It also leads to an interesting conclusion: Men and women become decidedly out of sync as they pass through midlife. Women get energized before the launching phase, generally around the age of 40. They begin by anticipating their children's leaving the home several years before the children actually leave—often fueled by the tumult of the teenage years. During this anticipatory period, women begin to envision new plans for themselves. By the time their children are being launched, women feel that there is a big world outside waiting for them. They are excitedly going back to school, beginning new jobs, or returning to full-time employment. By their fifties, midlife women are well on their way in their new or resumed jobs, careers, or personal pursuits.

Meanwhile, during the decade of their forties, usually while their children are still in the home, men begin a very gradual process of reevaluation. This process may be prompted by their noticing changes in their marriages as their wives begin looking outside the home for their new focus. However, men still remain focused primarily on their careers. Feeling that they have a last chance for success, they may actually develop a greater investment in work. It is not until later in midlife, some time in their fifties, that they begin to think differently about the meaning of work in their lives. Slowly, they become more introspective as they seriously reassess their lives. For some, this process is triggered by gradual physical signs of the aging process. For others, a specific incident—a promotion or failure at work, a retirement package, a personal or family illness, or death—may be the catalyst. Some may react to a feeling of being abandoned by their wives, or they may feel regret for not having spent more time with their children. Whatever the impetus, men begin to explore their inner selves, seeking greater meaning in life. However, it is usually not until the latter half of the launching stage, some time in their mid- to late fifties or perhaps early sixties, that men become noticeably less focused on work. They are finally willing to slow down and accept their current level of achievement at work, even if this level does not match their early dreams. They experience an increased awareness of relationships and interests that they may have previously suppressed. They tend to become less competitive and aggressive and more willing to listen and learn (Better Carter, personal communication, January, 1998).

Thus, during midlife, men and women are moving past each other in different directions and at different paces. As women develop autonomy and move toward outside commitments, men want more time for leisure and/or travel and expect their wives to be free to join them (Carter & Peters, 1996). These gender contradictions are often confusing and unsettling to the partners and may lead to significant shifts in the marriage, including a redefinition of what constitutes a good husband or wife. As women become more independent, there may be a change in the balance of power in the marriage and a renegotiation of marital expectations, plans, and dreams—or the viability of the marriage itself.

Launching Children: What It Feels Like

All in all, launching children is a very individual experience for both mothers and fathers. Some women cry for a week or two; some are surprised by how quickly they adjust. Some women feel worse with the departure of the first child; some, with the last. They may feel that the house is too quiet, especially if they are single parents. There may be mixed feelings of happiness and sorrow at the loss of active parenting. But what most mothers have in common is that after a short time, they may feel relieved, revitalized, and ready for their own launching. Men also feel the loss, especially if they have missed much of the child-rearing because of their earlier focus on work. Now, as their children are leaving, fathers are beginning to be ready to spend less time at work and more time with their families. Thus, men may actually find their adjustment to the launching experience more problematic than women do, since men often find themselves without either their wives or children at home when they want them.

> Gail (age 49), a single parent, entered treatment when her only child, Dana (age 18), left for college. Gail could not get through a day without repeated bouts of crying. She initially used treatment to mourn the loss of her early pictures of what her life would be like when Dana was launched—images that did not match her current financially constrained single life-style. Gail was also assisted in maintaining appropriate parental contact with Dana without drawing her daughter in as a confidante or caretaker. Recognizing that the loss of the full-time parenting role is particularly stressful for single women, Gail agreed to utilize her support system by reaching out to close family members and friends. Together, they planned a "mother's liberation ritual" to mark this life cycle passage. Like many women, Gail was adept at relationship skills, and she responded well to this intervention. She also found keeping a journal to be a useful tool for identifying neglected and new interests, not to be used as time fillers but as expressions of her own authentic self, which she now had the freedom to explore.

Midlife Marriages

Research has presented two contradictory facts about midlife marriages: (1) Midlife is the period of the peak of marital happiness (White & Edwards, 1993), and (2) midlife is the period during which two out of the three most dramatic divorce peaks of the life cycle occur (Shapiro, 1996). A number of interrelated factors account for the findings of both high marital happiness and high divorce rates at midlife, including launching children, women going into the workplace, and men's increased introspection and reassessment process. However, of all the factors related to the status of midlife marriages, the launching of children is the single most significant one.

Marital Happiness at Its Peak

Studies of the impact of launching children leave no doubt that launching children is good for marriages and good for the partners' general feeling of well-being. In fact, the presence of children in the home has not been found to correlate with marital happiness in any age group (White & Edwards, 1993). Therefore, marital happiness is described as having a first peak after the marriage, dropping off during the child-rearing phase, and peaking again in the launching stage, producing a U-shaped model. Although stress in the home is reduced as each child leaves, the full beneficial effect of the launching process occurs only after the last child moves out (Shapiro, 1996).

What are the reasons for this boost in marital happiness at the launching stage? The removal of stress and the simplification of household routines are certainly key factors. Partners are no longer so focused on their children and can think more about and spend more energy on their marriages; and with the awareness that time is moving on, partners expect more from their relationships. At the same time, women's new outward focus takes some of the pressure off marriage as the primary source of gratification after the children leave. Then, too, midlife partners have been together for many years and have developed the relationship skills with which they weathered the stressful child-raising years. Finally, the very nature of marriage tends to change during midlife. Relationships are increasingly characterized by friendship, companionship, equality, tolerance, and shared interests (Dowling, 1996).

White and Edwards (1993) identify two qualifiers to the positive correlation between launching children and marital happiness. First, it appears that the timing of the launch is critical. When children leave too early or too late, parents tend to remain child focused, question their parental effectiveness, and do not experience that marital boost. Second, parents need to stay closely connected to their children to experience the improvement in well-being. Without frequent telephone or personal contact, parents tend to feel that their parenting role has ended, and they actually report feeling worse than they did when the children were home. These two qualifying conditions usually indicate that other transitions were not adequately resolved and are resurfacing during the launching phase. Often, marital issues and conflicts are buried during the tumult of the child-rearing years and are revisited after the children leave.

Midlife Sexual Love

Midlife presents men and women with physical changes that will require adjustments in their sexual lives. Beginning some time in their fifties and continuing into their sixties, men's sexual responses gradually slow down. They experience decreased frequency and intensity of orgasm, less ease in achieving erection, and a longer refractory period. The men's reactions to these changes depend on their self-esteem and how well they can acknowledge their emerging need for tenderness. Women may notice physical changes in their sexual responses somewhat earlier in the life cycle than men, perhaps as early as 35, or with the onset of menopause, which generally occurs during the mid-forties to mid-fifties. Changes in sexual functioning during menopause may include decreased vaginal lubrication, painful intercourse, and changes in the appearance of the genitalia (Leiblum, 1990).

The bodies of both partners are showing obvious signs of age. Fortunately, because of the developmental and logistical shifts of this period, the partners are well-equipped to make the necessary adjustments. First, the children are launched. With the children out of the home, both partners, especially the woman, feel less inhibited and preoccupied, and they may become more responsive and passionate. The cessation of menstruation also has a disinhibiting effect. Men's increased expressiveness and vulnerability and women's greater willingness to express their needs further contribute to this positive outcome. Interestingly, midlifers tend to still perceive their bodies as more youthful than they are, so they are not significantly inhibited by the physical signs of aging bodies (Bergquist et al., 1993). Also, after so many years together, most partners find that they are more patient with and tolerant of each other (Apter, 1995). They also may bring a more mature sense of self to their sex lives, which can enhance their sexual potential (Schnarch, 1997).

Midlife Divorces

The High Divorce Rate at Midlife

While divorce is increasingly prevalent in all age groups, the increase is particularly noticeable in midlife: One dramatic divorce peak occurs after fifteen to eighteen years of marriage and another after twenty-five to twenty-eight years (Shapiro, 1996). According to the U.S. Census Bureau, the number of Americans who divorced between the ages of 40 and 54 in 1995 represents almost 14 percent of the population, up 11 percent from a decade ago (Rubin, 1997). In the 1950s, only 4 percent of divorces involved marriages of more than fifteen years. In the 1980s, the divorce rate for this group rose to 25 percent. This represents a very large group of unmarried people. In 1970, there were 1.5 million people in the United States who were divorced and not remarried. In 1991, the number had risen to 6.1 million (Dowling, 1996). However, despite the high divorce rate, it is important to bear in mind that 75 percent of midlifers are still in married or partnered relationships (Gallagher, 1993).

Why After All Those Years?

Sometimes the empty nest does not lead to the solidification of the marriage or to the acceptance of a familiar relationship. After many years of not dealing with differences, but instead burying feelings or distancing from each other or turning elsewhere, some couples realize that what is empty is the marriage. Some marriages simply cannot survive without the children present. Some couples hold onto their children to retain them as buffers; others decide to divorce. Two significant factors contribute to the timing of these midlife divorces. First, there is a change in the structure of the family and a freedom that comes with the end of the day-to-day responsibility for children. The couple has a newly available ration of time, finances, and emotional focus, which provides the opportunity and resources for change. Second, one or both of the spouses is motivated to seek a divorce by the unpleasant prospect of being left alone with a stranger or an adversary for the remainder of life. Both of these factors are magnified by the realization that time is running out.

Interestingly, 85 percent of divorces are initiated by women (Apter, 1995). Because women today are better educated than they were in the past, they are more marketable for employment. Sometimes, as women begin to experience their independence and develop their competence, they are less willing to remain in a relationship that they recognize as dead. The sense of empowerment that comes with making the decision to end an unsatisfying relationship helps to enhance women's self-confidence and their capacity for assertiveness. Though some women may be terrified of being alone and of handling finances, the emotion that most often accompanies the decision to divorce is relief (Apter, 1995). Despite their fears, women rarely regret their decision to divorce (Dowling, 1996).

When women turn outward, men take notice. They may experience a sense of confusion, vulnerability, and abandonment. Some men, as they go through the midlife process of reassessment, develop a renewed appreciation of their marital relationship, or at least they decide that remaining in the marriage is preferable to leaving, while some men respond to the questioning of an unhappy marriage by seeking a new, exciting romance. This decision may be fueled by their developing awareness of mortality and a desire for that last chance for happiness. However, a decision to end a long marriage is usually a protracted and painful one. People who are now at midlife were socialized in a time when divorce was less prevalent, and they are likely to experience their divorces as personal failures. This is especially true for women, as women tend to assume that it is their responsibility to make relationships work.

> After twenty-five years of marriage, Tina (age 47) and Ed (age 49) launched their second child from the home. Tina had returned to graduate school two years before this event and was deeply absorbed in her studies, while Ed was focused on his legal career. Despite these distractions, Tina found the silence between them to be a painful indicator of their long-term estrangement. She told Ed that if they did not enter marital therapy, she did not want to remain in the marriage. Ed then agreed to enter treatment. After completing the initial assessment, the couple's therapist suggested a nine-month plan: Both Tina and Ed would agree to put their maximum effort into being the best partners they could be for the next nine months; after that, they would reevaluate their relationship. During that period, in addition to couples work, each partner was individually coached to strengthen their own support systems and to identify and pursue their individual interests and needs. Despite this work, Ed and Tina remained disconnected. After five months, Ed disclosed that he was involved in a long-standing affair. With what she described as relief, Tina stated that she had had enough—The marriage was over. Both Tina and Ed agreed to remain in treatment for three months to handle the separation process as constructively as possible. They were given the names of local divorce mediators so that the separation and divorce process would be collaborative rather than adversarial. Individual therapeutic work with Tina focused primarily on her learning to manage her finances, while work with Ed primarily addressed developing plans to maintain contact with his children. Tina returned to treatment several months later to address the feelings of loss and failure that followed the initial sense of relief and hopeful expectation.

Women on Their Own

There is no question about it—although men have higher incomes and greater opportunity to find new mates, women do better on their own. As Terri Apter notes, "Whereas divorcing women are likely to discover their capacity for independence, divorcing men are likely to discover their dependence." (1995, p. 178) Divorced men have three times the mortality rate of married men and are more prone to stress-related alcoholism and suicide. By contrast, women tend to experience a wide range of psychological growth after divorce, including an increase in such qualities as self-esteem, assertiveness, and humor (Dowling, 1996). This is not to say that divorce is not a crisis; it is always a series of crises and disillusionments. There is usually an initial confusion, a feeling of "not knowing who I am" or of no longer being part of a family or part of a couple. But women recover more quickly than men and are more likely to use the experience as a jump start for personal growth, especially when they are the initiators of the divorce.

One of the reasons that midlife women do so much better after divorce is that they have more friends and close family ties. With their larger support systems, they are not as lonely as they had feared they would be. They are also not as frantic as men to enter new relationships, although the prospect of dating after so many coupled years can be as frightening as it is exciting. However, since midlife women have a more limited dating pool than midlife men, their potential for remarriage is dramatically lower. Therefore, it is functional that women tend to develop what Apter (1995) calls "a growing understanding that love is not a woman's whole existence, but an important part of a different whole" (p. 244). Women learn to challenge the assumption that they can be happy only by having a man, being married, and being a mother. However, this role shift is made more difficult by the fact that our society is organized around the status of couplehood, so much so that many singles complain of a feeling of invisibility. At first, women who have remained close to home tend to feel self-conscious eating alone in restaurants and are reluctant to travel alone; however, once they have experienced going off on their own, most find independence to be enriching and enjoyable (Anderson & Stewart, 1991). More problematic is the difficulty in finding ways to manage their need for physical affection and sexual gratification and the profound sense of deprivation they feel. This is one of the postdivorce losses that women talk about frequently with friends and in therapy. Some women pursue opportunities to meet eligible men, some engage in recreational sex, and some find gratification through masturbation. However, for many midlife single women, there is a grudging acceptance that they do not have a sexual partner now, and this reality may not change in the future. Therapists can provide useful support in helping women process this loss, while at the same cautioning them against using rebound relationships or hasty remarriages as a solution to this problem.

In their book *Flying Solo*, Anderson and Stewart (1991) state that the tasks midlife women are least prepared to master are those related to the ultimate indicator of power: money. Many women say that they are terrified to spend money after their divorce. This may be a realistic concern, as most women's standard of living goes down after divorce, while that of their ex-husbands goes up. Therefore, the authors suggest that dealing responsibly with money, especially making long-term financial plans, is the "final frontier" of women's independence (p. 265).

Midlifers at Work

Women Finding Meaning at Work

Current midlife women were socialized to expect that family life would be a higher priority than work. Nonetheless, changing social forces have led women into the work-force, so by age 50, over 67 percent of women are employed outside the home (U.S. Bureau of the Census, 1996). As they launch their children, women increasingly say that their career is what gives them a sense of meaning and pleasure (McCullough & Rutenberg, 1989), and this is not just true for professional women (Anderson & Stewart, 1991). Women who reenter the work force as their children begin to move out may initially just want to fill a void or address a financial need. However, they soon begin to change their perceptions and to see themselves as women with talents and opportunities, rather than as mothers without children at home. They also shift their view of work from just providing financial security to being a source of autonomy and independence. Work also provides midlife women with a new sense of community, and especially if they are single, work may become the center of their social lives (Bergquist et al., 1993; Hochschild, 1997). Furthermore, McQuaide (1998) identified a number of factors which contribute to the well-being of midlife women that are related to their working outside the home. These factors include an income above $30,000, a sense of effectance, and high self-esteem.

Sexual and Age Discrimination at Work

This positive picture of midlife women at work is clouded by the endurance of sexual discrimination in the workplace. Women were not a presence in the workforce until the 1960s and 1970s. During that time, the salaries of women stabilized at rates much lower than those of men's salaries. From 1960 to 1979, the median earnings of women work-ing full-time stabilized at approximately 59 percent of the earnings of men (Bergquist et al., 1993). Then, from 1979 to 1993, women's median earnings rose from 62 percent to 77 percent of men's (Lewin, 1997). However, a troubling new study indicates that after twenty years of a steadily narrowing wage gap, it is now widening again: The median earnings are now just under 75 percent of men's (Lewin, 1997). Women also continue to be underrepresented in power positions. For example, only 2 percent of chief execu-tive officers of major corporations and fewer than 10 percent of corporate board mem-bers are women (Bergquist et al., 1993). Furthermore, as midlife women enter the workforce and attempt to develop their careers by changing jobs, they find that age dis-crimination limits their ability to be hired or to move into new positions (Pogrebin, 1996). Thus, women remain about ten years behind their male cohorts in job develop-ment (Ackerman, 1990). This is indicative of the double discrimination that mature women face: first for being women and second for aging. Youthful appearance is not just about looks; it is about power. And when it comes to youth and power, there is a gender gap. While midlife women experience a sense of invisibility as they show signs of aging, men are considered to have character or wisdom. Nonetheless, some positive changes are occurring. Corporations are making accommodations to women who took the "mommy track." Corporate women who chose flexible work arrangements to raise their children are able to get back on track and are accepted by co-workers when they return to full-time employment (Shapiro, 1996).

Men Reassessing Priorities

Men in their forties are still strongly career focused, but by their early to mid-fifties, some men begin to reprioritize marital satisfaction as a central factor to their happiness (Julian et al., 1992). However, work remains important, and it is not until they approach 60 that they realistically assess what they have accomplished in their careers. As part of this reevaluation, men often decide that the price of their occupational success was too high. However, this does not necessarily mean that they willingly initiate a process of relinquishing or reducing the power and money that accompany their success. In a study of 4,000 male executives, 68 percent admitted they had neglected their families for their careers, and 50 percent said that they would have done it differently (Bergquist et al., 1993). When this realization occurs, it is usually hypothetical, but it may become very functional for the many midlife men who lose their jobs when companies reorganize. Some men report that the experience of being downsized pushed them into developing more balanced and fulfilling lives (Bergquist et al., 1993; Carter & Peters, 1996).

Regrouping after the Pink Slip

The numerous reorganizations in the corporate world have significantly affected midlife men and women through early retirement packages and layoffs. These job terminations may result in an initial sense of betrayal, disillusionment, and confusion, especially for men who had viewed themselves as good company men and fear that they may now be unemployable because of their age, type of experience, and high salary level. For women, the restructurings may mean that the middle management jobs that they had hoped to find have disappeared. For many men and women, the response to these challenges is a mobilization of their resiliencies and resources. For some, this may mean retraining or additional education, especially in the increasingly technological marketplace, and opportunities to meet new people and gain new perspectives and skills. For others, this may be an opportunity to start their own business. Entrepreneurship is a major phenomenon of the 1990s, with women-owned business representing the fastest growing segment of the economy (Bergquist et al., 1993). For those who remain employed, benefits such as medical plans, vested retirement plans, or profit-sharing plans provide the "golden handcuffs" that keep people employed at jobs that may be less than satisfying. This has particular significance for midlifers because the economic reality, especially for single women, is that they may be working past the age of 70. Even among married women, economic pressures may lead to a lengthening of the period of employment. Indeed, a new study indicates a shift in gender patterns of older married midlifers in the workplace. While the percentage of working married men age 55–64 has declined in the last fifteen years, the percentage of working married women in that age range has sharply increased. The study suggests that women, who lack the Social Security credits or pension savings of men their age, are continuing in the workforce after their husbands retire to secure their economic survival (Uchitelle, 1997). The stress of adjusting to changes in work status frequently motivates individuals and families to seek clinical assistance. In addition to attending to practical matters, such as budgetary concerns and reassignment of household chores, clients will need to address maintaining their support systems and reassessing the meaning of productivity at this stage in their lives.

Redefining Family Relationships at Midlife

The Sandwich Generation

Contrary to the image of aging parents being packed off to the nursing home, most elderly people are healthy enough and financially stable enough to live independently throughout their lives. Most of those who develop infirmities or illness are cared for by their children. Because people are living longer, the period of providing care for aging parents has moved from the forties to the fifties. Also, because child-bearing has been delayed and children are older when they leave home, midlifers may be caring simultaneously for aging parents and young adults—and perhaps for returning children and grandchildren as well. The group of adults caught in this competition of roles is called the "sandwich generation." Typically, the caregivers are midlife daughters and daughters-in-law, not sons. Women provide the day-to-day care for their aging parents and sometimes their in-laws, while their husbands and brothers provide financial support and supervise property and other assets. It is not that men do not care, but the tasks of caregiving have traditionally been distributed differentially between the sexes.

Fortunately, this system overload occurs when adults are at their peak of competence, control, and ability to handle stress (Gallagher, 1993). If the family views caregiving as normal rather than burdensome, the phase will be less stressful. These caregiving expectations are strongly influenced by ethnic values. For example, Latino, Asian American, African American, and Native American families tend to normalize the caregiving role, while Irish and Czech families are less likely to do so. Anglo Americans, who value independence and self-sufficiency to the extreme, tend to find provision of care to the elderly particularly problematic for both generations (McGoldrick et al., 1996). However, even in families in which caregiving is culturally supported, women caregivers are at high risk for stress-related illnesses and are sometimes called the hidden patients in the health care system. Greene (1991) has identified the following issues for midlife caregivers:

- *A shift in intimacy:* Caregivers become aware of personal details, and that breaks down generational boundaries.
- *A shift in power and responsibility:* Caregivers, who now give rather than receive nurturance and advice, feel like parents to their parents.

- *Financial burden:* The financial demands of caring for parents occurs around the same time midlife women are launching children, starting new careers, and/or going to school.

- *Role competition:* Caregivers may also be mothers, partners, employees, homemakers, and/or students.

- *Emotional ambivalence:* Caregivers feel anger and embarrassment about providing their parents with intimate physical care, but also guilt and responsibility. As a result, they may have difficulty setting limits on their level of participation.

- *Confrontation with one's own aging and mortality.*

As a result of these pressures and the potential for burnout, caregivers may need assistance with identifying their own needs and setting appropriate limits. This is particularly true for single midlife women, who are the most isolated but who are assumed to be free of other responsibilities and are the most overwhelmed. The more resilient caregivers are able to view this period as an opportunity to resolve old issues with parents that have persisted through previous life cycle phases. For those who had managed their intergenerational issues as they occurred and moved more smoothly through earlier life cycle transitions, the postlaunch phase provides an opportunity for both generations to continue to adjust their relationship in ways that are mutually satisfying.

> Meryl (age 48) and Steve (age 50) called for an appointment in response to Meryl's complaint of depression. At intake, it was apparent that Meryl was worn out. According to the couple, her main problem was the pressure of visiting her widowed mother five times a week, doing all the shopping and household chores, and chauffeuring her mother to her medical and other appointments. Meryl had not complained until the previous fall, when the couple's youngest child, Amy (age 18), had gone off to college. At that point, Meryl's resentment spilled over, and she complained that Steve was not supportive. Steve stated that he held up his end by being the family's sole wage earner, and now he was doubly burdened by bills for Amy's tuition and for his mother-in-law's home health aide. Upon further probing, it became apparent that Meryl's sense of isolation was a longstanding marital issue that had surfaced with such urgency only when their daughter was no longer in the home. The first phase of treatment addressed the couple's presenting problem: Meryl's urgent sense of burden, burnout, and isolation. As a typical oldest daughter, Meryl had assumed the overresponsible role in her family of origin. She was coached to call her younger sister and brother to express her need for them to assume a more equitable role in caring for their mother. With some prodding, both siblings agreed to increase their visits and phone contacts with their mother. Meryl was also coached to begin setting limits on her unconditional availability to her mother. These interventions began to challenge Meryl's previously unquestioned assumption that she alone was responsible for the smooth running of the family.

Just as midlifers have the opportunity to redefine their relationships with their parents, they may also feel able to establish a more comfortable relationship with in-laws if they are not caught up in old conflicts with them. With their recognition of their own mortality, midlifers may now see themselves as peers with in-laws. Feeling on a more equal footing, midlifers' constraints of surface politeness or resentment may drop away, and they are better able to express their own wishes.

The Death of Parents

Dealing with the death of parents is now considered a normative task of midlife. However, normative does not mean easy. The death of a parent at any time is a major loss, but at midlife, there are special developmental tasks that are related to, and may have an impact on, the resolution of their grief. As described by Scharlach and Fredricksen (1993), these tasks include the following:

- *Acceptance of one's own mortality:* This is seen as the critical task of this life cycle phase. Midlifers are aware that they are now the executive generation and can no longer look to their parents for guidance. They may become more attentive to their own health, draft their wills and make their own funeral arrangements. Along with freedom from child care, this awareness of mortality is a prime trigger for the life reassessment process.

- *Redefinition of family roles and responsibilities:* Midlifers are now the heads of the family. The role of maintaining family contacts, continuing family rituals and values, and guiding the next generation now falls to them. This redefinition also includes attending to unresolved issues with siblings without the impetus of the older generation to prod them.

- *Change in self-perception:* Midlifers who experience the death of a parent may become more self-reliant and autonomous, while at the same time more responsible toward others. This flowering of autonomy and emotional connectedness is viewed as an indicator of midlife maturity.

Unresolved grief following the death of a parent is usually related to longstanding unresolved issues, such as feelings of dependency, criticism, guilt, or ambivalence. The experience of death and mourning rituals may provide an opportunity to readdress these issues, even after the parent's death. As with all unresolved issues, if they are not addressed now, they will find ways of resurfacing later in life.

Redefining Relationships with Adult Children and Boomerang Kids

It is one thing to have children move out of the home. It is another to view them as adults and relate to them accordingly, and still another for young adults to see their parents as people with a history, life, and concerns of their own. Fortunately, parents and children tend to stay closely connected after launching, often speaking several times a week (White & Edwards, 1993). This validates the parental role and makes the launch less wrenching. If they see that their children are becoming more and more independent in their new roles as young adults both inside and outside the family, parents feel that their job was well done and are able to relinquish some of their parental oversight. If the young adults are not harboring major unresolved issues, then parents and children are increasingly able to interact on an adult, mutually supportive basis. In fact, parent-child relationships have been found to become more affectionate and close after the children leave home (Troll, 1994), and parents often come to view their children as close friends (Shapiro, 1996), especially after the children marry and have children of their own.

More and more frequently, young adult children, especially sons, remain home or return home after a brief period on their own. This may be due to financial concerns, lengthened years of education, delayed marriage plans, or marital breakups. The phenomenon of adult children, and perhaps grandchildren, residing at home is most likely to occur under three conditions: if the parent-child relationship has been positive, if the family has positive attitudes about continuing to provide children with support, and if the family is "intact," rather than being a step-family or a single-parent household. Another factor that encourages adult children to reside with parents is the tendency of couples in unhappy marriages to triangulate their children and hang onto them as a source of emotional support or as a means of maintaining equilibrium in the home. Additionally, parents may want to maintain an immature adult child in their home because of their concern about that adult child's ability to function independently (Aquilino, 1991).

Parents, especially middle-class parents, anticipate the freedom that comes after children leave. Therefore, having adult children in the home produces stress. This is related partly to the frustration of their expectations, but also to the fact that the household is simply more complicated with children present. However, the crucial factor in the parents' response is the way in which they interpret the children's presence. Parents view the situation more negatively if their children are unemployed or move back after a marital breakup than if the children remain home while working or going to school or if they never had been married. The more autonomous and less dependent their children are, the better the parents feel about having adult children in the home. Here again, class and ethnicity influence the family's responses. For example, because of their beliefs about adult development, upper-middle-class parents may find their children's presence worrisome (Aquilino, 1991). By contrast, poor or working-class African American midlifers are more accepting of the tradition, born of necessity, of having their adult children reside in their homes and/or assuming the role of parenting their grandchildren (McGoldrick et al., 1996).

Redefining parent-child relationships as adult-to-adult personal relationships does not happen automatically when grown children leave home, or even when they marry and have children. It is quite common for unresolved emotional issues or differences in the wish for close involvement to create situations of polite, dutiful distance instead of a warm and eager sharing of lives between generations. Resolving old issues is the central emotional task of the younger generation, but parents can help or hinder the process. Their shift from hands-on direction of adolescents to on-call consultant to young adults may not be easy. Some parents also find it difficult to be more open and personal with "children" whom they have always shielded from "adult" problems.

Accepting the Expansion of Family through Marriage and Grandchildren

While midlife is a period of family contraction because of the launching of children and the illness or death of aged parents, it is also a time of expansion and regeneration through marriage and the birth of grandchildren. Families must change their usual relationships with their grown children and also learn to incorporate their children's new spouses and their families. Although some families experience antagonism with in-laws, parents often form close relationships with sons-in-laws and/or daughters-in-law (Bergquist et al., 1993). This process is facilitated if children have chosen spouses who are compatible with their parents' ethnic, class, and religious values or, alternately, if the family is flexible and open to differences. Family of origin traditions and beliefs regarding the appropriate degree of inclusion of in-laws also govern the melding process. On the other hand, if the choice of a marriage partner is seen as a reactive challenge to the parents or if the spouse is selected as a way for the child to distance from the parents, the blending of the two families will be more problematic. Conflicts may develop around such issues as holiday plans or acceptable terms of address. Parents may feel unwanted and attempt to be either overinvolved or under-involved with the young couple or, in extreme cases, cut them off. In general, these difficulties are actually displacements for unresolved family issues that are reenacted through the children's marriage. Because women are typically assigned the role of being responsible for the family's emotional life, the most difficult of these problems usually involve the women in the family: sisters-in-law, mothers with their sons or daughters, and mothers-in-law with daughters-in-law. Betty Carter and Joan Peters (1996) note that the target of mother-in-law jokes is invariably the husband's mother. In this drama, the son is caught in the middle as family history is repeated. Carter and Peters advise that the players who are responsible for handling the problem be the family members, not the in-laws.

> Joan (age 54) and Frank (age 55) prided themselves on their close Italian Catholic family and were disappointed when their son Perry (age 24) married Kathy (age 24), a German Methodist. Nonetheless, Joan continued her daily calls to Perry and still prepared large Sunday dinners, which the new couple increasingly began to miss. A crisis occurred when Perry spent Thanksgiving and then Christmas Eve with his wife's family. Joan reacted angrily with Perry. Their distress and bewilderment about the ensuing estrangement led Joan and Frank to seek therapy. At intake, it was apparent that Joan's intensity was balanced by Frank's affable distancing. Their traditional roles—homemaker and wage earner—had worked well when the children were home, especially since Joan's overresponsible parental role was culturally sanctioned. After first normalizing their dilemma in the context of their life cycle stage and ethnic expectations, the therapist challenged the couple to refocus on their marital relationship (a normative midlife task) and suggested that they get "remarried." They were coached to begin dating and eventually to invite Perry and Kathy out on a double date. They were cautioned to avoid making demands on the younger couple or to refer to past disappointments. Joan was also encouraged to reexamine her expectation of daily contact with her son and her lack of acknowledgment of his married status. This proved to be extremely challenging for Joan until Frank recalled his feeling of being discounted by Joan's mother when he and Joan were newlyweds.

One of the supreme rewards of midlife is grandparenthood. Grandparents say that the pleasure of seeing their own children parent the next generation is a joy that defies description. Family identity is solidified as the family reenacts meaningful life cycle rituals and ceremonies. Grandparents have an opportunity to revisit and perhaps redo their experience as parents without the day-to-day responsibility of child care.

On the other hand, Bergquist et al. (1993) have identified the following potential problems of grandparenthood:

- If grandparents are divorced, conflict may arise around who gets invited to parties or, if they are remarried, who are the "real grandparents."
- If adult children divorce, custody agreements may need to include grandparents' visitation rights. This may be a potentially critical issue if the relationship between the two adult generations, especially with the in-laws, has not been good.
- If the adult children are incapacitated by drug abuse or illness, grandparents may be recruited to raise their grandchildren.

Relations with Siblings and Other Kin

The sibling relationship is the family relationship of longest duration—longer than with parents, spouses, or children. While levels of closeness vary at different periods, the sibling relationship tends to be sustained throughout life. Despite distances or differences, siblings often come together to share holidays and special occasions. Midlife siblings draw together as aunts and uncles, parents, and grandparents become ill and die, leaving them to assume their place as the older generation. They also face the stressor of distributing the tasks of providing care to their aging parents. Typically, a sister, either the oldest or the closest, will assume the role alone if a family therapist has not been involved to help the sister get support from her siblings. After a parent's death, the primary caregiver may feel resentment with her siblings for their lesser involvement. As part of the grief process, siblings should be encouraged to address this issue and find a way to adequately express their appreciation to the caregiver. Failure to do so may lead to a disruption of relations. There also may be other issues that have been chronic sources of conflict through other life phases. After the parents' deaths, if there is no outside help, siblings may distance themselves or cut off rather than work at resolving these conflicts. If the discord persists, the siblings risk losing a significant source of practical and emotional support that they may need in later life.

Friendships at Midlife

Friendships take on new importance at midlife. During the child-raising years, friendships were often diluted by the omnipresence of children at most social gatherings, but at midlife, they matter again in a profound and personal way. Midlifers are reinventing themselves. Their families look different. They may be suddenly single. For all the special concerns of midlife, long-term friends are there to provide a sense of belonging and continuity, while new friends are needed to address new interests and realities. With their heightened awareness of life's fragility, midlifers consciously value and appreciate their friends.

For single women in particular, friends are needed to provide a sense of connection and community. Just after divorce or widowhood, women tend to turn to their married friends. This soon shifts, and single women find that they need to develop a network of single friends. Developing this network requires exploring new depths of self-confidence and assertiveness, but the effort pays off. Friends function almost like a new extended family that provides resources, support, and opportunities for developing purpose and meaning in life through connection. The connection between female friendships and the well-being of midlife women has been supported by research (McQuaide, 1998). Therefore, clinicians should offer treatment to midlife women that helps them enhance their social networks.

For men, forming or maintaining friendships may be a new experience, since they were not socialized to develop relationship skills, and their wives had performed that role during earlier life stages. Now, it is more important than ever for men to take responsibility for the work of maintaining relationships, including friendships. However, men's friendships continue to conform to the cultural norms of "masculinity," which prescribes superficial and competitive connections, rather than the more intimate, disclosing friendships of women (Julian et al., 1992). Friendships do become more important to men at midlife, especially if they are divorced or widowed; however, true to their upbringing, which emphasized financial and work success, men still tend to rely primarily on the close partnership of a one-to-one relationship with a woman, who is expected to make it work out. The emotional isolation of men at this stage of life should be treated by therapists as a serious crisis waiting to happen. A good place to help men start to learn how to maintain relationships is to coach them on relating to their grown children.

> When John (age 55) was told by his wife that she was leaving him, he moved into a condo and began dating, but he still felt unremittingly lonely. At the urging of his sister, John entered therapy. His lack of relationship skills was indicated by his humorous yet poignant expression of surprise at his wife's decision to end the marriage: "I didn't know we were unhappy until she told me!" An exploration of his support system revealed superficial relationships with his children and friends. John reported that he had not yet disclosed to his closest friends at work that he was living on his own. His difficulty with emotional closeness was normalized in the context of the socialization of men in our culture. The therapist suggested to John that before he could develop a truly intimate relationship with a woman, he must first learn to connect with family members. The therapist began by coaching him to schedule dinners with his son Dan (age 31), who lived locally, and to maintain phone contact with his daughter Emily (age 28), who was away at graduate school. John was cautioned to take care not to attempt to put his children in a caretaking role, but rather to reconnect around his desire to know more about their lives, interests, and memories.

Gays and Lesbians at Midlife

The tasks of midlife are egalitarian. Gays and lesbians, bisexuals, and heterosexuals are all challenged by the same developmental and life cycle issues. However, gays and lesbians have unique midlife concerns that require special attention, some of which are addressed below.

Midlife Gay and Lesbian Parents

There has always been a minority of gays and lesbians—often an invisible minority—who have parented and launched children. There is no single route to this role. Sometimes when heterosexual couples divorce, one of the partners identifies him or herself as homosexual. Other gays and lesbians become parents after coming out by using alternative means of insemination, surrogacy, sexual intercourse, or adoption. Gay males who are parents overwhelmingly became fathers during an earlier heterosexual marriage, while deciding to become parents after coming out is primarily a lesbian phenomenon and has been called the "lesbian baby boom" (Patterson, 1996).

Gays and lesbians who leave marriages at midlife are influenced by the same life reevaluation process experienced by midlife heterosexuals who decide to divorce, including the sense of time running out and the postlaunch boost. The timing of their decision to leave their marriages and begin living openly as homosexuals is also frequently due to the sensitivity of these parents to their children's needs. Most children of homosexuals are nonreactive about their parents' sexuality until they reach adolescence. At that time, because of their own developmental issues, some adolescents may experience anger and embarrassment at having a parent who is "different" and stigmatized. Therefore, many gay parents wait to come out until their children reach young adulthood, with the expectation that their children will then be more able to accept their sexual orientation. Parents may also delay their decision to live openly as gays or lesbians because of the ongoing homophobia of the court system and the possibility of losing visitation rights with their children during divorce proceedings (Bigner, 1996).

> Cheryl (age 46) had been married for eighteen years to Stan (age 49), a successful businessman, and their daughter Jill (age 17) was starting to plan for college. Cheryl had given up a teaching career to be a stay-at-home mom and was involved in several volunteer activities in her upper-middle-class community. Before her marriage, she had experienced romantic feelings for women but never acted on them. When she married Stan, she immersed herself in her roles as wife and mother and put those feelings out of mind. Then, after fifteen years of marriage, she met Elaine (age 42) at a tennis game and felt drawn to her. The two women developed a close friendship and eventually became romantically involved. Because of Stan's frequent business trips, Cheryl was able to keep the relationship a secret. As devoted as she came to feel to Elaine, Cheryl felt equally committed to her family's stability and could not leave her marriage. Feeling torn between two lives and becoming increasingly depressed about her struggle to maintain the pretense of stability, Cheryl entered therapy. Cheryl stated that she had no intention of leaving her family, but she needed help with her depression. Treatment initially addressed the stress of managing the logistics of her situation. As Cheryl felt more relaxed about talking about her dilemma, her therapist helped her look at her own homophobia—at stereotypical images she held of gay people, her early concepts of homosexuality, and her family's attitudes. Cheryl was then able to identify her own sense of shame that added to her need to maintain the secret. Cheryl was then encouraged to look at her social network to identify those friends who would accept her as a gay woman. She was coached to firm up those relationships and then to slowly share her dilemma. She was also assisted in moving closer to her daughter, as that

relationship was most important to her. When her level of comfort was clearly established, Cheryl was assisted in preparing to disclose her relationship to her husband and daughter through extensive use of role play.

The process of simultaneously launching children, divorcing, and coming out complicates three processes that are already major life transitions when experienced separately. Each of these transitions requires major role shifts and life-style changes, with feelings that range from liberation to loss. Furthermore, gay parents and their children are engaged concurrently in the processes of individuation and the development of new adult identities. However, for the parents, there is an additional issue of developmental lag. Bigner (1996) notes that gay men who come out at midlife are off-time in terms of their development of a stable, positive homosexual identity compared with gays who come out earlier in life. These men may prematurely seek to replicate the exclusive, committed relationship model of heterosexual marriages, which may complicate their integration into gay culture.

Aging Bodies and Confronting Mortality

Coming to terms with aging is a key developmental task of midlife. Among gay men, concern about body image is particularly strong, as they fear that signs of aging will mean that they are less sexually desirable. The critical midlife task of accepting one's own mortality is also drastically heightened among gay men. A large proportion of men living with HIV/AIDS are now in midlife; some of these men have been HIV-positive for ten years or more. In addition to their acute personal awareness of mortality, gay men have buried and grieved for numerous friends and partners. Therefore, rather than just beginning to confront mortality at midlife as heterosexuals typically do, gay men have been living with a heightened awareness of death on a daily basis for many years.

Midlife lesbians are more tolerant of the body changes that come with age than midlife gay men. Women in general tend to focus more on the emotional than the physical aspects of intimacy. Therefore, with two women in a relationship, the partners are much less prone to equate desirability and beauty with youth, thinness, or any of the other usual male criteria of female beauty (Cole & Rothblum, 1990). However, women in lesbian partnerships may find the transition of menopause to be more problematic than heterosexual women do. Human sexuality researcher Sandra Leiblum (1990) suggests that the couple's adjustment to the physical and psychological effects of menopause may be exacerbated by their experiencing menopause together, as both women's sexual interest and performance may decline at the same time. Furthermore, lesbian partners undergoing menopause at the same time may respond more acutely to their mutual cessation of fertility if they were prevented from having children because of their lack of access, as lesbians, to donor insemination or adoption options. In this case, the association between menopause and loss will be compounded for lesbian partners (Slater, 1995). Nonetheless, it has also been reported that lesbian women complain much less of menopausal symptoms than do heterosexual women (Pogrebin, 1996).

As with midlife heterosexual couples, midlife gays and lesbians are more companionable and less passionate. At this stage of life, both gays and lesbians report that while they remain sexually active, sex does not have the urgency it did in their youth. This is particularly true of lesbians, who are typically less sexually active (though not less affectionate or expressive) than either gay male or heterosexual couples (Green, Bettinger, & Zacks, 1996; Leiblum, 1990). However, while sex may be less frequent, gays and lesbians report sex to be more satisfying in midlife (McWhirter & Mattison, 1984; Tully, 1989). Johnson and Keren (1996) note that gay couples are much less likely than heterosexual couples to view infrequent sex with their partners as an indicator of a relationship problem.

Support Systems

Gays and lesbians who are now in midlife were raised in an even more homophobic society than today's younger generation and may not have felt able to disclose their sexual orientation or their partnerships to family members; or if they did disclose, they may have been rejected or kept at a distance. Therefore, friends are overwhelmingly important sources of support and come to serve as more accepting quasi-families. These "families of choice" may include homosexual friends, heterosexual friends, co-workers, children from former marriages, and selected family members. As gays and lesbians age, especially those without children, the expectation is that they will be turning to members of their families of choice to care for them in sickness or old age (Tully, 1989).

Summary

Midlife, the longest phase of the life cycle, is a time of major family restructuring. The family shrinks when children are launched from the home or when parents of midlifers are lost through the death. Additionally, many families experience loss through midlife divorce or the death of a spouse. Women also "leave" voluntarily by joining the workforce or other outside involvement, while midlife men may suddenly experience the loss of employment if their company is restructured. On the other hand, the family expands through the marriage of adult children and the birth of grandchildren. Families may also expand when launched children return home, some with their own children, or if aged parents join the household. Any one of these events is a stress point that might motivate families to seek a family therapist for help.

With or without treatment, families will need to adjust to the realignments and redefinitions of roles that result from these restructurings. While women typically lead the way toward change, men frequently join the process by being jolted into an awareness that they are at risk of losing relationships they had taken for granted. Making a decision about working on or ending unsatisfying relationships or reconnecting with estranged family members becomes more urgent when an individual is aware of being closer to death than birth. Accomplishing these shifts requires midlifers to reexamine and alter the rigid role definitions that have defined their relationships during the child-rearing years. Admittedly, this is a tough job in a culture that still supports traditional gender roles, but midlifers know that it is "now or never." Therefore, they may be more accessible to clinical intervention than at earlier stages in their life cycle. Thus, rather than being a time of winding down, midlife is a long life cycle stage that can be a fertile time for new options, growth, and change.

References

Ackerman, R. (1990). Career developments and transitions of middle aged women. *Psychology of Women Quarterly, 14,* 513–530.

Anderson, C. M., & Stewart, S., with Dimidjian, S. (1991). *Flying solo.* New York: W. W. Norton.

Apter, T. (1995). *Secret paths: Women in the new midlife.* New York: W. W. Norton.

Aquilino, W. S. (1991). Predicting parents' experience with coresident adult children. *Journal of Family Issues, 12,* 323–342.

Bergquist, W. H., Greenberg, E. M., & Klaum, G. A. (1993). *In our fifties: Voices of men and women reinventing their lives.* San Francisco: Jossey-Bass.

Bigner, J. (1996). Working with gay fathers: Developmental, postdivorce parenting, and therapeutic issues. In J. Laird and R. -J. Green (Eds.), *Lesbians and gays in couples and families: A handbook for therapists,* (pp. 370–403). San Francisco: Jossey- Bass.

Carter, B., & Peters, J. K. (1996). *Love, honor and negotiate: Making your marriage work.* New York: Pocket Books.

Cole, E., & Rothblum, E. (1990). Commentary on "Sexuality and the midlife woman." *Psychology of Women Quarterly, 14,* 509–512.

Dowling, C. (1996). *Red hot mamas: Coming into our own at fifty.* New York: Bantam Books.

Friedan, B. (1963). *The feminine mystique.* New York: W. W. Norton.

Gallagher, W. (1993, May). Midlife myths. *The Atlantic Monthly,* 551–568.

Green, R. -J., Bettinger, M., & Zacks, E. (1996). Are lesbian couples fused and gay male couples disengaged? Questioning gender straitjackets. In J. Laird and R. -J. Green (Eds.), *Lesbians and gays in couples and families: A handbook for therapists,* (pp. 185–230). San Francisco: Jossey-Bass.

Greene, C. P. (1991). Clinical considerations: Midlife daughters and their aging parents. *Journal of Gerontological Nursing, 17,* 6–12.

Hochschild, A. (1997). *Time binds: When work becomes home and home becomes work.* New York: Metropolitan Books.

Johnson, T. W., & Keren, M. S. (1996). Creating and maintaining boundaries in male couples. In J. Laird and R. -J. Green (Eds.), *Lesbians and gays in couples and families: A handbook for therapists,* (pp. 231–250). San Francisco: Jossey-Bass.

Julian, T., McKenry, P. C., & McKelvey, M. (1992). Components of a man's well-being at midlife. *Mental Health Nursing, 13,* 285–298.

Leiblum, S. (1990). Sexuality and the midlife woman. *Psychology of Women Quarterly, 14,* 495–508.

Levinson, D. J. (1978). *The seasons of a man's life.* New York: Ballantine Books.

Lewin, T. (1997, September 15). Women losing ground to men in widening income difference. *New York Times,* pp. A1, 12.

McCullough, P. G., & Rutenberg, S. K. (1989). Launching children and moving on. In B. Carter & M. McGoldrick (Eds.), *The changing family life cycle: A framework for family therapy* (2nd ed.) (pp. 285–309). Boston: Allyn and Bacon.

McGoldrick, M., Giordano, J., & Pearce, J. K. (Eds.) (1996). *Ethnicity and family therapy.* New York: The Guilford Press.

McQuaide, S. (1998). Women at midlife. *Social Work, 43,* 21–31.

McWhirter, D. P., & Maattison, A. M. (1984). *The male couple: How relationships develop.* Englewood Cliffs, NJ: Prentice-Hall.

Mitchell, V., & Helson, R. (1990). Women's prime of life: Is it the 50's? *Psychology of Women Quarterly, 14,* 451–470.

Neugarten, B. (1968). The awareness of middle age. In B. Neugarten (Ed.), *Middle age and aging: A reader in social psychology*, (pp. 93–98). Chicago: University of Chicago Press.

Patterson, C. J. (1996). Lesbian mothers and their children: Findings from the Bay Area Families Study. In J. Laird and R. -J. Green (Eds.), *Lesbians and gays in couples and families: A handbook for therapists*, (pp. 420–437). San Francisco: Jossey-Bass.

Pogrebin, L. C. (1996). *Getting over getting older.* New York: Berkley Books.

Rubin, N. (1997, December 7). In middle age and suddenly single. *New York Times*, Westchester Regional Section, pp. 1, 8.

Scharlach, A. E., & Fredricksen, K. (1993). Reactions to the death of a parent during midlife. *Omega*, 27, 307–319.

Schnarch, D. (1997). Passionate marriage. *Family Therapy Networker*, 21, 42–49.

Shapiro, P. G. (1996). *My turn: Women's search for self after children leave.* Princeton, NJ: Peterson's.

Slater, S. (1995). *The lesbian family life cyle.* New York: The Free Press.

Troll, L. (1994). Family connectedness of old women: Attachments in later life. In B. F. Turner & L. E. Troll (Eds.), *Women growing older*, (pp. 169–201). Thousand Oaks, CA: Sage.

Tully, C. T. (1989). Caregiving: What do midlife lesbians view as important? *Journal of Gay and Lesbian Psychotherapy, 1*, 87–103.

Uchitelle, L. (1997, December 14). She's wound up in her career, but he's ready to wind down. *New York Times*, Section 3, pp. 1, 13.

U.S. Bureau of the Census. (1996). *Statistical abstract of the United States.* Washington, DC: U.S. Government Printing Office.

Warga, C. L. (1997, August 30). Estrogen and the brain. *New York Magazine*, 26–31.

White, L., & Edwards, J. N. (1993). Emptying the nest and parental well-being: An analysis of national panel data. *American Sociological Review, 55*, 235–242.

11

Families in Later Life

Challenges and Opportunities

Froma Walsh

> For age is opportunity no less
> than youth itself, though in another dress,
> and as the evening twilight fades away
> the sky is filled with stars invisible by day.
>
> —Longfellow

The major demographic changes over the coming decades concern the aging of societies worldwide. What passes unnoticed is that families are aging as well, as they are also becoming more diverse. This chapter examines the emerging challenges and opportunities for families in later life associated with retirement and financial security; grandparenthood; chronic illness and caregiving; and death, loss, and widowhood. Clinical guidelines are offered to encourage the many possibilities for personal and relational resilience and growth and for meaningful connection, reconciliation, and transformation of intergenerational relationships.

The Graying of the Family

Declining birth rates, health care advances, and increasing longevity are contributing to the rise in the number and proportion of elderly people in the United States, as in other parts of the world (Kausler, 1996). Family networks

Taken from: *The Expanded Family Life Cycle: Individual, Family, and Social Perspectives,* Third Edition, edited by Betty Carter and Monica McGoldrick.

are becoming smaller and top-heavy, with more older than younger family members. Life expectancy has increased from 47 years in 1900 to over 76 at present. The baby boom generation, now entering its fifties, will soon swell the over-65 population to record levels: 13 percent of our population by the year 2000, up from 8 percent in 1950. By 2040, over one in five Americans will be over 65 (one in four people in most of the Western world). With medical advances and healthier life-styles, a growing number of people are living into their 80s, 90s, and even past 100. Later life is being redefined in terms of the "young old," persons age 65 to 85 who are mostly healthy and vibrant, and the "old old" or "fourth age" of elders over 85, the fastest-growing segment of older people and the group most vulnerable to serious illness and disability.

The Varying and Extended Family Life Cycle Course

As societies age, the family life course is becoming ever more lengthened and varied (Hareven, 1996; Walsh, 1993). Four- and five-generation families add complexity in balancing members' needs and family resources. With fewer young people to support the growing number of elders, threats to Social Security and health care benefits will likely fuel greater insecurity and intergenerational tensions. More "young old" people at retirement age, with diminishing resources, are involved in caring for their elderly parents. At the same time, the trend toward having few or no children will leave elders with fewer intergenerational connections. The declining proportion of younger people and increasing workforce involvement of women exacerbate family strain in providing financial and caretaking support. New technologies prolonging life and the dying process pose unprecedented family challenges. With impersonal, inadequate health care systems and the loss of community in our society, the family is more important than ever in providing not only caregiving, but also a sense of worth, lasting emotional ties, and human dignity at life's end.

Pathways through later life are increasingly varied. Our aging population is becoming more racially and ethnically diverse (Johnson & Barer, 1990). Changes in family life-styles also present new challenges with aging. The growing number of single older adults (Anderson & Stewart, 1994) and couples who are unmarried or without children forge a variety of significant kin and friendship bonds. With greater life expectancy, couples may have thirty to forty years ahead after launching children; increasing numbers are celebrating fifty and sixty years of marriage. Although nearly 50 percent of marriages end in divorce, remarriage is becoming the most common family form. Two or three marriages over a long lifetime, along with periods of cohabitation and single living, are likely to become increasingly common, creating enlarged and complicated family networks in later life. As Margaret Mead (1972) noted, it's difficult for one relationship to meet the changing developmental priorities of both partners over a lengthened lifetime. In view of these challenges, perhaps it's remarkable that over 50 percent of couples do *not* divorce.

The family and social time clocks associated with aging are also becoming more fluid. As many become grandparents and great-grandparents, others are beginning or extending parenthood. With new fertility methods, women in middle age are bearing children. Men, whose remarriages are often to women many years younger than themselves, are increasingly starting second families in later years.

Aging gay men and lesbian women meet needs for meaning and intimacy in varied ways (Berger, 1996; Reid, 1995), with developmental challenges strongly influenced by their present life circumstances and social environment (Cohler, Hostetler, & Boxer, 1998). In the context of the current HIV/AIDS epidemic, many experience their life course as doubly out of time from the social norm (Hagestaad, 1996): Not only do they confront mortality and loss earlier than most others, but also it is difficult to plan for an uncertain future. Concerns of middle and later life tend to be compressed in a present focus, with a foreshortened sense of time (Borden, 1992).

To be responsive to the growing diversity in society, our view of "family" must be expanded to the lengthened and varied course of the life cycle and therapeutic objectives must fit the challenges and preferences that make each individual and family unique. We will need to learn how to help family members live successfully in complex and changing relationship systems, buffer stressful transitions, and make the most of their later life course.

Ageism and Gerophobia

As a society, we are not readily confronting the challenges of later life or seeing the opportunities that can come with maturity. Our gerophobic culture holds a fearful, pessimistic view of aging as decay. The trajectory theory of human development depicts an upswing during the early years, with gains in competency and achievements. Aging is seen as unmitigated deterioration, decline, and loss, until the downslope ends in death. The elderly have been stereotyped as old-fashioned, rigid, senile, boring, useless, and burdensome. In a culture that glorifies youth, we cling to it, strive to recapture it, and face aging with either dread or denial. As Letty Cottin Pogrebin (1996) observes, many people continue to think of themselves as "thirty-something" until they realize that's what their children are.

The clinical literature on aging has been predominantly a discourse on illness, disability, and declines in functioning, neglecting the positive changes that can occur with maturity. The prevailing biomedical view pathologizes later life, focusing on disease and treatment. The mental health field has given scant attention to the later phases of life other than noting that adults over age 65 are the group most vulnerable to mental illness, particularly organic brain disease and functional disorders such as depression, anxiety, and paranoid states (Butler & Lewis, 1983). Suicide rates also rise with age, the highest rate being among elderly white men. A grim picture of later life is indeed portrayed. Institutionalized forms of ageism and sexism make it especially difficult for women to thrive and prosper.

Pessimistic views of the family hold that most elders either have no families or, at best, have infrequent, obligatory contact; that adult children don't care about their elders and dump them in institutions; and that families in later life are too set in their ways to change long-standing interaction patterns. In fact, family relationships continue to be important throughout later life for most adults (Hughson, Christopherson, & Bonjean, 1996). Contrary to popular belief and stereotype, families provide most direct caregiving assistance, psychological support, and social interaction for elderly loved ones (Brody, 1985; Cohler, 1995; Sorenson, 1977; Sussman, 1976). The vast majority live with spouses or other relatives, including children, siblings, and aged parents.

Couples who weather the storms that are inevitable in longlasting relationships and childrearing report high marital satisfaction in their postlaunching years, as they have more time and resources for individual and shared pursuits. In later life, needs for companionship and caregiving come to the fore. Although sexual contact may be less frequent, intimacy can deepen with a sense of shared history and connection over time.

The importance of sibling relationships often increases over adulthood (Cicirelli, 1995). The centenarian Delany sisters, born into a southern African American family, pursued careers and lived together most of their lives, crediting their remarkable resilience to their enduring bond. They watched over each another and saw their differences as balancing each other out. They also shared enjoyment in conversation and laughter. When Dr. Bessie Delany, who lived to the age of 103, was asked how she accounted for their longevity, she quipped, "Honey, we never married; we never had husbands to worry us to death!" (Delany & Delany, 1993, p. 24).

Although most older Americans and their adult children prefer to maintain separate households, they sustain frequent contact, reciprocal emotional ties, and mutual support in a pattern aptly termed "intimacy at a distance" (Blenkner, 1965; Spark & Brody, 1970). Research finds a strong link between social contact, support, and longevity. Elders who visit often with friends and family and maintain a thick network of diverse relationships are likely to live longer than those with few kin and social resources (Litwin, 1996). The proximity of family members and contact by telephone are especially important to those who live alone, 80 percent of whom are more elderly women, typically widowed. Adult children and grandchildren also benefit in many ways from frequent contact and support. However, in our mobile society, uprooting for jobs or retirement can bring enormous strain in the ability to provide mutual support and caregiving in times of crisis.

Negative stereotypes of older people and their families have led clinicians to pessimistic assumptions that they are less interesting than younger clients, a poor investment for therapy, and too resistant to change. Elders are most often treated custodially, given a pat on the hand and a medication refill, or expected to fit into programs geared to younger adults. Functional problems may be discounted as merely a natural, irreversible part of aging and deterioration. In a social context of gerophobia, it is perhaps not surprising that a recent survey of family therapy literature over the past decade found a paucity of journal articles on family issues in later life and the concerns of older adult members (Van Amburg, Barber, & Zimmerman, 1996), concluding from this lack of attention that the family therapy community is still engaged in "coming of age."

A normal life course perspective of family development and aging is needed, emphasizing the potential for growth and meaning as much as negative aspects of change. The family as a system, along with its elder members, confronts major adaptational challenges in later life. Changes with retirement, grandparenthood, illness, death, and widowhood alter complex relationship patterns, often requiring family support, adjustment to loss, reorientation, and reorganization. Many disturbances are associated with difficulties in family adaptation. Yet such challenges also present opportunities for relational transformation and growth.

Later-Life Transitions and Challenges

Each family's approach to later-life challenges evolves from earlier family patterns. Systemic processes that develop over the years influence the ability of family members to adapt to losses and flexibly meet new demands. Certain established patterns, once functional, may no longer fit changing life cycle priorities and constraints.

For most families in the dominant culture, launching of children from home sets the stage for relationships in middle and later life. With the structural contraction of the family from a two-generational household to the marital dyad or single parent alone, parent-child relationships are redefined and parental involvement shifts to refocus on individual and couple life pursuits. Most parents adjust well to this "empty nest" transition (Neugarten, 1991) and are more likely to have trouble when children return to the nest for financial considerations. When a child has filled a void in a marriage or a single parent's life, it can complicate a family's subsequent ability to deal with later-life challenges, as in the following case:

> Luis (age 66) was brought by his wife, Maria, for treatment of serious alcohol abuse since his retirement. Living with the couple was their 42-year-old son Raul, who had never left home. Longstanding close attachment between the mother and son had stabilized a chronically conflictual marriage over the years, when Luis had worked long hours outside the home. Retirement shifted the balance as Luis, now home all day, felt like an unwanted intruder. Lacking job and breadwinning status as sources of self-esteem, he felt like an unworthy rival to his son for his wife's affection at a time in his life when he longed for more companionship with her. Competitive struggles fueled Luis's drinking, erupting into angry confrontations. His wife sided protectively with the son.

In Latino families, as in many ethnic groups, ties between a mother and her children are commonly stronger than the marital dyad. However, in this family, a pattern that provided a workable balance over many years became a dysfunctional triangle when retirement disrupted the relationship system.

Retirement

Retirement represents a significant milestone and adjustment for individuals and couples. For the retiree, particularly for men in our society, there is a loss of meaningful job roles, status, productivity, and relationships that have been central to traditional male standards for identity and self-esteem throughout adult life. Whether retirement was desired or forced will affect adjustment. Loss of a role as financial provider along with income reduction may bring significant stress. Residential change, a common occurrence at retirement, adds further dislocation and loss of connectedness with nearby family, neighbors, and community. A successful transition involves a reorientation of values and goals and a redirection of energies and relationships (Atchley, 1992).

For women in the workforce, retirement can be a financial disaster. A recent survey (U.S. Department of Labor, 1994) found that 40 percent of employed women over age 55 have no pension plan and 34 percent have no health insurance. Furthermore, divorced women may find that they have no rights to their former spouse's pension benefits at his death. For such reasons, many women continue working past retirement age. As our society grapples with the coming crisis in Social Security and retirement benefits, the retirement age for most workers is likely to rise from 65 to 70, which will require a major shift in expectations and later-life plans.

In traditional marriages, couples may have difficulty with the husband's retirement, accompanied by losses of his job-related status and social network, especially if they have repeatedly been uprooted from kin and social networks to accommodate career moves. Another challenge involves the retired husband's incorporation inside the home, with a change in role expectations, time together, and the quality of interaction (Szinovacz & Harpster, 1994). It can be problematic if the husband tries to take over the household, making the wife feel displaced or under his thumb. At the other extreme, if a retired husband feels that he has earned full leisure while his wife is expected to continue to take care of the household, her resentment is likely to build. For successful adaptation to retirement, couples need to renegotiate their relationship to achieve a new balance. With needs and concerns shared through open communication, relational resilience is strengthened as partners pull together to reshape their lives, plan financial security, and explore new interests to provide meaning and satisfaction together and on their own.

Grandparenthood

As people live longer, increasing numbers are becoming not only grandparents, but also great-grandparents. The experience can hold great significance, as Margaret Mead (1972) remarked on her own response to becoming a grandparent: "I had never thought how strange it was to be involved at a distance in the birth of a biological descendant . . . the extraordinary sense of having been transformed not by any act of one's own but by the act of one's child" (p. 302). Grandparenthood can offer a new lease on life in numerous ways. First, it fulfills the wish to survive through one's progeny, thereby assisting in the acceptance of mortality. As Mead (1972) experienced, "In the presence of grandparent and grandchild, past and future merge in the present" (p. 311). Grandparenthood also stimulates the reliving of one's own earlier child-rearing experiences. Such reminiscence and new perspective can be valuable in coming to accept one's life and one's parenting satisfactions and achievements as well as any regrets or failure.

Grandparenthood is a systemic transition that alters intergenerational relationships (Spark, 1974). When adult children become parents, this can be an opportunity for reconnection and healing of old relational wounds with their parents, as they begin to identify with the challenges inherent in parenting and develop more empathy for their parents' positions.

Grandparents and grandchildren may enjoy a special bond that is not complicated by the responsibilities, obligations, and conflicts in the parent-child relationship. A common saying is that grandparents and grandchildren get along so well because they have a common enemy. Such an alliance can become problematic if a grandchild is triangulated in a conflict between parent and grandparent, as in the following case.

> After the death of her father and her own divorce, Sharleen (age 32) and her son Billy (age 8) moved in with Sharleen's mother to consolidate limited resources. The family was seen in therapy when Sharleen complained that Billy was behaving badly and was

disrespectful to her. At the first session, Billy went to his grandmother for help in taking off his boots. The grandmother quickly took over the discussion while Sharleen seemed passive and helpless. Billy, sitting between them, glanced frequently to his grandmother for cues. Each time Sharleen and her mother started to argue, Billy drew attention to himself. Sharleen's attempts to quiet him were ineffectual, whereas Billy responded immediately to a raised eyebrow from his grandmother.

The grandmother complained that she was overburdened by having to take care of "both children." Sharleen felt that her mother undercut her efforts to assume more responsibility by criticizing everything she did as "not right," meaning not her way. We explored how the grandfather's sudden death from a heart attack had left the grandmother feeling devastated by the loss and uncertain how to go on with her own life. Taking charge to help her daughter raise Billy filled the void. Therapy focused first on family losses—both the death and the divorce—for all three generations. Then attention was directed to work out more balanced relationships so that Sharleen could be a more effective mother to her son while the grandmother's role as head of the household was redefined from a position of control to honored-elder status. Sharleen agreed to respect her mother's wishes about how she wanted her home kept. Her mother agreed to respect Sharleen's ways of child-rearing and support her parental leadership.

While most grandparents are relieved not to have primary caretaking demands, expectations to be a resource and yet not an interference can be burdensome (Cherlin & Furstenberg, 1986). As Mead (1972) asserted, "I think we do not allow sufficiently for the obligation we lay on grandparents to keep themselves out of the picture—not to interfere, not to spoil, not to insist, not to intrude" (p. 303). When a widowed parent moves in with adult married children, conflicts of loyalty and primacy can erupt in triangles involving both partners and the parent/in-law.

In poor and minority communities with high rates of early pregnancy, grandparenting typically occurs early. Grandmothers, often only in their thirties and forties, and great-grandparents provide care for the children, particularly when single parents must work. While this provides a vital lifeline for the youngsters and their parents, it often takes a toll on their own health, when combined with other heavy job and family responsibilities or increasing frailness (Burton & Dilworth-Anderson, 1992; de Toledo, 1995).

Foster grandparenting can enrich later life, serve as a resource for single and working parents, and provide connectedness across the generations, especially where more informal connections are lacking in age-segregated living arrangements. Seniors can also be encouraged to volunteer in child care centers. Youngsters benefit from the attention, companionship, and wisdom of their elders.

Chronic Illness and Family Caregiving

As our society ages, the number of people with chronic conditions is increasing dramatically and those impaired are living longer with disabilities than ever before. Even though most elders do maintain good health, fears of loss of physical and mental functioning, chronic pain, and progressively degenerating conditions are common preoccupations. Health problems and severity vary greatly. Among seniors age 65 to 84, arthritis, high blood pressure, and heart disease are most prevalent. For people over 85, the risk of cancer and the extent of disabilities increase, combined with intellectual, visual, and hearing impairment. Physical and mental deterioration may be exacerbated by depression and helplessness, reverberating with the anxiety of family members.

Because our society lacks a coherent approach to caring for people with disabling chronic conditions, growing numbers live with deteriorated health and lack access to appropriate and affordable services. Families in poverty, largely members of minorities, are most vulnerable to environmental conditions that heighten the risk of serious illnesses, permanent disabilities, and caregiver strain, as well as early mortality (Lockery, 1991). Diseases such as asthma, diabetes, high blood pressure, and heart disease are most prevalent among the poor.

Family caregiving is a major concern. The increasing numbers of frail elderly people over 85 pose growing demands for long-term care and financial coverage (Baltes, 1996). By 2020, there will be twice as many elderly (14 million) needing long-term care as today. In 1970, there were twenty-one potential caregivers (defined as people age 50 to 64) for each person 85 or older; by 2030, there will be only six such potential caregivers, severely straining intergenerational relations. As average family size decreases, fewer children are available for caregiving and sibling support. With more people marrying and having children later, those at midlife—the so-called sandwich generation—are caring simultaneously for children and adolescents, as well as for aging parents, grandparents, and other relatives. Finances can be drained by college expenses for children just as medical expenses for elders increase. Adult children who are past retirement and facing their own declining health and resources must assume responsibilities for growing numbers of infirm parents. The likelihood of being caregivers for one or more aging family members is rapidly increasing.

Growing numbers of elders with chronic conditions are receiving care at home, producing a crisis in caregiving. Only 5 percent of the elderly are maintained in institutions, yet chronic health problems require increasing hospitalizations, medical costs, and home-based care for daily functioning. Family and friends are the front lines of support. Nearly three quarters of disabled people over 65 rely exclusively on these informal caregivers. As the pool of caregivers diminishes, caregivers themselves are badly strained by multiple pressures.

Women at midlife are especially burdened, as job demands are juxtaposed with expectations to maintain traditional responsibilities for homemaking, child-rearing, and elder care. Caregiving responsibilities have been almost exclusively the domain of women, mostly daughters and daughters-in-law; three out of four primary caregivers are women. Their average age is 57, but one fourth are 65 to 74, and 10 percent are over 75. As women have become fuller participants in the workforce and their income essential in two-parent as well as single-parent families, rebalancing of work and family roles is needed. Yet few employers offer schedule flexibility or consider men to be caregivers.

Prolonged caregiving takes a heavy toll. Eighty percent of caregivers provide help seven days a week, averaging four hours daily. In addition to housekeeping, shopping, and meal preparation, two thirds also assist with feeding, bathing, toilet, and dressing. The lack of useful management guidelines by most medical specialists adds to the confusion, frustration, and helplessness family members commonly experience. Some aspects of chronic illness are especially disruptive for families, such as sleep disturbance, incontinence, delusional ideas, and aggressive behavior. One symptom and consequence of family distress is elder abuse, which is most likely to occur in overwhelmed families, stretched beyond their means and tolerance.

Among the most difficult illnesses for families to cope with are dementias, progressive brain disorders. Alzheimer's disease, accounting for 60 percent of dementias, is one of the most devastating illnesses of our times. It affects one in ten people over 65 and nearly half of those over 85. The disease is often not correctly diagnosed; cognitive losses are erroneously assumed to be a natural part of aging. The irreversible course of the disease can last anywhere from a few years to twenty years or more, becoming an agonizing psychosocial and financial dilemma for families. Over time, Alzheimer's disease strips away mental and physical capacities in gradual memory loss, disorientation, impaired judgment, and finally loss of control over bodily functions. People with Alzheimer's may repeatedly ask the same questions, forgetting earlier answers, or prepare a meal and forget to serve it. They may get lost easily and forget where they live. With impaired memory and judgment, they may forget entirely about a boiling pot or a child under their care or make disastrous financial decisions. It is most painful for loved ones when they are not even recognized or are confused with others, even with those long deceased.

Since medical treatment of the illness is limited, a custodial bias has prevailed in its management. Individuals who are kept at home on low-dose or drug-free regimens do not show as severe decrements as those in institutions, where they tend to be highly medicated and isolated from familiar people and surroundings (Zarit, Anthony, & Boutselis, 1987). Adult daycare can partially relieve family burden. Family psychoeducation and support networks are helpful in meeting caregiving challenges, coping with stress, and dealing with confusion and memory lapses. Useful illness-related information and management guidelines reduce the risk of caregiver depression, particularly with ambiguity in the illness course (Bonjean, 1989; Boss, 1991; Henderson & Gutierrez-Mayka, 1992; Light, 1994). Family members can be helped in grieving for the loss of a loved one's family roles and relationships.

In approaching all serious illness in the elderly, clinicians and researchers need to expand the narrow focus on an individual female caregiver to encourage the involvement of all family members as a caregiving team. It is important for clinicians not to assume that family distress indicates a family causal role in deterioration of a chronic illness. Family intervention priorities should include (1) stress reduction; (2) information about the medical condition, functional ability, limitations, and prognosis; (3) concrete guidelines for sustaining care, problem solving, and optimal functioning; (4) linkage to supplementary services to support family efforts. To meet caregiving challenges, communities must support families through a range of services, from day programs to assisted living and commitment to full participation of elders, including those with disabilities, in community life (Pinkston & Linsk, 1984).

Family dynamics also require attention. For couples, chronic illness and disability can skew the relationship between the impaired partner and caregiving spouse over time (Rolland, 1994). In some cases, a caregiving partner may overfocus on the other's disability to avoid facing his or her own vulnerability, anxiety, or longings to be taken care of. Couples therapy can help each to gain empathy for the other's position, address such issues as guilt and blame, and rebalance their relationship to live and love as fully as possible.

Intergenerational dependency issues come to the fore as aging parents lose functioning and control over their bodies and their lives. Handling increased dependency of aging parents is not a parent-child role reversal as some imply. Even when adult children give financial, practical, and emotional support to aging parents, they do not become parents to their parents. It should be kept in mind that despite childlike appearance or functioning, the aged parent has had over fifty years of adult life and experience (Spark & Brody, 1970). Family therapists can open conversation about dependency issues with sensitivity and a realistic appraisal of strengths and limitations. An elderly father may be driving with seriously impaired vision, unwilling to admit the danger or give up his autonomy to be driven by others. Older parents often fail to tell their adult children that they are financially strapped because of the shame and stigma of dependency in our society, with its ethos of the rugged individual. Adult children can be coached on ways to develop a filial role (Blenkner, 1965), taking responsibility for what they can appropriately do for aging parents and recognizing their own constrains (Boszormenyi-Nagy & Spark, 1973; Brody, 1974).

If an aging parent becomes overly dependent on adult children, who become overly responsible through anxiety or guilt, a vicious cycle may ensue: The more the children do for the parent, the more helpless the parent may become, with escalating neediness, burden, and resentment. Ambivalent overattachment and dependence are common (Kahana & Levin, 1971). Siblings may go to opposite extremes in meeting filial responsibilities, as in the following case:

> Mrs. Z., a 74-year-old widow, was hospitalized with multiple somatic problems and secondary symptoms of disorientation and confusion. She complained that her two sons, Tim (age 46) and Roger (43) didn't care whether she lived or died. The sons reluctantly agreed to come in for a family interview. On the phone, Roger offered his belief that his mother's hospitalization was merely a ploy for sympathy, to make him feel guilty for not being at her beck and call as Tim was. He said that he had learned years ago that the best relationship with her was none at all. In contrast, Tim had become increasingly responsible for his mother, particularly since she had been widowed. Yet the more helpful he was, the more helpless she became in managing her own life. He felt drained by his mother's growing neediness.
>
> The overresponsible son was coached to be more helpful by challenging his mother to function maximally rather than doing for her. The underinvolved son was encouraged to join his brother and to relieve him of some limited, specific burdens. Both sons were helped to communicate their feelings and concerns directly with their mother and to be patient in listening to her. They were advised not to be put off if their mother initially resisted the changes. With anxiety in the system reduced and the family working together, Mrs. Z.'s thinking and functioning improved markedly.

Caregiving challenges can be burdensome; yet they can become opportunities for healing strained relationships and forging new collaboration as a caregiving team, building relational resilience. When family conflict has been intense and persistent, where ambivalence is strong, or when relationships have been estranged, caregiving for aging parents is more likely to be complicated. Life-and-death decisions become more difficult, as in the following crisis situation:

> Joellen, a 38-year-old single parent, was deeply conflicted when her father, hospitalized for long-term complications from chronic alcohol abuse, asked her to donate a kidney needed to save his life. She felt enraged to be asked to give up something so important when he had not been there for her as a father over the years. He had been a mean drunk, often absent and many times violent. She was also angry that he had brought on his deteriorated condition by his drinking and had refused to heed his family's repeated pleas to stop. Further, she was hesitant to give up a vital organ when she had to think about caring for her children and their possible future needs. Yet, a dutiful daughter and a compassionate woman, she also felt a sense of obligation and guilt. She did not want her father to die because she denied him her kidney.
>
> When I suggested that Joellen talk with her mother about her dilemma, she learned that her father had also asked her siblings for the kidney donation. Estranged from them, Joellen feared that old rivalries would be stirred up as to who would be seen as the good giving child or the bad selfish ones. I encouraged her to overcome her reluctance to meet with her siblings to grapple with the dilemma, and to persevere when the meeting proved hard to schedule. When the siblings finally met, they were surprised to learn how torn each of them felt. Old rivalries shifted as they began to reach out to one another.
>
> I suggested that they begin to plan together about how they might collaborate to share the many challenges likely to come up in caring for both of their aging parents. As each envisioned taking a part of future responsibilities, the elder brother, who was healthy and had no plans for a family of his own, volunteered his kidney for their father. The decision was less conflictual for him because he had experienced better times with his father in earlier years before the problem drinking. As the others offered to support him and agreed to contribute to their parents' future well-being in ways that fit their abilities and resources, a new solidarity was forged.

The point at which failing health requires consideration of nursing home placement is a crisis for the whole family (Tobin & Kulys, 1981). Contrary to myth, placement is usually turned to only as the last resort, when family resources are stretched to the limit, and most often in later stages of mental or physical deterioration. Nevertheless, feelings of guilt and abandonment and notions of institutionalization can make a placement decision highly stressful for families, particularly for adult daughters, on whom the caretaking expectations typically concentrate.

> Mrs. Arletti called for help, stating that she felt helpless to control her teenage son and feared that he needed to be institutionalized. A family assessment revealed that the problems had developed over the past eight months, since Mrs. Arletti's mother had been brought into their home. She wept as she described her mother's Parkinson's condition and her difficulty in providing round-the-clock attention, on top of a full-time job. She was alarmed by her mother's occasional loss of balance and falling, especially since finding her on the floor one morning. Her worry about institutionalization concerned her mother: At her father's deathbed, a year earlier, he had asked Mrs. Arletti to promise that she would always care for her mother. She felt alone with her dilemma, her husband preoccupied by his work.

This case underscores the importance of inquiry about elderly family members even when problems are presented elsewhere in the system, which may express concerns of the family crisis. It's also crucial to attend to a spouse's distancing and lack of support, in this case due to the husband's lingering guilt over having left the care of his dying mother to his sisters.

Family sessions can be helpful in assessing needs and resources, weighing the benefits and costs of options, and sharing feelings and concerns before reaching a decision together. Often, through discussion, new solutions emerge that can support the elder's remaining in the community without undue burden on any member. Organizations such as the Visiting Nurses Association can provide home services and inform families of community backup. Respite for caregivers is crucial to their well-being. When placement is needed, therapists can help families to see it as the most viable way to provide good care and help them to navigate through the maze of options.

We must also re-vision chronic care, which is often thought of narrowly in terms of medical services and nursing home placement. A report commissioned by the Robert Wood Johnson Foundation (Institute for Health and Aging, 1996) takes a broader view to address chronic care challenges for the twenty-first century. The report envisions a system of care: a spectrum of integrated services—medical, personal, social, and rehabilitative—to assist people with chronic conditions in living fuller lives. A continuum of care is needed to ensure that individuals receive the level and type of care that fit their condition and their changing needs over time and to support independent living, optimal functioning, and well-being as long as possible.

Dealing with terminal illness is perhaps the family's most painful challenge, complicated by agonizing end-of-life decisions. The rising rate of suicide among the elderly involves not only a desire for control over their own dying process but also is a response to unmet needs for pain control and palliative care and worries about laying financial and emotional burdens on loved ones. Clinicians need to work with families to reduce suffering and make the best arrangements to keep the seriously ill person comfortable and comforted, while balancing the needs of family members.

Family adaptation to loss involves shared grieving and a reorganization of the family relationship system (Walsh & McGoldrick, 1991). Avoidance, silence, and secrecy complicate mourning. When patient and family hide knowledge of a terminal illness to protect one another's feelings, communication barriers create distance and misunderstanding, prevent preparatory grief, and deny opportunities to say goodbyes. Therapists can assist family members with feelings of helplessness, anger, loss of control, or guilt that they could not do more. It may be easier for younger family members to accept the loss of elders whose time has come, than for elders to accept the loss—and their own survival—of siblings or their own children who die first. The death of the last member of the older generation is a milestone for a family, signifying that the next generation is now the oldest and the next to face death. It is important, also, to address the impact of an elder's death on grandchildren, often their first experience with death and loss.

Widowhood

Widowhood is a highly stressful transition, with a wide diversity of responses in adaptation. Women are four times as likely as men to be widowed and are widowed at an earlier age with many years of life ahead. Those in traditional marriages, who are more dependent on their husbands, begin in midlife to anticipate the prospect of widowhood (Neugarten, 1991). Research finds that 5 percent of bereaved spouses become severely depressed; 10 to 17 percent become depressed to a clinically significant degree. The initial sense of loss, disorientation, and loneliness contributes to an increase in death and suicide rates in the first two years, especially for men. Social contact is often more disrupted for men, since wives traditionally link their husbands to the family and community, especially after retirement. Yet the long-term hardships for widowed women tend to be greater, with more limited financial resources and remarriage prospects. Widows over age 75 are at highest risk of poverty; currently, over 50 percent have incomes of $10,000 or less.

Despite initial problems with the challenges in daily living, most older surviving spouses are quite resilient over time. The profound loss may even be accompanied by positive feelings associated with pride in coping. Most widows view themselves as having become more competent and independent; only a small portion view the changes entirely negatively (Lopata, 1996). Older people are at highest risk when adult children have moved away and when they have lost most of their friends and siblings through death or relocation.

The psychosocial challenges in the transition to widowhood involve grief over the loss and reinvestment in future functioning (Lieberman, 1995; Lopata, 1996). A realignment of relationships in the family system also occurs (Walsh & McGoldrick, 1991). The initial task is to take in the fact of death, transforming shared experiences into memories. Encouragement of expression of grief with family members and through meaningful rituals is most helpful. Attention must also turn to the reality demands of daily functioning and self-support. Wherever possible, clinicians and adult children should help both partners to anticipate widowhood, preparing for the challenges each would face. Many need to acquire new skills for independent living, such as managing finances, returning to the job market, or arranging household maintenance. The adjustment to being physically alone, in itself, may be difficult.

Within one to two years, adjustment shifts to new activities and interest in others. The label of "widow" can be harsh, defining a person in terms of spousal loss. This identity can interfere with the process of reengaging in life. Reentry is also impeded by distancing of family and friends who have not faced their grief or come to terms with their own mortality or possibility of widowhood. Further dislocation may occur if one's home is given up or if financial problems or illness block independent functioning. In such cases, widows are likely to move in with adult children, siblings, or even very aged parents. One woman prepared for the imminent loss of her husband by reassuring herself that she could go home to her mother. Her mother's death shortly after the death of her husband was devastating.

Remarriage is becoming an increasingly common option for older adults, although less so for women. Economic and legal constraints lead many elderly couples to live together without formal marriage. Critical to the success of remarriage is the relationship with adult children and their approval of the union. Problems can arise when a child views remarriage as disloyalty to the deceased parent. Adult children may be shocked by remarriage of an aged parent—especially when they cannot conceive of the elderly as attractive or sexually active—and may assume that the new spouse is interested only in money. Concerns about a will may arise, particularly if children view inheritance as compensation for earlier disappointments or as evidence that they will still come before the new partner.

Cross-Generational Interplay of Life Cycle Issues

Within every family, the later-life challenges of the elderly interact with salient concerns of children at their own concurrent life phases. With increasing diversity in family patterns and the tendency toward later marriage and child-rearing, different pressures and conflicts may be generated. The issues that come to the fore between an older adult parent and young adult child will likely differ from those that arise between a parent, a middle-aged child, and an adolescent grandchild. Tensions are heightened when developmental strivings are incompatible, as in the following case:

Julia, in her mid-twenties, was beginning a social work career and engaged to be married when her 63-year-old mother, who lived 2000 miles away, developed cardiovascular disease, with a long and painful deterioration. Julia, who had always been close to her mother, felt torn. Her sense of obligation was countered by reluctance to put her own new job and marriage plans on hold indefinitely. The situation was complicated by Julia's recently emerging separation and identity issues. She had always been close to her mother and dependent on her direction and support. The geographic distance from home that she had established bolstered her self-reliance. Like many of her peers, she had absorbed the cultural ethos confusing differentiation with distancing and disconnection. Now, just at the time her social world pushed her to be independent and self-directed, her mother needed her most; and Julia feared losing her.

Phone contact became increasingly strained. Julia's mother saw her failure to return home as uncaring and selfish. Deeply hurt, she struck back: "What kind of social worker can you be if you can't even care about your own mother?" Julia made a brief visit home, feeling guilty and upset. The uncertain course of the prolonged illness made it difficult to know how long her mother would live or when to plan trips. Julia sent her mother gifts. One, picked with special care and affection, was a leather-bound book for her memoirs. On her next visit, Julia discovered the book, unopened, on a closet shelf. Deeply hurt, she screamed at her mother to explain. Her mother replied, "If I wrote my memoirs, I'd have to write how much you've let me down." Julia cut her visit short. When she returned to her own home, conflict erupted with her fiance, and the wedding plans were canceled. Deeply upset by the breakup, Julia phoned her parents for consolation. Her mother expressed her own disappointment, saying that she now had nothing to live for. A few hours later, she had a stroke. Julia's therapist interpreted this as her mother's narcissism and manipulation. Furious, Julia did not return home again before the long-anticipated call came one night from her father informing her, "Mom is dead."

Julia scarcely grieved. She got married within weeks to someone she hardly knew. It was not until the marriage broke up that tremendous grief at the loss of her mother surfaced, with guilt and regret over the final alienation and the fact that it was too late to change the past. Working with a family therapist, she determined to learn from that experience to repair her strained relationship with her father—whom she had not visited since her mother's death—before it was too late. With the therapist's coaching, she also initiated new connections with her mother's family, learning more about her mother's life and coming to understand her more fully as a person. She also learned that her mother's own mother had cut her off because of disappointment with her shortly before Julia's grandmother's death. With new compassion and emotional reconnection, Julia arranged a memorial service to honor her mother on the anniversary of her death.

The mother's developmental needs at the end of life occurred "off-time" from the perspective of the daughter's developmental readiness and out of sync with her age peers. Terminally ill, the mother needed to draw her family close and to feel that she had successfully fulfilled her role as a mother. The young adult daughter was threatened by the closeness and dependency at a time of impending loss, when she was not yet secure in her own personhood and felt her culture's pressure for autonomy. In this case, cross-generational anniversary reactions complicated the picture as unresolved issues from the mother's relationship with her own mother were revived, adding fuel to the conflict, disappointment, and estrangement at life's end.

As Erikson (1959) noted, young adults in our culture are emerging from the search for identity into issues of commitment. The fear of ego loss in situations calling for self-abandon may lead to isolation and self-absorption. This may heighten preoccupation with making initial choices and commitments, especially marriage, career, and residence, that define one's place in the adult world. Responding to caregiving needs and threatened loss of aging parents at this life stage may be fraught with conflict. Clinicians need to help young adults offset the cultural push for family disconnection and prioritize relationships with their elders at the end of life.

Successful Aging

The aging process is more variable and malleable than was long believed (Posner, 1995). Elders can enhance their own successful development in their approach to their challenges and by making the most of their options. Baltes and Baltes (1990) have posited that successful aging is accomplished by "selective optimization with compensation" as a means of coping with reduced functioning. They cite the example of the pianist Arthur Rubinstein, who described how he dealt with the weaknesses accompanying aging. First, he selectively reduced his repertoire, playing a smaller number of pieces. Second, he practiced them more often (an optimizing strategy). Third, he slowed down the speed of his playing just before the fast movements, producing a contrast effect that heightened the impression of speed (a compensating strategy). By these means, he sustained a successful concert career into old age.

Studies of normal adult development and family functioning indicate that a variety of adaptive processes, rather than one single pattern, contribute to successful later-life adjustment (Bengtson, 1996; Birren & Schaie, 1995; Schulz & Heckhausen, 1996). This diversity reflects differences in family structures, individual personality styles, gender roles, and ethnic, social class, and larger cultural influences (Gelfand, 1982; Gibson, 1982). Traditional gender role distinctions of earlier adulthood tend to shift as older men show increasing passivity and accommodation in response to environmental challenges and greater needs for nurturance and affiliation, whereas older women become more assertive and active in meeting their own needs (Gutmann, 1997). The development of more androgynous modes of response, of aspects of life that were earlier constrained, can enable a greater role flexibility that may be related to longevity and greater life satisfaction in old age.

Likewise, successful family functioning in later life requires flexibility in structure, roles, and responses to new developmental needs and challenges (Caspi & Elder, 1986; Walsh, 1993). As patterns that may have been functional in earlier stages no longer fit, new options must be explored. With the loss of functioning and death of significant family members, others are called upon to assume new roles, responsibilities, and meaning.

Strengths That Have No Name

Betty Friedan's (1993) analysis of international studies reveals that older adults may actually integrate problems at a higher level than the young, in particular attending to ethical and contextual issues. Also, the degree of mental acuity varies depending on the environment: The more autonomy, the more acuity. In discovering "strengths that have no name," from a number of studies of different populations, Friedan concludes that women experiencing the most profound change and discontinuity were the most vital in later life. The women who were most frustrated, angry, and depressed were those who held on most rigidly to the early roles—or had been forced to stay in or repeat the "cluttered nest" past its time and thereby were kept from moving on (p. 143). In the anthology *If I Had My Life to Live over I Would Pick More Daisies* (Martz, 1992), women reflect on the choices they have made and wish to make from childhood to old age, their alternatives both extended and limited by personal belief systems, ethnic and cultural identity, class and economic status, age, and gender. Personal choices are never simple; more often, they are complex, conflictual, and intertwined with the decisions of others because of their strong relational orientation. Friedan found that what distinguished women who were vital was not which roles they played in earlier adulthood, but whether or not they had developed a quest, creating a sense of purpose and structure for making life choices and decisions.

In contrast to the redefinition of self that many women must move through with menopause, widowhood, or divorce, most men's identities continue to be based in career and sexual potency. As these paths to self-expression close off, aging men who continue to invest in these two "proofs" of masculinity experience uncertainty, decline, and a void. Friedan proposes that men choose meaningful work, not give up and retire as we've been taught to do. Intimacy can become more basic and ultimately more rewarding than sexual intercourse, as an emotional intercourse that is shared in more authentic ways than in gender games of youth.

Heilbrun (1997) approaches maturity with celebration, finding possibilities in aging for enrichment and unexpected pleasures. For her, the greatest reward of parenting has been delight in her fully grown progeny, considering them to be friends with an extra dimension of affection. She finds it powerfully reassuring at this time to think of life, and each day, as borrowed time to be fully savored. As May Sarton wrote in her essay *At Seventy*, this can be the best time of life because we are more ourselves than ever: We have less conflict and are more balanced; we are better able to know and use our powers; we are surer of what counts in life and have less self-doubt to conquer.

Wisdom of the Elders

The notion that the later years may have a significance of their own is scarcely considered. In Erikson's theory of human development, old age is viewed as a critical period, during which resilient individuals may review earlier life experiences and their meaning in the quest to achieve integration and overcoming despair at the end of life's journey. In this process, the new adaptive strength of wisdom may be gained. The task of achieving integration is challenging, as older adults are faced by the finiteness of life and knowledge of past imperfections. More recent extension of Erikson's work (Erikson, Erikson, & Kivnick, 1986) emphasizes the importance of vital involvement in the present for the ultimate achievement of integration. Interviews with octogenarians revealed many pathways for integration and reconciliation of earlier life issues. Some look for models of aging in parents or grandparents; others look to friends or even media personalities. Some achieve a sense of integrity from displaying such attributes as humor, compassion, continual growth, and commitment. For the most resilient aged people, past traumas and inescapable missteps are ultimately put into perspective. Even those who have not achieved integration are actively involved in attempts to reach some resolution. A priority for clinicians is to recognize the sources of meaning in late life and understand how older adults integrate the varied experiences of a lifetime into a coherent sense of self and life's worth.

What is notable about this life stage is the search for life's transcendent meaning. A common thread that emerges through the accounts of study participants is the dynamic portrait of older people, not as victims of life forces but as resilient, possessing the capacity to shape as well as to be shaped by events. Transcendence involves the freedom to risk, with courage, seeing aging as a personal and spiritual evolution and, instead of focusing on limits, seeking new horizons for learning, adventure, and change.

Spiritual faith, participation in religious services or activities, and congregational support are wellsprings sustaining resilience for most elderly people (Walsh, 1998; in press). Medical studies suggest that faith, prayer, and spiritual rituals can actually strengthen health and healing by triggering emotions that influence the immune and cardiovascular systems. One study of elderly patients after open-heart surgery found that those who were able to find hope, solace, and comfort in their religious outlook had a survival rate three times higher than those who did not. What matters most is drawing on the power of faith to give meaning to precarious life challenges.

The search for identity and meaning is a lifelong process. Individuals and their families organize, interpret, and connect experiences in many ways. We must be sensitive to the culture and time in which individuals have lived and the contribution of structural sources of meaning. At the same time, we need to recognize the diverse ways in which people are influenced by common background. For some, religion is salient in making meaning of their experience; for others, it might be ethnic heritage or the education that enabled them to rise out of poverty. Many elders show enormous potential for continual self-renewal. They are vital and potent as they create their own meanings by interpreting and reformulating experiences, values, structural forces, and elements of their own particular contexts.

Clinical Challenges and Opportunities: A Resilience-Based Approach

A resilience-based approach to practice (Walsh, 1996, 1998) engages elders collaboratively, affirms their strengths and personhood, encourages their optimal functioning, and builds social network resources to support independent living to the fullest extent possible. This orientation rebalances the traditional clinical focus on patient deficits, which too often leads professionals to objectify the elderly, become unduly pessimistic, underestimate their resourcefulness, and make plans for them, based on what professionals think is best, as in the following case:

> Rita, a 78-year-old widow, was admitted to a psychiatric unit with a diagnosis of confusional state and acute paranoia after an incident in which she accused her landlord of plotting to get rid of her. Rita's increasing blindness was making independent living more difficult and hazardous. Her apartment was in disarray, and she had trouble managing simple daily tasks. She was socially isolated, stubbornly refusing assistance from "strangers." Her only surviving family member was a sister who lived in another state. The hospital staff, doubting that Rita could continue to function independently, worked out a nursing home placement for her. Rita vehemently objected, insisting that she wanted only to return to her own apartment. Hospitalization was extended to "deal with her resistance" to the their plan.
>
> A family therapist's strength-based interviews with Rita led to a new appreciation of her as a person and to a plan that was reached collaboratively with her. When asked what most distressed her, Rita replied that it was her failing vision. Asked how she felt about living alone, she responded, "I'm not alone; I live with my books." Rita had been a teacher, happily married, without children, until her husband's death sixteen years earlier. Her beloved father died the same year. After those painful losses, she withdrew from family and friends, determined never to become dependent on anyone again. Rita centered her life on her work; she was known as a "tough cookie," respected by colleagues for her perseverance with challenging students. Since retirement, she had immersed herself in her books, which became a vital source of her resilience. They enhanced her knowledge, imagination, and pleasure, transporting her beyond her immediate circumstances. The books held special meaning because she had inherited many of them from her father, a scholar. They revived her close childhood relationship, when he had spent countless hours reading to her. Now Rita's loss of vision was cutting her off from her most valued connections.
>
> In Rita's strong identification with her father was an intense pride in his part-Indian heritage, carrying a sense of hardiness in adversity, a toughness, and a will to survive and adapt. These strengths were found in the therapist's visit with Rita to her apartment. At first glance, all appeared chaotic: piles of books, clothing, and food containers everywhere. However, a closer inspection revealed that Rita had carefully ordered her environment in a system that made sense to adapt to visual impairment. With a magic marker, she had color-coded food containers; clothes were arranged according to function; books were stacked by subject. Almost blindly, she could easily locate everything she needed.

Rita's stubborn "resistance" had been viewed as a pathological denial of dependency needs. Yet self-reliance had served Rita well over many years. It was the breakdown of her primary mode of adaptation—her vision—that brought confusion and anxiety. Still, realistically, Rita would require some assistance to maintain independent living. Her reluctance to become dependent on caretakers made her reject any aid with one exception: She herself had contacted a religious organization that sent Brothers to read to her whenever she called. She could allow help when she took initiative and had some control in determining the nature and boundaries of the relationship. This positive experience became a model for building a social resource network to support Rita's objective of independent living. Her ability to take responsibility for herself and her determination to function as autonomously as possible were reinforced. She was encouraged to select, and initiate contact with, a few neighbors and shopkeepers she trusted who could provide occasional backup service. Setting up a routine of weekly phone contact with her sister became a source of meaningful touchpoints for both.

Applying the concept of resilience to the family as a functional unit, a family resilience approach affirms the potential in all families for healing and growth, by tapping into their strengths and building resources as they confront life challenges (Smith et al., 1995; Walsh, 1998). Multigenerational and couple relationships in later life encompass a variety of situations that are potentially stressful and may benefit from this approach, as illustrated above. Given the potentially destructive impact of unresolved conflicts and cut-offs (Bowen, 1978), the fallout of hurt, misunderstanding, anger, alienation, sense of failure, and guilt may accompany children and grandchildren into their future relationships. Strains can be prevented and repaired by helping multiple family generations to redefine and reintegrate their roles and relationships as they age and mature.

Family Life Review

I have found the application of life-review therapy (Lewis & Butler, 1974) to couples and families to be of great benefit in later life. It extends the process of the aging person's reminiscence, which facilitates acceptance of one's life and approaching death, to include the perceptions and direct involvement of significant family members who are central to such resolution. Hearing and sharing the varied perspectives on life experiences and relationships enlarge the family story, build mutual empathy, and can heal old wounds for all family members.

In the case of Mrs. Z. and her sons Tim and Roger (described earlier in the chapter), the mother and sons were encouraged to share reminiscences of their family life history. They were helped to explore developmental periods of particular emotional import, evoking crucial memories, responses, and new understanding. The brothers' longstanding rivalry was put into perspective. Roger's cut-off became better understood in recalling a late adolescent conflict over autonomy that he handled by leaving home in anger, severing contact, and vowing to remain self-sufficient. His relationship with his parents had become frozen at that point but now could be brought up to the present. Mother and sons shared their grief at the death of the father for the first time together. Most important, a healing reconciliation among the surviving family members was achieved.

The resolution of later-life issues rests on the foundation of all earlier life stages. Conflicts or disappointments in earlier stages that may have resulted in cut-offs or frozen images and expectations can be reconsidered from a new vantage point and from the many viewpoints of family members. People in later life are often able to be more open and honest about earlier transgressions or shame-laden family secrets. Past mistakes can be more readily owned and forgiven. Misunderstandings and faulty assumptions about one another can be clarified. Successive life phases can be reviewed as relationships are brought up to date. Family albums, scrapbooks, genealogies, reunions, and pilgrimages can assist this work. Precious end-of-life conversations can be videotaped and preserved. The transmission of family history to younger generations can be an additional bonus of such work (Myerhoff, 1992).

Looking Ahead

Families should be encouraged to consider and prepare together for such challenges as transitional living arrangements and end-of-life decisions, discussions that are commonly avoided. Future-oriented questions can also open up new possibilities for later life fulfillment. One son carried concern about how each of his parents would manage alone on the family farm if widowed, but he dreaded talking with them about their death. Finally, on a visit home, he got up his courage. First he asked his mother, tentatively, whether she had ever thought about what she might do if Dad were the first to go. She replied, "Sure, I've thought about it for years. I know exactly what I'd do: I'd sell the farm and move to Texas to be near our grandkids." Her husband shook his head and replied, "Well if that isn't the darndest thing! I've thought a lot about it too, and if your mother weren't here, I'd sell the farm and move to Texas!" This conversation led the couple to sell the farm and move to Texas, where they enjoyed many happy years together.

Making the Invisible Visible

The invisibility of the elderly and ageism have contributed to the unresponsiveness of mental health services to the needs of older adults and their families. Clinical training programs must expand from preoccupation with early developmental stages and offer greater exposure to elders and their families. I once assigned a group of medical students to interview a couple in later life about their life course. The students looked stunned. One acknowledged that he had never had a real conversation with an older person, including his parents. This led us to a valuable discussion of age segregation in our society and professional ageism stemming largely from avoidance of the personal reality of our own aging, losses, and death. Clinicians need to develop awareness of our apprehensions, a perspective on the whole life course, and appreciation of what it is like to be old.

Developmental models for understanding growth and change in later life are needed, for example, to include wisdom and integrative understanding. Current theory, research, and practice are biased to the extent that they fail to include values and meanings that are salient to elders. Clinical services must be flexible to fit the diversity of older people and their significant relationships and to support optimal functioning and integration in the community. Clinicians can foster a growing sensitivity to people who are attempting, with courage, to adapt to losses and challenges of later life in ways that fit needs for identity, connectedness, and meaningful experience.

Problems involving family relationships with elderly members are often hidden. Older adults are more likely to present somatic problems than emotional or relational problems (Qualls, 1991). In a medical assessment, such functional problems as depression, confusion, and anxiety may not be detected or may be assumed to be merely part of old age. Even in cases of organic disease, family relationships can exacerbate or alleviate suffering. The stressful impact of chronic illness on the family also requires attention to family needs for support, information, caregiving guidelines, respite, and linkage to community resources. Clinicians have an ethical responsibility to ensure that interventions respect the developmental needs of all family members. Families are our most valuable resources in treating serious illness. Our clinical interventions can strengthen their resilience in coping with persistent stress. We must encourage their collaboration, understand their caregiving challenges, and support them in our social policies and provision of health care.

The complexity and diversity of family networks in later life require careful clinical assessment. Clinicians shouldn't mistakenly assume—or accept an older adult's initial claim—that there is no family or that the family is not important in later life. Given the prevalent pattern of intimacy at a distance, we must look beyond the sharing of a household to identify significant relationships. Emotionally meaningful bonds with siblings, a daughter-in-law, a nephew, cousins, or a godchild can be valuable resources. The very statement that one has "no family left" may indicate continuing emotional significance of recent deaths or unresolved losses. Longstanding cut-offs may hold potential for repair. Drawing a genogram with an elder can be particularly useful in identifying those who are significant and or could be drawn upon for support.

Another problem of visibility occurs when younger generations present themselves or their children for treatment. Problems involving elderly family members may be hidden behind complaints or symptoms elsewhere in the system. Diagnostic evaluation commonly includes past family-of-origin history with little or no mention of current ongoing extended family relationships or recent changes that may be connected to distress. Whatever the age or problem of the symptom bearer, it is important to inquire about elder members and relationships in the extended family.

Clinicians who are trained to view families from a model based on early developmental stages, with family structure, roles, and functioning geared to child-rearing imperatives, must be careful not to transfer assumptions to families in later life. Moreover, reification of the nuclear family model has pushed the extended family to the margins, much to the detriment of us all. Family assessments should explore how each family, given its particular composition, modes of adaptation, and needs of its members, has responded to later-life challenges. When it has broken down, we need to consider the options for reorganization and transformation of relationships to fit each family situation. Clearly, the later-life challenges and the diversity in family networks require that we develop new, more flexible conceptualizations and approaches to understand and strengthen family functioning to master challenges and seize opportunities for enriched relationships.

Conclusion

The diversity, complexity, and importance of family relations in later life can be expected to become even greater in the coming years. Because more people are living longer than elders did in the past, we lack role models for later-life family relations, just as we lack appropriate labels and role definitions. The term "adult children" is loaded with attributions of dysfunctional childhood families. The term "postparental" is unfortunate, as parents never cease to be parents. Instead it is the *nature* of parent-child relationships that changes over the years. We need to explore and expand possibilities for growth in that transformation. Elders can be encouraged to draw on their rich history and experience to inform both continuity and innovation, as society's futurists. The wisdom of our elders, linked with the energy and new knowledge of the young, can be the basis for rich interchange and planning for the future. Important in the resilience of our society is a sense of pride in age, the value of history and life experience, and the capacity to adapt courageously to change.

More people today are living longer than at any time in history, generating a shift in the population that some regard as the "aging revolution." What will we do with this gift of long life? How can we contribute to people's ability to live with vitality and meaning into advanced old age? Our society and all helping professionals will need to prepare for these challenges. Clinicians' interface issues with our aging families—and with our own aging and losses—may contribute to anxiety, avoidance, overresponsibility, or empathic difficulties with elders and their adult children. As we reach out to become better acquainted with the elders in our own families, as we attempt to resolve our own losses and grievances, and as we explore new relational possibilities with growing maturity, therapeutic work with families in later life will take on new meaning and possibilities for growth.

References

Anderson, C., & Stewart, S (1994). *Flying solo: Women at midlife and beyond.* New York: Norton.

Atchley, R. C. (1992). Retirement and marital satisfaction. In M. Szinovacz, D. J. Eckert, & B. H. Vinick (Eds.), *Families and retirement.* Newbury Park, CA: Sage.

Baltes, M. M. (1996). *The many faces of dependency in old age.* New York: Cambridge University Press.

Baltes, P. B., & Baltes, M. M. (1990). Psychological perspectives on successful aging: The model of selective optimization with compensation. In P. B. Baltes & M. M. Baltes (Eds.), *Successful aging: Perspectives from the behavioral sciences* (pp. 1–34). New York: Cambridge University Press.

Bengtson, V. (1996). *Adulthood and aging: Research on continuities and discontinuities.* New York: Springer.

Berger, R. (1996). *Gay and gray: The older homosexual man* (2nd. ed.). New York: Haworth.

Birren, J., & Schaie, K. W. (1995). *Handbook of the psychology of aging* (4th ed.). San Diego: Academic Press.

Blenkner, M. (1965). Social work and family relationships in later life with some thoughts on filial maturity. In E. Shanas & G. Strieb (Eds.), *Social structure and the family: Generational relations.* Englewood Cliffs, NJ: Prentice-Hall.

Bonjean, M. (1989). Solution focused psychotherapy with families caring for an Alzheimer's patient. *Journal of Psychotherapy and the Family, 5,* 197–210.

Borden, W. (1992). Narrative perspectives in psychosocial intervention following adverse life events. *Social Work, 37*, 153–141.

Boss, P. (1991). Ambiguous loss. In F. Walsh & M. McGoldrick (Eds.) *Living beyond loss*. New York: Norton.

Boszormenyi-Nagy, I., & Spark, G. (1973). *Invisible loyalties: Reciprocity in intergenerational family therapy*. Hagerstown, MD: Harper & Row.

Bowen, M. (1978). *Family therapy in clinical practice*. New York: Jason Aronson.

Brody, E. (1974). Aging and family personality: A developmental view. *Family Process, 13*, 23–37.

Brody, E. (1985). Parent care as normative family stress. *Gerontologist, 25*, 19–29.

Burton, L. M., & Dilworth-Anderson, P. (1992). The intergenerational family roles of aged black Americans. *Marriage and Family Review*.

Butler, R., & Lewis, M. L. (1983). *Aging and mental health: Positive psychosocial approaches* (3rd ed.). St. Louis: Mosby.

Caspi, A., & Elder, G. (1986). Life satisfaction in old age: Linking social psychology and history. *Journal of Psychology and Aging, 1*, 18–26.

Cherlin, A. J., & Furstenberg, F. F. (1986). *The new American grandparent: A place in the family, a life apart*. New York: Basic.

Cicirelli, V. (1995). *Sibling relationships across the life span*. New York: Plenum Press.

Cohler, B. J. (1995). The family in the second half of life: Connecting theories and findings. In R. Blieszner & V. Hilkevitch Bedford (Eds.), *Handbook of aging and the family*. (pp. 59–94). Westport, CT: Greenwood Press.

Cohler, B. J., Hostetler, A., & Boxer, A. (1998). Generativity, social context, and lived experience: Narratives of gay men in middle adulthood. In D. McAdams & E. de St. Aubin (Eds.), *Generativity and adult development: Psychosocial perspectives on caring and contributing to the next generation*. Washington, DC: American Psychological Association Press.

Delany, S. & Delany A. E.(1993). *Having our say: The Delany sisters' first 100 years*. New York: Dell.

deToledo, S. (1995). *Grandparents as parents: A survival guide for raising a second family*. New York: The Guilford Press.

Erikson, E. H. (1959). *Identity and the life cycle*. New York: International Universities Press.

Erikson, E. H., Erikson, J. M., & Kivnick, H. (1986). *Vital involvement in old age: The experience of old age in our time*. New York: Norton.

Friedan, B. (1993). *The fountain of age*. New York: Simon & Schuster.

Gelfand, D. (1982). *Aging: The ethnic factor*. Boston: Little, Brown.

Gibson, R. (1982). Blacks at middle and late life: Resources and coping. *The Annals of the American Academy*, 79–90.

Gutmann, D. (1997). *The human elder in nature, culture and society*. Boulder, CO: Westview.

Hagestaad, G. (1996). On-time, off-time, out of time? Reflections on continuity and discontinuity in an illness process. In V. Bengston (Ed.), *Adulthood and aging* (pp. 204–222). New York: Springer.

Hareven, T. K. (Ed.). (1996). *Aging and generational relations over the life course: A historical and cross-cultural perspective*. New York: Aldine de Gruyter.

Heilbrun, C. (1997). *The last gift of time: Life beyond sixty*. New York: Dial Press.

Henderson, J. N., & Gutierrez-Mayka, M. (1992). Ethnocultural themes in caregiving to Alzheimer's disease patients in Hispanic families. *Clinical Gerontologist: Special Issue on Hispanic Mental Health, 11*, 59–74.

Hughson, G. A., Christopherson, V. A., & Bonjean, M. J. (Eds.). (1996). *Aging and family therapy: Practi-tioner perspectives on Golden Pond*. New York: Haworth.

Institute for Health & Aging, University of California, San Francisco. (1996). *Chronic care in America: A 21st century challenge*. Princeton, NJ: Robert Wood Johnson Foundation.

Johnson, C. L., & Barer, B. M. (1990). Families and networks among older inner-city blacks. *The Gerontologist, 30*, 726–733.

Kahana, R., & Levin, S. (1971). Aging and the conflict of generations. *Journal of Geriatric Psychiatry 4*, 115–135.

Kausler, D. L. (1996). *The graying of America: An encyclopedia of aging, health, mind, and behavior*. Urbana: University of Illinois Press.

Lewis, M. I., & Butler, R. N. (1974). Life review therapy. *Geriatrics, 29*, 165–173.

Lieberman, M. (1995). *Doors close, doors open: Widows, grieving, and growing.* New York: Grosset/ Putnam.

Light, E. (1994). *Stress effects on family caregivers of Alzheimer's patients: Research and interventions.* New York: Springer.

Litwin, H. (1996). *The social networks of older people: A cross-national analysis.* Greenwood, CT: Praeger.

Lockery, S. (1991, Fall/Winter). Family and social supports: Caregiving among racial and ethnic minority elders. *Generations,* 58–62.

Lopata, H. (1996). *Current Widowhood: Myths and realities.* Thousand Oaks, CA: Sage.

Martz, S. H. (Ed.). (1992). *If I had my life to live over / I would pick more daisies.* Watsonville, CA: Papier-Mache Press.

Mead, M. (1972). *Blackberry winter.* New York: William Morrow.

Myerhoff, B. (1992). *Remembered lives: The work of ritual, storytelling, and growing older.* Ann Arbor: University of Michigan Press.

Neugarten, B. (1991). Successful aging in 1970 and 1990. In E. Pfeiffer (Ed.), *Successful aging: A conference report.* Raleigh, NC: Duke University.

Pinkston, E., & Linsk, N. (1984). *Care of the elderly: A family approach.* New York: Pergamon.

Pogrebin, L. C. (1996). *Getting over getting older.* New York: Little, Brown & Company.

Posner, R. A. (1995). *Aging and old age.* Chicago: University of Chicago Press.

Qualls, S. H. (1991). Resistence of older families to therapeutic intervention. *Clinical Gerontologist, 11,* 59–68.

Reid, J. D. (1995). Development in late life: Older lesbian and gay lives. In A. D'Augelli & C. Patterson (Eds.), *Lesbian, gay, and bisexual identies over the lifespan.* (pp. 215–245). New York: Oxford University Press.

Rolland, J. R. (1994). *Families, illness, and disability.* New York: Basic Books.

Schulz, R., & Heckhausen, J. (1996). A life span model of successful aging. *American Psychologist, 51,* 702–714.

Sorensen, E. M. (1977). Family interaction with the elderly. In P. Watzlawick & J. Weakland (Eds.), *The interactional view.* New York: Norton.

Smith, G., Power, P., Robertson-Tchabo, E., & Tobin, S. (1995). *Strengthening aging families.* Thousand Oaks, CA: Sage.

Spark, G. (1974). Grandparents and intergenerational family therapy. *Family Process, 13,* 225–238.

Spark, G., & Brody, E. M. (1970). The aged are family members. *Family Process, 9,* 195–210.

Sussman, M. (1976). The family life of old people. In R. Binstock & E. Shanas (Eds.), *Handbook of aging and the social sciences.* New York: Van Nostrand Reinhold.

Szinovacz, M., & Harpster, P. (1994). Couples' employment/retirement status and the division of household tasks. *Journal of Gerontology: Social Sciences, 49,* 125–136.

Tobin, S., & Kulys, R. (1981). The family in the institutionalization of the elderly. *Journal of Social Issues, 37,* 145–157.

Van Amburg, S. M., Barber, C. E., & Zimmerman, T. S. (1996). Aging and family therapy: Prevalence of aging issues and later family life concerns in marital and family therapy literature (1986–1993). *Journal of Marital and Family Therapy, 22,* 195–203.

Walsh, F. (1993). Conceptualization of normal family processes. In F. Walsh (Ed.), *Normal family processes* (2nd. ed.). New York: Guilford Publications.

Walsh, F. (1996). The concept of family resilience: Crisis and challenge. *Family Process, 35,* 261–281.

Walsh, F. (1998). *Strengthening family resilience.* New York: Guilford Publications.

Walsh, F. (Ed.)(In press). *Spiritual resources in family therapy.* New York: Guilford Publications.

Walsh, F., & McGoldrick, M. (1991). *Living beyond loss: Death in the family.* New York: Norton.

Zarit, S., Anthony, C., & Boutselis, M. (1987). Interventions with caregivers of dementia patients: Comparison of two approaches. *Psychology and Aging, 2,* 225–232.

12

Culture and the Family Life Cycle

Paulette Moore Hines
Nydia Garcia Preto
Monica McGoldrick

Rhea Almeida
Susan Weltman

Culture interacts with the family life cycle at every stage. Families differ in their definition of "family"; in their definition of the timing of life cycle phases and the tasks appropriate at each phase; and in their traditions, rituals, and ceremonies to mark life cycle transitions. When cultural stresses or transitions interact with life cycle transitions, the problems inherent in all change are compounded.

The consciousness of ethnic identity varies greatly within groups and from one group to another. Families vary in attitude toward their ethnicity, often as a result of pressures on them from the larger cultural context, at times regressively holding on to past traditions, at others denying any relevance of their ethnic heritage at all. In groups that have experienced discrimination, such as Jews and African Americans, family attitudes about allegiance to the group may become conflicted, with members turning against themselves or each other, reflecting the prejudices of the outside world. Some people have a choice about ethnic identification; others, because of their color or physical characteristics, do not. Ethnicity intersects with class, religion, politics, geography, the length of time a group has been in this country, the historical cohort, and the degree of discrimination the group has experienced. Generally speaking, Americans tend to move closer to the dominant American value system as they move up in class. People in different geographic locations evolve new cultural norms. Religion also motivates or reinforces certain cultural values. Families that remain within an ethnic neighborhood whose work, community and religion reinforce ethnic values are likely to maintain their ethnicity longer than those who live in

Taken from: *The Expanded Family Life Cycle: Individual, Family, and Social Perspectives,* Third Edition, edited by Betty Carter and Monica McGoldrick.

heterogeneous settings without reinforcers of their cultural traditions. The degree of ethnic intermarriage in the family also plays a role in cultural patterns (McGoldrick & Preto, 1984). Nevertheless, there is burgeoning evidence that ethnic values and identifications are retained for many generations after immigration and play a significant role in family life throughout the life cycle (McGoldrick, Giordano, & Pearce, 1996). Second-, third-, and even fourth-generation Americans differ from the dominant culture in values, behavior, and life cycle patterns. While we are well aware of the problems of stereotyping and generalizing about groups in ways that may lead to prejudice and in no way mean to contribute to that tendency, we have taken the risk of characterizing intergenerational patterns over the life cycle for several groups to sensitize clinicians to the range of values that different people hold. Of course, each family must be dealt with as unique, and the characterizations used here are meant to broaden the therapist's framework, not to constrict it.

When we talk of families moving through the life cycle together, it is important to note how our clients themselves define "family." For example, the dominant American (Anglo) definition has focused on the intact nuclear family, often including other generations only to trace family genealogy to distinguish ancestors who were in this country before 1776 or, for southern Anglo families, noting family members who took part in the Civil War (McGill & Pearce, 1996). For Italians, by contrast, one might even say there is no such thing as the "nuclear family." For this group, family has tended to refer to the entire extended network of aunts, uncles, cousins, and grandparents, who are involved in family decision making; who share holidays and life cycle transition points together; and who tend to live in close proximity, if not in the same house (Giordano & McGoldrick, 1996). African American families tend to focus on a wide informal network of kin and community in their even broader definition of family, which goes beyond blood ties to close long-time friends, who are considered family members (Hines & Boyd-Franklin, 1996; Stack, 1974). The Chinese go even further, including all their ancestors and all their descendants in their definition of family. However, women traditionally moved into their husbands' family at the time of marriage, and their names disappear from the family tree in the next generation, leaving only the males as permanent members of the family (Kim, 1981). Thus, in a sense, Asian families consist of all one's male ancestors and descendants.

Life Cycle Stages

Groups differ in the importance given to different life cycle transitions. For example, the Irish have always placed great emphasis on the wake, viewing death as the most important life cycle transition, which frees human beings from the suffering of this world and takes them, it is hoped, to a happier afterlife. African Americans, perhaps as a result of similar life experiences with suffering, have also emphasized funerals. Both groups go to considerable expense and have traditionally delayed services until all family members can get there. Italian and Polish families have placed the greatest emphasis on weddings, often going to enormous expense and carry on the celebration and feasting for lengthy periods of time, reflecting the importance these groups place on continuation of the family into the next generation. Jewish families give special emphasis to the bar mitzvah and bat mitzvah, a transition to adulthood for boys and girls, respectively, reflecting the value placed on intellectual development, a transition that most other Western groups do not mark at all.

Families differ also in their intergenerational struggles. Anglo families (families of British extraction) are likely to feel that they have failed if their children do not move away from the family and become independent. Indeed, in Britain, many of those who can afford it send their children away to school by age 7. Even in this country, upper-middle-class Anglos often send their children away to boarding school by age 14. By contrast, Italian families may feel that they have failed if their children do move away. Jewish families will expect a relatively democratic atmosphere to exist in the family, children being free to challenge parents and to discuss their feelings openly (Rosen & Weltman, 1996). Greek families, by contrast, do not expect or desire open communication between generations and would not appreciate a therapist's getting everyone together to discuss and resolve their conflicts. Greek children are expected to respect parental authority, which is maintained by the distance parents keep from their children. Irish families are generally embarrassed to share feelings and conflicts across generations and cannot be expected to do so to any great extent.

Any life cycle transition can trigger ethnic identity conflicts, since it puts families more in touch with the roots of their family traditions. How the rituals of transition are celebrated can make an important difference in how well the family will adjust to the changes. All situational crises—divorce, illness, job loss, death, retirement—can compound ethnic identity conflicts. causing people to lose a sense of who they are. The more sensitive a therapist is to the need to preserve continuities, even in the process of change, the more he or she can help the family to maintain maximum control of its context and build upon it.

Groups differ not only in parent-child relationships in childhood, but also in the degree of intergenerational sharing and dependence expected between adult children and their aging parents. For example, whereas Italians or Greeks are likely to grow up with the expectation that they will eventually take care of their parents, Anglo parents' worst nightmare might be that they will eventually have to depend on their children for support. Minimal interdependence is expected or fostered, so adult children feel relatively guiltless when they have to put their parents in a nursing home. Conversely, adult children avoid asking their parents for support beyond paying for their education.

Groups differ in their definitions of responsibilities and obligations according to gender roles, in their expectations of motherhood and fatherhood, and in their treatment of sons and daughters. Marriage, child-rearing, leaving home, and caring for the elderly demand changes in relationships that are inherently stressful, especially when ascribed cultural rules for dealing with these stages are devalued or impossible to carry out in the new context. When conflict erupts, younger members may be most influenced by society's dominant values, while the older generations of a family usually attempt resolution by drawing on the strengths and legacies passed down from one generation to the next.

The portraits that we offer here are suggestive, not complete, and readers should consider the many other factors that may influence the particular values and behavior of each family they work with, including:

- the number of generations since the family came to the United States,
- their reasons for coming,

- socioeconomic factors that influence class status and class change,
- racial experiences in the United States and elsewhere,
- gender roles,
- migration history,
- religious influences, and
- the culture of the locale where the family lives.

African American Families

African traditions, the experience of slavery, assimilation into the U.S. mainstream, the psychological scars of past and current discrimination, age, education, religion, and geographic origins make for great heterogeneity within African American culture. However, survival issues based on interdependence and oppression due to racism are commonalities that transcend individual and group differences. The legacy of slavery, racism, and oppression is a common bond for all African Americans, regardless of differences in educational or economic status (Hines & Boyd-Franklin, 1996; Mahmoud, 1998, Pinderhughes, 1998).

Despite conscious and consistent efforts by members of the dominant culture to erase all remnants of African culture from the memories and practices of African slaves and their descendants, the sense of oneness, exemplified in the practice of greeting one another as "sister" or "brother," is critical to understanding the dynamics of relationships among African Americans.

Family relationships, more than bank accounts, represent wealth and guarantee emotional and concrete support in the face of negative feedback from the larger society. The emotional significance of relationships is not determined solely by the immediacy of blood ties. In fact, "family" is an extended system of blood-related kin and people who are informally adopted into this system (Boyd-Franklin, 1989; Hines & Boyd-Franklin, 1996). Extended family systems tend to be large and constantly expanding as new individuals are incorporated through marriage and informal adoptions of children and fictive kin. Commonly, three or four generations live in proximity, sometimes residing in the same neighborhood.

Strong value is placed on loyalty and responsibility to others. This value is reinforced through the belief that everything one does in the public domain reflects on one's family and on other African Americans. Similarly, African Americans often believe that one does not succeed just for oneself, but for one's family and race as well. In essence, African Americans believe that "you are your brother's keeper." Personal accomplishments are considered the dual consequence of individual effort and the sacrifice of others. Success is to be acknowledged and celebrated but not overemphasized, as positive outcomes cannot be guaranteed despite one's efforts in a racist environment. Furthermore, even when success is achieved, it may be short lived. Intelligence and education without character and common sense have little value. Good character involves respect for those who helped one succeed and survive difficult circumstances. Family members are expected to stay connected and to reach out and assist others who are in need (McGoldrick, Garcia-Preto, Hines, & Lee, 1989).

The elderly are held in reverence. Older women, more than men, are called upon to impart wisdom as well as to provide functional support to younger family members. Older adults are testimony to the fact that one can not only survive, but even transcend difficult circumstances. They serve as models for self-sacrifice, personal strength, and integrity. By example, they show that although suffering is inevitable, one can grow from hardship and adversity. Children and adults are expected to show verbal and nonverbal respect to the elderly. Titles such as Mr., Mrs., Aunt, and Uncle are used to convey respect, deriving from the slavery and postslavery eras during which African American men and women, irrespective of their age, were treated and referred to as objects or children.

Children and adolescents may express their feelings and opinions but are not allowed to argue with adults after a final decision has been made. Although adults have the liberty to voice dissenting opinions to those who are older, younger adults are expected to acknowledge respectfully the older adult's opinion and perspective. To fail to do so shows disrespect for the life experience of the older person. Use of profanity in an intergenerational context is generally considered disrespectful and unacceptable.

Young adulthood for African Americans is a critical period during which poor decisions and impulsive behavior can have lifelong consequences. The usual stressors on intergenerational relationships during this phase of the life cycle can be both eased and complicated by the numerous adults who may be intensely concerned about a young adult's well-being. Young adults who have few employment possibilities and who find it difficult to achieve adult status while living at home may move in with relatives until they become economically self-sufficient. However, they remain subject to older family members' collective efforts to protect them from life's hardships.

Intergenerational issues may surface in families with young children and adolescents. The role flexibility (exchange of responsibilities) that is characteristic of African American families allows adults to help children thrive in an environment with many minefields (Hines, 1990). The proverb "It takes a village to raise a child" works well as long as roles are clearly defined, rules are consistent, and ultimate authority is clearly established. However, when distinctions between their functions and the process for decision making among various caretakers is not clearly delineated, confusion is likely to result. Intergenerational conflicts are most likely to arise when a child exhibits disrespectful behavior at home or school, poor academic functioning, and behavior that may put the youth at risk of compromising his or her personal freedom. More specifically, the primary concerns are that male adolescents will get into trouble with legal authorities and that female adolescents will act out sexually or, worse, become pregnant. Parents may resort to overfunctioning (i.e., become inflexible) and turn to relatives for help. Male adolescents in female-headed households are particularly inclined to rebel against the power and influence of their mothers and other females in positions of authority as they struggle to concretize their male identity (Hines, 1990).

Although African Americans have the capacity to be openly expressive of their feelings, such expression may be held in check in an effort to minimize intergenerational conflicts. Such conflicts threaten unity and diminish energy needed to deal with everyday life. Parent-child conflicts frequently occur, nevertheless, when individuals violate cultural norms by exhibiting hopelessness and a lack of self-respect. Tensions also are likely to arise when individuals are perceived to be wallowing in their sorrows, engaging in self-destructive behaviors, or pursuing individual interests without concern for significant others, particularly children and older adult family members.

Intergenerational conflicts may arise between family members over two, three, or even four generations based on differences as to whether children are being taught the traditional values that are considered critical to the survival of African American people. Youths who are oppositional in response to adults' push for their church involvement are seen as more vulnerable and defenseless in dealing with adverse circumstances. Conflicts may also surface between adults across generations as to how best to teach survival skills to youths without exposing them to hardships and depriving them of the fruits of the previous generation's labor. It is not uncommon for youths to have major differences with their parents and other adults in their extended families about their choices of clothing and/or hairstyles. While these issues are common sources of intergenerational conflict across ethnic groups, African American parents are likely to become upset not because of power and control issues but because such choices may limit their children's employment opportunities and further expose them to discrimination and problems with the police. African American youths may respond with equal intensity because they are not just rejecting adult authority, but struggling to express their racial identity and, often, anger at racist attitudes and practices. When the stakes are perceived to be so high, adult family members are reluctant to relax their positions; therapists must validate their goals before challenging them to shift maladaptive behavior.

Therapists are likely to encounter difficulty if they label any family member as a "villain" or "bad," regardless of how angry, disappointed, or rejecting family members may be because of that person's behavior. To attack one family member is to attack the entire family, which will arouse resistance. This does not mean that family members absolve one another of responsibility for problematic behaviors. However, families can become resentful or furious at the tendency of Whites to ignore the pernicious effects of racism and poverty. Families will gauge their therapist's attitude toward such issues before they are willing to share personal information and subject themselves to the therapist's influence. African Americans are highly attuned to nonverbal as well as verbal communication, and therapists should be careful about what messages they convey at both levels. Giving family members permission to express their concerns facilitates trust so that the family can devote their attention to problem solving.

Because they are so invested in maintaining family unity, some family members may need encouragement to address topics that they anticipate might lead to intergenerational tension or cut-offs. One way to accomplish this is to offer examples that highlight how failure to discuss important issues can lead to damaged relationships that affect a family for generations. Family members are more likely to take the risk of bringing conflicts to the surface if they are clear that doing so is for the ultimate good of the family.

Family members often are inclined to make personal sacrifices "for the good of the family." Therapists should avoid suggesting that clients focus on their own needs before those of significant others (Hines, 1990). Behavioral changes can be encouraged by asking clients to consider the short- and long-term negative effects on significant others if they persist in their old behavior(s) while simultaneously emphasizing the individual's responsibility to self and the personal benefits of behavioral change.

When several people share caretaking responsibility for a child, the therapist should attempt to involve family members in clarifying who makes which decisions and how other family members can be supportive. Single mothers, especially those raising male adolescents, may benefit greatly when others within their social support systems are recruited to serve as mentors rather than as additional disciplinarians for their children.

When making referrals to self-help groups, therapists should be aware that the client may be uncomfortable if he or she is the sole African American participant. Clients should be offered the opportunity to discuss such concerns, and alternative options for seeking support should be made available if needed. For example, young adults, struggling under the weight of unrealistic family- or self-imposed expectations and/or challenged by the inherent stress of working in a bicultural setting can be encouraged to develop peer or professionally led support groups within their work and social environments.

Latino Families

The web of relationships that extends across generations in Latino families provides a support network that is sustained by rules of mutual obligation. These rules are perpetuated by patterns of caretaking that fulfill expectations of emotional, physical, and economic support for those who need it from those who are capable of providing it. Rules of respect also play an important role in preserving this intergenerational network of close, personal relationships. For example, children learn to relate to others according to their age, sex, and social class. When the system works, that is, if sacrifices do not border on martyrdom, the support and emotional acceptance that are provided can be healthy and nurturing as well as reassuring and validating.

The sense of responsibility and mutual obligation can be so ingrained among Latinas and Latinos that individuals with few resources run the risk of self-sacrifice. Women, in particular, are expected to assume caretaking roles in the family and tend to experience more pressure than do men to devote their lives to the welfare of others. Becoming martyrs gives women special status, in that family members often see their sacrifice as exemplary. However, the price they pay for "carrying this cross" is often too high (Garcia-Preto, 1990). This behavior is reinforced by the cultural concepts of marianismo and hembrismo, a term derived from "hembra" and literally meaning "female" in Spanish, which contribute to the complexity of Latino gender roles.

Marianismo stems from the cult of the Virgin Mary, whereby women are considered morally superior to men and therefore capable of enduring the suffering inflicted by men (Stevens, 1973). Also implicit in the concept of marianismo are women's repression or sublimation of sexual drives and consideration of sex as an obligation. The cultural message is that if a woman has sex with a man before marriage, she will lose his respect, he will not marry her, and she will bring dishonor to herself and to her family. Traditionally, the line separating *doñas* (a respectful term for "Mrs.") from *putas* (whores) has been quite clear: no sex before marriage and afterward an accepting attitude without much demonstration of pleasure (Garcia-Preto, 1994).

Marianismo has been reinforced by the acclaim that the culture gives to mothers. Motherhood has been romanticized in Latino literature and their music, and the association made between mothers and the Virgin Mary is so strong that the mere mention of the word "mother" tends to evoke an almost religious response. Having children also raises the status of women in society and is a rite of passage into adulthood, eliciting respect from family members and friends. Mothers are glorified when they put their children's welfare above everything else and protect them. This sacrificial role is reinforced by the admiration of society. Feeling pressured and obligated to sacrifice themselves to be good mothers, women may assume positions of martyrdom in the family. Keeping the family together under all circumstances becomes their devotion, their cross to bear (Garcia-Preto, 1990).

Hembrismo, on the other hand, connotes strength, perseverance, flexibility, and the ability to survive. Within a historical context, hembrismo shares elements with the women's movement in the areas of social and political goals (Gomez, 1982). Also, in the same way that feminists have been perceived as men haters in this culture, Latinas who behave like hembras are sometimes viewed as trying to act like men or as challenging them. For instance, in the literature about Latinas, reference has been made to hembrismo as being a cultural reaction to machismo, or a frustrated attempt to imitate males. However, culturally, hembrismo can also translate into a woman's attempt to fulfill her multiple role expectations as a mother, wife, worker, daughter, and community member—in other words, the "superwoman" working a double shift, at home and on the job (Comas-Diaz, 1989). In therapy, we often see women presenting with symptoms related to pressure and conflict that they experience when they try to act like *marias* at home and *hembras* at work. At work, they assume responsibility and try to be flexible, strong, and assertive; at home they sacrifice themselves and suffer under the oppression of male dominance.

Men, for their part, are expected to assume financial responsibility for elderly parents, younger siblings, and nephews and nieces. This behavior, too, is admired and respected. Grandparents and other elderly relatives, although not expected to con-tribute financially to the family, often serve as caretakers for grandchildren, enabling parents to work or go to school. In return for this assistance, it is expected that the elderly will be cared for by their adult children. If such expectations are not met, intergenerational conflicts are likely to occur throughout the family system.

A common source of intergenerational conflict in Latino families who enter therapy is the struggle between parents and children who have grown apart while trying to adapt to American culture. Traditionally, Latino children tend to have closer relationships with their mothers than with their fathers. Perhaps because women are responsible for holding the family together, they tend to develop very strong relationships with their children and other family members. This central position in the family system yields them a degree of power that is reflected in the alliances mothers often build with children against authoritarian fathers, who are perceived as lacking understanding of emotional issues. Relationships between sons and moth-ers often are particularly close and mutually dependent, and it is not uncommon to see a son protecting his mother against an abusive husband. A family therapist

working with this type of family may think that it is helpful to get the son to separate from the mother. The problem, however, is not the closeness between the mother and son, since strong loyalty ties between children and mothers are within the cultural norm among Latinos, but the lack of power that women in these positions　　　　　　　　　　　　　　　　　　　　　　　　　　　　experience.
A more useful approach would be to empower women to stop the abuse by linking them up with an antiviolence program and to address the alienation that is often created between fathers and children when men are uninvolved or abusive at home. Mothers and daughters also have close relationships, but these are more reciprocal in nature. Mothers teach their daughters how to be good women who deserve the respect of others, especially males, and who will make good wives and mothers. Daughters usually care for their elderly parents, often taking them into their homes when they are widowed, even though sons may provide financial support.

Relationships between Latinos and their fathers vary according to family structure. In families in which fathers assume an authoritarian position, there tend to be more distance and conflict. While attempting to be protective, fathers may become unreasonable, unapproachable, and highly critical of their daughters' behavior and friends. In contrast, they expect their sons to protect themselves, and they support sons' moves toward independence. On the other hand, in families in which fathers are more submissive and dependent on mothers to make decisions, they may develop special alliances with their daughters, who in turn assume a nurturing role toward them. With the increasing number of Latino families being headed by single women (for complex reasons including colonialist oppression of Latino cultures and the breakdown of patriarchal social structures), common scenarios are for fathers to be absent and distant or for daughters and sons to grow up having memories of their fathers' violent, abusive, and addictive behavior (Garcia-Preto, 1994).

When Latino families arrive in the United States, the children usually find it easier to learn English and adapt to the new culture than parents do. The parents may find English too difficult to learn and the new culture unwelcoming and dangerous. They may react by taking refuge in the traditional culture, expecting their children to do the same. When this occurs, children typically rebel against their parents' rigidity by rejecting parental customs, which are viewed as inferior to the American way of life.

Children may become emotionally distant from their parents, who often feel that they have lost control. Parents usually react by imposing stricter rules. Corporal punishment may be used. Commonly, parents will demand respect and obedience, cultural values that are traditionally seen as a solution to misbehavior. Parents may become very strict and highly protective of adolescents, especially if the family lives in a high-crime community. Daughters in particular may be overprotected because they are most vulnerable than males in a society with loose sexual mores. Such patterns of overprotection are most characteristic of families that are isolated or alienated from support systems in the community and when extended family members are not available (Garcia-Preto, 1996).

Children who are caught in the conflict of cultures and loyalties may develop a negative self-image, which can inhibit their chances for growth and accomplishment. Parents, then, may feel thwarted at every turn and consequently give up on their children. In therapy, it may be useful to see adolescents alone if they are unable to speak freely in front of their parents. Issues of respect and fear about their parents' reactions may inhibit adolescents from speaking about sex, drugs, incest, problems at school, or cultural conflicts at home and in the community. In such instances, obvious goals include helping adolescents to define and share with their parents personal issues that affect their relationship in an effort to find compromises. Discussing a family's migration history and acculturation process may help to clarify conflicts over cultural values. The therapist can also encourage parents to redefine privileges and responsibilities and to discuss their genuine concern for the child. By encouraging parents to express their love, concern, and fear to their children, therapists help parents and children to relate in a more positive manner (Garcia-Preto, 1996).

Disagreements that parents have with their own parents about child discipline can become another source of intergenerational conflict. This is especially true when grandparents live in the household with adolescents, who show disrespect toward them and reject Latino values. Parents often find themselves caught between two generations that pull them in opposite directions. Adolescents may feel that their grandparents are too old-fashioned and resent their attempts at discipline. Both adolescents and grandparents may complain to parents, who may try to mediate by explaining cultural differences but end up feeling powerless and confused about their own values.

Asking grandparents to attend therapy sessions to discuss adolescence and cultural values is sometimes helpful. The therapist might ask the family to identify the values that cause the most conflict at home. Ensuing discussions might lead to intergenerational compromise. For female adolescents, dating usually presents the greatest source of conflict. In traditional Latino culture, dating begins much later than it does in the United States. When dating is allowed, it is generally chaperoned by family or friends. Dating a number of boys is frowned upon, and girls gain bad reputations if they violate this rule of behavior. Once parents and grandparents recognize the difference between these rules and what is considered acceptable adolescent behavior in this culture, they are more willing to make compromises, especially when they realize the extent to which their children are affected by peer pressure. For instance, parents and grandparents may be more willing to accept their daughter's dating if, instead of going out alone with a boy, the dating is done with a group of friends. Meeting the girl's friends and their parents also helps them to feel less anxious about her going out.

As was stated earlier, intergenerational conflict is often caused by the inability of one generation to provide care for another. Adult children who are unable to care for their elderly parents, especially if the parents are ill, may experience stress and guilt. Conflicts with siblings and other family members may result. Practitioners need to encourage communication among family members to help them find ways to contribute to the care of elderly parents. Women who devote themselves to caring for elderly parents may express their stress and resentment through somatic complaints and or depression. Therapists can help these women to express their resentments openly as well as assist them in finding support from other family members or community resources.

Leaving the family system (e.g., through divorce or separation) is extremely risky for both men and women because it implies loss or control, support, and protection. For couples who are still adjusting to American culture, the loss of the family system can be devastating. For example, women usually depend on other women in the extended family to help with child-rearing and domestic tasks because men are not expected to share these responsibilities. Without the help of their mother, mothers-in-law, grandmothers, aunts, or sisters, Latinas may become overburdened and begin demanding assistance from their husbands. The husband may, in turn, resent these demands and become argumentative and distant, perhaps turning to alcohol, gambling, or extramarital affairs. The extended family can provide a measure of control for aggression and violence by intervening in arguments and providing advice to couples. Helping couples to make connections with relatives, friends, or community supports may be the therapist's most crucial task.

Irish Families

Intergenerational relationships among the Irish often are not terribly intimate. Unlike groups that tend to view the extended family as a resource in times of trouble, the Irish often take the attitude that having a problem is bad enough, but if your family finds out, you have two problems: the problem and your embarrassment that your family knows. It is said of the Irish that they suffer alone. They do not like others to see them when they are in pain. It is not so much a fear of dependence, which it might be for Anglos, as a sense of embarrassment and shame at not being able to keep up appearances. Intergenerational secrets are common. The Irish would often rather tell almost anything to a stranger than to a family member. If they do share it with a family member, it is usually told to someone of the same sex and same generation as the teller. Intergenerational boundaries are strongly maintained, even if this is very hurtful for everyone involved.

Within the family, intergenerational relationships throughout the life cycle were traditionally handled primarily by the mother. She cared for both the old and the young. Everyone is likely to view caretaking as her responsibility (McGoldrick, 1991). Her main supporters are her daughters, though she might also call on her sisters when she needs help. The therapist may have to teach both her and her husband how to involve him in handling problems.

The Irish sense of duty is a strong resource. Parents want to do the right thing for their children. It is not a lack of caring but a lack of attention to detail that most often interferes with appropriate nurturing of their children. This is the legacy of a history of oppression that forced parents to be overly vigilant about their children's behavior and left them often unable to attend adequately to their children's emotional needs because of their own deprivations. The Irish have tended to focus more on their children's conformity to rules than on other aspects of their child's development, such as emotional expression, self-assertiveness, or creativity. Traditionally, the Irish have believed that children should be seen and not heard. They should not bring outside notoriety to the family, especially for bad behavior. Less emphasis was placed on being a star student than on not standing out from the group for misbehavior. Irish parents traditionally tended to have little sense of child psychology. They hoped that keeping their children clean and out of trouble and teaching them right from wrong would get them through. When children develop psychological symptoms, Irish parents may be mystified. When children act out, parents tend to blame outside influences, although inwardly they blame themselves.

During the child-rearing phase, the greatest problem in Irish families occurs if a child gets in trouble with outside authorities, such as the school system. When parents have problems during this phase, for example, if the father is an alcoholic, Irish children can be remarkably inventive in developing strategies to obey family rules of denial while appearing to function well. However, they may later pay a high price emotionally for having learned at an early age to suppress their disallowed feelings.

During the adolescent phase and the launching years, drinking may become a major, often unidentified, problem that the parents do not know how to handle. They may ignore it, often with disastrous consequences. Parents do not want to be intrusive as long as the problem is not obvious and may not know how to talk through conflicts. They may hardly mention their concern at all until things reach an extreme.

Irish fathers have tended to play a peripheral role in intergenerational family relationships, whereas Irish mothers were always at the center (McGoldrick, 1996). Although Irish mothers have provided outstanding female role models of strong-minded, commanding, indomitable women, the stereotype of the "sainted Irish mother" is not totally positive (Diner, 1983; McGoldrick, 1996; McKenna, 1979; Rudd, 1984; Scheper-Hughes, 1979). She might be sanctimonious, preoccupied with black-and-white categories of right and wrong and with what the neighbors think, consciously withholding praise from her children for fear it would give them "a swelled head." Of course, this pattern makes sense in a culture with such a long history of foreign domination, in which the mother sought control through whatever means were available to her and felt the need to keep her family in line to minimize the risk of their being singled out for further oppression.

Sons and daughters rarely voice resentment toward their mothers. To do so is to risk guilt and to undermine their admiration for her stoic self-sacrifice. For generations, Irish women held a certain moral authority in their families, including control of the family money, even while being powerless in the larger context of the church and being unable to earn much money, except in low-paying jobs as caretakers or servants. Children tend to speak of "my mother's house," dismissing the role of the father (Diner, 1983). Irish mothers often fail to recognize their own strength or ability to intimidate their children, whether through teasing, ridicule, a disapproving glance, or a quick hand.

Perhaps because of their history of oppression, the Irish tend to communicate indirectly, often believing that putting feelings into words only makes things worse. They can also be uncomfortable with physical affection (Barrabe & von Mering, 1953; McGoldrick, 1996; Rudd, 1984) and tend to relate to their children through fixed labels: "Bold Kathleen," "Poor Paddy," and "That Joey." Children are loved, but not intimately known (Rudd, 1984).

What are we to make of these stereotypes of the Irish mother, who seems to be to blame for all sorts of problems—contempt for her husband, spoiling her sons and binding them in a love from which they will never be free while teaching her daughters to rely only on themselves, become overresponsible, and repeat these skewed patterns? We must take into account the very ancient tradition of Irish women, celebrated as formidable, tenacious, and powerful rulers from the time of ancient Irish legends (MacCurtain & O'Corrain, 1978). This tradition must be combined with awareness of the 900-year history of Irish oppression, which was focused especially on Irish men, who were systematically deprived of any sense of power and often turned to drink to blot out what was happening to them. Drink became institutionalized in the culture as an acceptable form of escape. Women were forced to run their families, and it is no wonder that they turned to their sons with the dreams their beaten-down husbands could not fulfill. They turned to their daughters to carry on with and after them.

As a result of the need of the Irish for ambiguous communication and ambivalence about self-assertion, parents may indirectly belittle a child for "putting himself ahead" while in the same breath chiding him for not being more aggressive and achievement oriented. Irish mothers tend to dote on their sons, overprotecting them and drawing them into powerful bonds, more intense than their marital tie. Sons might be pampered and protected much longer than daughters, and in traditional Irish families, they were called "boys" way into adulthood, probably largely because of the economic oppression that gave them no avenue to leave the parental home. A very high percentage of Irish men never married at all, and those who did were sometimes thought of as "married bachelors," more loyal to their mothers than to their wives (Connery, 1970). Conversely, Irish parents have tended to underprotect their daughters, treating them like sisters and often not allowing them much of a childhood by raising them to be overresponsible and self-sufficient, like the mothers themselves (Byrne & McCarthy, 1986). This failure to protect daughters teaches them to repress personal needs and contributes to an ongoing fatalism, emotional repression, and stoicism in the next generation of women. Irish women have little expectation of, or interest in, being taken care of by a man. Their hopes are articulated less often in romantic terms than in aspirations for self-sufficiency. They are often reluctant to give up their freedom and economic independence for marriage and family responsibilities. Generally, father-daughter relationships are distant, possibly because the father fears that closeness will be confused with trespass of sexual boundaries. Moreover, Irish families are not very good at differentiating among anger, sexuality, and intimacy. A father may maintain distance from his daughter or perhaps be sarcastic and teasing, not because such behavior reflects his true feelings but because he does not know how to approach her.

With a son, a father may share sports, work, and jokes, although the teasing and ridicule that are so common in Irish parent-child relationships may be very painful to sons as to daughters. Some Irish fathers remain silent, almost invisible, in the family. Another common pattern is the father who is jovial or silent except when drinking, at which time he becomes a fearsome, intimidating, larger-than-life antagonist, who returns to his gentler self when sober with no acknowledgment of this transformation. Children are kept off guard in such relationships. They may be drawn to the humor and fun, yet terrified of the unpredictable and violent moods.

Resentment over class differences may surface when Irish children marry. The Irish tend to measure others hierarchically as being "better than" or "inferior to" themselves. Thus, parents may criticize children for "marrying up" and putting on airs (which usually means marrying an Anglo) or may criticize them for "marrying down." Both of these parental reactions are deeply rooted in tensions stemming from the Irish history of oppression by the British, which left them with a deep sense of inferiority. When Irish children reach their mid-twenties or older, they may begin to resent the family's patterns of denial and emotional suppression. Such resentments may be evident in their young adult relationships with others. The resentments that Irish children have buried since childhood often continue into adulthood without realization that resolution is possible.

Resentments and distancing may become more intense throughout the adults' life, especially if parents' subtle disapproval continues or if adult children assume caretaking responsibilities for their parents. Unlike other children who are freer to express their resentments, Irish children may be extremely sensitive to perceived slights, such as favors shown to siblings, or other imagined wrongs. They may never confront the parent or the sibling with their feelings, dutifully continuing their caretaking responsibilities while maintaining tense silence with regard to their emotional wounds.

As parents age, intimacy may not increase. Even unmarried children who continue to be emotionally and physically tied to their parents while outwardly denying this dependence may be shut down in terms of their emotional connectedness. The mother may maintain her matriarchal role while being unaware of the hold she has on her family because inwardly she feels that hold slipping. Placing a parent in a nursing home may be acceptable to both children and parents because the parents prefer to "suffer alone" and not become a burden to their children.

It is also extremely important to frame observations, especially regarding family members' intentions, as positively as possible while gently helping them to move beyond denial. A little assistance will go a long way with Irish family members in dealing with intergenerational problems. The Irish are generally cooperative, especially if therapy gives them a concrete sense of what they can do. It is often preferable to interview the generations, and even sometimes each parent, separately to help them avoid embarrassment in telling their story.

Asian Indian Families

In the past ten years, Asian Indian immigration to the United States has been opened to nonprofessional classes. Twenty years ago, families immigrating here were primarily of the professional class. Today, however, the influx of uneducated families settling into menial jobs has created many problems similar to those experienced by earlier groups of immigrants from other countries.

Despite the intersecting influences of caste, region, and religion, predictable intergenerational conflicts emerge among family members. Relationships within and across generations are influenced by beliefs in caste and karma. These beliefs are pervasive despite the diversity among Asian Indians in the "old country" and in the United States (Malyala, Kamaraju, & Ramana, 1984). However, the degree to which these beliefs affect adaptation to life in Western society is influenced by level of education and acculturation (Matsuoka, 1990; Segal, 1991). For example, an educated family living in this country for ten to twenty years will adapt to Western values around education and socialization for their children. However, they frequently revert back to Indian values as the marriage of a child approaches.

Hindu culture portrays women in paradoxical positions. Women are sacred in the afterlife, yet they are devalued in present life (Almeida, 1990; Bumiller, 1990; Wadley, 1977). Although men share power with women in the scriptures, in present life the male-centered family system exerts enormous social and economic power over women and children. With its concepts of "purity" and "pollution," the caste system shapes both intragenerational and intergenerational relationships. Prejudices related to lighter versus darker shades of skin color are deeply embedded within the culture, light skin symbolizing purity and dark skin symbolizing pollution. In fact, advertisements for brides place a high price on light-skinned women who have a green card. These ideals are carried into the acculturation process. Thus, Asian Indian immigrants move more readily toward white Americans than nonwhites and teach their children to passively learn to succeed in work. This response to obedience, which is a deeply held value, works against children and adults in many aspects of their lives. One example is the commonly held view that Asians embrace the work ethic. This pits these families against other minorities and immigrants in ways that isolate them further in the acculturation process. Asian Indian experiences of racism are generally not talked about, as though acknowledgment of racism might connect them with others who are similarly discriminated against. Although work and educational opportunities are available to all, women and lower-caste men have fewer choices regarding marriage partners and economic choices. Such contradictions are pervasive and are explained in terms of karma.

Karma focuses on past and future life space. Current life dilemmas are explained in terms of karma. For example, a wife who is mistreated by her in-laws might say, "I must deserve this for something bad I did in a past life. If I endure my current life, I know I will be taken care of by God in a future life." Making choices to alter current life struggles is possible within this belief system but often occurs in extreme forms. Such choices consist of sacrificial actions that alter one's current life and thus are meaningful. Fasting, praying, somatic complaints, head shaving, and suicide alter karma and move one toward a better life. In work with Asian Indian clients, therapists might suggest culturally appropriate constructions of less destructive solutions such as limited fasting, praying, meditating, or even haircutting.

Intergenerational patterns are embedded and negotiated within a collective consciousness. For example, a young woman leaving for college thinks about her decision as pleasing to her parents, grandparents, siblings, and, lastly, herself. Therefore, any exploration of her ambivalence toward this decision must include discussion of the implications of the decision for family and community relationships. Relationships are other-directed rather than self-centered. Spirituality and simplicity are applauded, and family-centered decisions take priority over individual preferences. Within the family of origin, older men assume decision-making authority over all members of the family. Fathers are responsible for the education, economics, and values of their male children and for the care of their elderly parents. Emotional connectedness between sons and fathers, as well as among other extended family members, is not expected. However, intimacy between the son and mother is emphasized. Fathers are responsible for their daughters' dowry and marriage; uncles or older male siblings take on this responsibility in the event of a father's death. Mothers expect their sons to control their wives with regard to money, work, and social activities. Older women gain status and power through the mother-in-law role; younger women are socialized by their mothers and sisters to idealize the role of mother-in-law. The cultural system (i.e., caste and karma with their values of tolerance and passivity), supported by the male family lineage (endorsing tolerance and passivity), embraces this process. In this system, women realize power by exerting control over women of lesser status. Care-taking of grandchildren and food preparation are used as covert means of gaining power in family relations. A mother-in-law, in charge of preparing food while the daughter-in-law works, might cook only according to her son's desires. Young children are generally overprotected by grandparents while being taught to respect their elders. Children are taught to avoid direct eye contact with their elders and to avoid disagreeing with them. Older sisters-in-law assume a degree of power over younger women entering the male-centered family system.

Education of male children is considered necessary for the economic needs of the entire family; education for female children increases their marketability as brides. Aging parents are cared for within the family by adult married male children and, in rare instances, by female children who have families of their own. The son provides economically and administratively for parents, but it is always his wife who does the actual caretaking in the home.

Child-rearing is a shared responsibility of the women in the male-oriented extended-family system. These women can be aunts or friends of the family from India who visit for extended periods during the family's initial years of child-rearing. When young mothers are forced to parent without this extended-kinship system, children are more at risk because family conflicts tend to be expressed in the mother-child dyad rather than in the marital dyad.

Power in Western marriages is directly connected to the economic resources of each partner. This notion of power and relationships is less applicable to Asian Indian families because a couple's economic resources are distributed across the extended male-oriented family system (Conklin, 1988). Unlike the white, American, middle-class nuclear family, in which marriage stands at the center of the family system, men and their mothers are at the center of the Asian Indian family system. The mother-son tie is prominent in both Hindu and Christian Asian Indian families (Almeida, 1996; de Souza, 1975). Sons provide their mothers and grandmothers with the ultimate pride and status afforded women in this life (Issmer, 1989). Young wives do not participate in this system of power, even when they contribute economically to the family unit (Chakrabortty, 1978).

Marriage is complicated by overarching problems of caste, dowry, expensive weddings, and arranged marriages, which are common among Indians in the United States as well as in India. When the family chooses to emphasize college education over marriage, or if the child asserts his or her personal rights over the parents' choice of mates or chooses career and money over marriage, major conflicts arise within the family system. Parents expect daughters to be married between 18 and 22 years of age and sons between the ages of 22 and 26. Many social gatherings by parents are spent planning and choosing possible mates for their children. Weddings are showcases for future brides and their grooms. When marriage does not occur, parents lack a clear role in their adult child's life. This can be a devastating loss for parents, because this transition is so important for them. Marriage rather than education is the primary marker of the transition to adulthood. The process of differentiation of self from family, which has various implications for Asian Indians as a result of their cultural norms, is particularly problematic at this stage. Despite their efforts to create choices for their sons and daughters, cultural expectations for arranged marriages take precedence.

An Asian Indian family entered therapy because of the 21-year-old daughter's difficulty completing her last semester of college. They expressed their helplessness in dealing with her launching. The mother said, "Shiva is very immature and irresponsible; it worries me that she does not know the meaning of money or getting a job, and yet she is about to graduate. I think of her as a selfish brat sometimes. She says she is not ready to think about marriage, and I believe it sometimes, but all of our friends and relatives think I am being neglectful in my responsibility to find her a nice man. If she waits until she is 30, then by the time she is 40, when she should be taking care of us, she and her husband will still have the responsibility of young children. I might be too old to be the kind of grandparent I have to be. Of course, I know that if Shiva gets married, then I will be pushing her to give me grandchildren, so I suppose I have to trust that my husband's and my choice to provide her with some independence will keep her loyal to our expectations as well."

An Asian Indian woman's status within the family is determined by the gender order of her children. First-born males are preferred. First-born females are vulnerable to conflict between the mother and her in-laws and are perceived as diminishing the father's status with the deities. However, a second-born male child helps to normalize the situation. For many families a second-born female child following a first-born female child is at risk for premature death through malnutrition and abuse, even in the United States, if the family does not have sufficient emotional, social, and economic support. Many female children in homes where there is a physically or developmentally delayed male child may present a range of psychological problems. The girls are often given an excess of adult responsibilities, not rewarded for their achievements, and isolated from their peers. Male children offer the family greater economic support and thereby lead to better marital opportunities for the female children in the family. A woman's relationship with her mother-in-law may become strained and the marriage may suffer if she is infertile and thus does not meet the family's role expectations. Sons who cannot support the elderly family members, widowed mothers, or unmarried sisters extort large dowries from their brides as solutions to this intergenerational legacy (Ramu, 1987).

These intergenerational patterns often conflict with Asian Indian acculturation (Sluzki, 1979). Although most Asian Indians accommodate to the work ethic and value of education, they maintain strong cultural ties to Asian Indian concepts of marriage, child-rearing, parenting, and the sharing and allocation of economic resources.

Western values of privacy and individualism conflict with Indian values of collectivity and family-centeredness. In the context of separation, less acculturated families view adolescent and young adult struggles around independence as disloyal cutting off from the family and culture. When Asian Indians speak of respect, they mean obedience to the family and culture. Similarly, it is difficult for them to comprehend that some aspects of the Western ideal of love includes separation and independence from the family of origin. For Asian Indians, the concept of love includes loyalty and control (Mukherjee, 1991).

Families are most likely to enter treatment through referral by outside organizations, such as schools and physicians, although in recent years, couples have entered therapy because of troubled marriages. Practitioners need to determine how the presenting problem fits with the belief system of the dominant culture by considering the following factors:

- Life-style in India before coming to the United States, to assess similarity to and difference from current life-style as well as status and story of immigration.
- Household composition, social organization, and domestic functioning and activities. (Concept of household may include relatives in India and in-laws here.)
- Religious affiliation.
- Details and status of arranged marriage as it relates to current intergenerational anxieties (marital satisfaction, as defined by dowry status, negotiation of "second-shift" responsibilities) when women work out of the home, money, child-rearing, emotional nurturing, and social activities.
- Relationship of couples to the in-law system, especially that of the husband.
- Young men's and women's, as well as children's, sense of physical beauty in a culture that values and often eroticizes white-skinned beauty and a caste system that embraces these values.

Clinical observations reveal that Asian Indians do not remain in therapy for long (six to nine months is typical). Therapists can help families with children to work through intergenerational conflicts by helping them to examine the underlying assumptions of individualism and self-determination as they relate to success and achievement and eliciting examples of individualism that demonstrate disregard for others (e.g., talking back, visiting friends whose parents are unknown to the family, not accounting for small amounts of money spent, talking on the telephone) in contrast with examples of individualism that are positive (e.g., good study habits, doing chores, spending allowances wisely, using good judgment with friends and recreation). Such work allows parents to promote their children's success while simultaneously addressing concerns regarding family disloyalty. Work with couples and in-law systems must empower women and help men to find constructive solutions that will support their nurturing of their partners while they maintain loyalties toward their families of origin.

Asian Indians address their problems within the hierarchy of "father knows best" and "mothers and daughters should obey." The emotional difficulties of sons are ignored even when they are severe. Since emotions are neither identified nor acknowledged, families should be encouraged to speak about their problems within the context of their immigrant story and cultural heritage. Therapists must address family members' sense of loss over leaving home while struggling to be successful in their new country. Engaging the women in stories and myths about strong Asian Indian women can help them to achieve balance in their new culture (Almeida, 1996). Therapists should encourage families to discuss these experiences and identify their feelings so that families do not split their emotions from real life. Splitting has allowed men and women to uphold values of tolerance and passivity even when such values are not in their best interests. Therapists must inquire into the family's beliefs about tolerance (caste) and fate (karma). Asian Indians will not freely discuss these cultural beliefs unless they are specifically asked about them. Their responses might be couched in laughter, denial, or awkwardness. Gentle and respectful persistence will facilitate engagement of the family.

Jewish Families

Judaism has the unusual distinction of being both a religion and an ethnic identity (Farber, Mindel, & Lazerwitz, 1988). Jews, who have a long tradition of intellectual debate and dialogue, carry on a never-ending discussion about who is a Jew and what it means to be a Jew. This debate has been engendered in part by the Jewish history of exclusion, discrimination, and wandering, culminating in the Holocaust and the founding of Israel. As waves of Jewish immigrants entered the United States, including early settlers from Germany who were relatively wealthy and assimilated, the poor and less assimilated (more observant) Eastern Europeans before and after World War I, Holocaust survivors, and, most recently, Russian and Israeli Jews, the question of essential Jewishness has continued to be debated. This is a legacy that has led to sensitivity over issues of discrimination and a sense of being "other." Although "Jewishness" may not be apparent to the outsider, most Jews are sensitive to interactions that might be perceived as anti-Semitic and may adopt a defensive posture that seems inexplicable to non-Jews.

Jews in the United States have been both fearful of and fascinated by assimilation into mainstream culture (Rosen & Weltman, 1996). Many families are overwhelmingly concerned that family members marry within the faith or, if members marry outside the faith, that they maintain their Jewish traditions. A primary concern for many parents who move to a new community is whether their children will have other Jewish children with whom to play and date. The issue is further complicated by the diversity of Jewish religious practice; acceptable Jewishness in one family may be considered too assimilated or too religious in another.

Families often enter treatment to deal with conflicting feelings with regard to intermarriage, which may be perceived as destroying the integrity of the family and the faith. Generally, the families' most immediate concerns revolve around who, if anyone, will be expected to convert, who will perform the wedding, and how the grandchildren will be raised. Intermarriage is often felt to be a failure on the part of the parents, who somehow should have prevented it from happening. Such feelings exist even in families that are culturally rather than religiously observant Jews and are not affiliated with a synagogue.

When intermarriage is an issue, it is important that the therapist attempt to gather concerned family members together. The parent or grandparent who is most upset may be the most difficult to engage. Because Jews traditionally have had a high regard for discourse and the transmission of cultural tradition and history, it can be helpful to review family history and to engage the family in searching for others within the extended family for whom intermarriage did not result in leaving the faith. Jewish families respond well to information and the sharing of stories; therefore, referral to a support group and/or interfaith classes run by Reform synagogues or other Jewish organizations can be effective.

Regardless of geographic distance, maintaining close family ties is important to Jewish families. It is useful for the therapist to identify family members who are critical to the treatment process but who are not immediately available. Soliciting their involvement as consultants (through inclusion in family sessions, a joint phone call, or a letter) can help to promote change.

Jewish families' focus on children, particularly their education and nurturing, can be a mixed blessing. Children are expected to be a source of pride and pleasure for parents and grandparents. However, children may find it difficult to be the focus of so much attention, with so many people having an expressed point of view. Young people may find it difficult to operate independently in their own interests. Separation and individuation are difficult to achieve if the family has rigid definitions of acceptable and successful behaviors. Young Jewish men and women often enter treatment because they are having difficulty dealing with issues of enmeshment. Parents may perceive themselves as being generous and supportive and feel hurt by their children's efforts to become more independent. Reframing and relabeling their adult children's need to separate as successful and productive behavior can be an effective treatment approach.

The changing mores of late twentieth-century American life have been stressful for Jewish families. Traditionally, Jewish women were expected to stay home, complying with the dictum to "be fruitful and multiply." Jewish law has rigidly defined rules for men's and women's behavior, women having a minor function in religious ritual in the synagogue. Reform and Conservative congregations have opened all aspects of religious observance to women, including being ordained as a rabbi; in contrast, Orthodox Jews continue to maintain strict adherence to the teachings of the Talmud, the traditional compendium of Jewish law that was written over a 500-year period during the first millennium. Although many Jewish laws concerning gender roles are barely observed in all but Orthodox families, these laws still have a subtle influence on role definition and expectations.

In Jewish families, women have traditionally held power at home while the husband faced the work world and the synagogue. Jewish mothers have been responsible for maintaining religious tradition and culture. However, because many Jewish women were employed outside the home during the Depression in the 1930s, many families remember grandmothers or other female relatives who worked, generally out of necessity. Their daughters were primarily homemakers, and their granddaughters now expect themselves to be "supermoms" (Hyman, 1991). The dilemma faced by all three generations (and now the fourth) has been how to reconcile social expectations with cultural expectations. Women who saw their mothers struggling to support the family during the Depression came to value their homemaker role. Their granddaughters have aspired to raise their family while participating in the professional world. Issues faced by American women in the 1980s and 1990s have been especially complicated for Jewish women because of the emphasis Jewish culture places on education, social consciousness, and tradition. In some situations, it may be the grandmother or great-grandmother who can serve as a role model for both working and maintaining a family.

Significant shifts in the role of the Jewish husband/father have also occurred. Jewish men have experienced discrimination and violence in the larger community. Traditionally, their home has been the place where they expected to achieve respect and authority. When both spouses work, the father may be called upon or may wish to be a more active parent than was his father. However, when he does take an active role, he risks the disapproval of his own parents, who may be uncomfortable in seeing him in an unconventional role. The extended family may also not be supportive of these changes.

Religious observance is another source of intergenerational conflict. The majority of Jews in the United States are affiliated with Reform congregations, which do not follow many of the laws (for example, keeping kosher, not driving or working on the Sabbath) that Orthodox and Conservative Jews follow. Intergenerational conflict may arise over the perceived religious laxity or conservatism of family members. Parents may be disappointed if their adult child chooses not to be affiliated with a synagogue or chooses not to have a bar mitzvah for their grandson or a bat mitzvah for their granddaughter when they turn 13.

Conversely, some young people have become more observant of the Jewish faith than their families, perhaps joining an Orthodox congregation and living in a style that is foreign to their families. Grandchildren's being unable to eat in their grandparents' non-kosher home can have a profound effect on intergenerational relationships. Conflicts in some families may occur if younger family members emigrate to Israel, thus separating parents from their children and grandchildren. Families may enter treatment to deal with feelings of loss and may need help in developing new ways to interact and to develop rituals that accept the differences in religious observance and practice.

The influx of immigrants from the former Soviet Union that began in the mid-1970s has significantly changed the face of the American Jewish community. Many of these families have come to the United States with little knowledge of Judaism, having been victims of anti-Semitism and State-declared atheism. Because of financial and living conditions it was not unusual for three generations of the family to live together and depend on each other; this pattern has frequently persisted in the United States and can lead to complex intergenerational patterns of relating (Feigen, 1996).

Jewish families tend to seek expert opinions and may ask a therapist many questions about professional degrees and competence. Although such inquiries may make practitioners feel uncomfortable and challenged, they may help clients to feel more comfortable in therapy. Directing Jewish families to appropriate reading materials about problems can be helpful because Jews tend to value being well-informed.

Jews have been avid consumers of psychotherapy, in part as a result of their comfort with discourse, their search for solutions, and the expectation that family life should follow predefined rules (Rosen & Weltman, 1996). However, extensive analysis does not always lead to resolution of problems. The therapist may find structural interventions and assigned tasks helpful in challenging verbal interactions that have not led to change. Families may need to be reminded that the goal of therapy is not to tell a good story or to be "right" in the eyes of the therapist, but to resolve the conflict or assuage the pain that brought the family to therapy.

References

Almeida, R. V. (1990). Asian Indian mothers. *Journal of Feminist Family Therapy, 2*(2): 33–39.

Almeida, R. V. (1996). Asian Indian families. In M. McGoldrick, J. Giordano, & J. K. Pearce (Eds.), *Ethnicity and family therapy* (2nd ed.). New York: The Guilford Press.

Barrabe, P., & von Mering, O. (1953). Ethnic variations in mental stress in families with psychotic children. *Social Problems, 1,* 48–53.

Boyd-Franklin, N. (1989). *Black families in therapy.* New York: The Guilford Press.

Bumiller, E. (l990). *May you be the mother of a hundred sons: A journey among the women of India.* New York: Random House.

Byrne, N., & McCarthy, I. (1986, September 15). Irish women. Family Therapy Training Program Conference, Robert Wood Johnson Medical School, Piscataway, NJ.

Chakrabortty, K. (1978). *The conflicting worlds of working mothers.* Calcutta, India: Progressive Publishers.

Comas-Diaz, L. (1989). Culturally relevant issues for Hispanics. In V. R. Koslow & E. Salett (Eds.), *Crossing cultures in mental health.* Washington, DC: Society for International Education, Training and Research.

Conklin, G. H. (1988). The influence of economic development and patterns of conjugal power and extended family residence in India. *Journal of Comparative Family Studies, 19,* 187–205.

Connery, D. S. (1970). *The Irish.* New York: Simon & Schuster.

de Souza, A. (1975). *Women in contemporary India.* New Delhi, India: Manohar.

Diner, H. R. (1983). *Erin's daughters in America.* Baltimore, MD: Johns Hopkins University Press.

Farber, B., Mindel, C. H., & Lazerwitz, B. (1988). The Jewish American family. In C. H. Mindel & R. W. Habenstein (Eds.), *Ethnic families in America: Patterns and variations.* New York: Elsevier.

Feigen, I. (1996). Soviet Jewish families. In M. McGoldrick, J. Giordano, & J. K. Pearce (Eds.), *Ethnicity and family therapy,* (2nd ed.), (pp. 631–637). New York: The Guilford Press.

Fogelman, E. (1996). Israeli families. In M. McGoldrick, J. Giordano, & J. K. Pearce (Eds.), *Ethnicity and family therapy* (2nd ed.). New York: The Guilford Press.

Garcia-Preto, N. (1990). Hispanic mothers. *Journal of Feminist Family Therapy, 2*(2), 15–21.

Garcia-Preto, N. (1994). On the Bridge. *Family Therapy Networker, 18*(4), 35–37.

Garcia-Preto, N. (1996). Puerto Rican families. In M. McGoldrick, J. Giordano, & J. K. Pearce (Eds.). *Ethnicity and family therapy* (2nd ed.), (pp. 183–199). New York: The Guilford Press.

Giordano, J. & McGoldrick, M. (1996). Italian families, in M. McGoldrick, J. Giordano, & J. K. Pearce (Eds.). *Ethnicity and family therapy* (2nd ed.), (pp. 567–582). New York: The Guilford Press.

Gomez, A. G. (1982). Puerto Rican Americans. In A. Gaw (Ed.), *Cross cultural psychiatry* (pp. 109–136). Boston: John Wright.

Habach, E. (1972). Ni machismo, ni hembriso. In *Coleccion: Protesta.* Caracas, Venezuela: Publicaciones EPLA.

Hines, P. (1990). The family life cycle of poor Black families. In B. Carter & M. McGoldrick (Eds.). *The Expanded Family Life Cycle: Individual, Family and Community Perspectives.* Boston: Allyn & Bacon.

Hines, P. (1990). African American mothers. *Journal of Feminist Family Therapy, 2*(2): 23–32.

Hines, P., & Boyd-Franklin, N. (1996). African American families. In M. McGoldrick, J. Giordano, & J. K. Pearce (Eds.), *Ethnicity and family therapy* (2nd ed.). New York: Guilford Press.

Hyman, P. (1991). Gender and the immigrant Jewish experience. In J. R. Baskin (Ed.), *Jewish women in historical perspective.* Detroit, MI: Wayne State University Press.

Issmer, S. D. (1989). The special function of out-of-home care in India. *Child Welfare, 68,* 228–232.

Kim, B.-L. C. (1981). *Women in the shadows: A handbook for service providers working with Asian wives of U.S. military personnel.* La Jolla, CA: National Committee Concerned with Asian Wives of U.S. Servicemen.

Mahmoud, V. (1998). The double bind dynamics of racism. In M. McGoldrick (Ed.), *Revisioning family therapy: Race, culture and gender in clinical practice.* New York: The Guilford Press.

Malyala, S., Kamaraju, S., & Ramana, K. V. (1984). Untouchability: need for a new approach. *Indian Journal of Social Work, 45*, 361–369.

Matsuoka, J. K. (1990). Differential acculturation among Vietnamese refugees. *Social Work, 35*, 341–345.

MacCurtain, M., & O'Corrain, D. (Eds.). (1978). *Women in Irish society: The historical dimension.* Dublin: Arlin House.

McGill, D. & Pearce, J. K. (1996). American families with English ancestors from the Colonial Era: Anglo Americans. In M. McGoldrick, J. Giordano, & J. K. Pearce (Eds.). *Ethnicity and family therapy* (2nd ed.). New York: The Guilford Press.

McGoldrick, M. (1991). Irish mothers. *Journal of Feminist Family Therapy, 2*(2).

McGoldrick, M. (1996). Irish families. In M. McGoldrick, J. Giordano, & J. K. Pearce (Eds.), *Ethnicity and family therapy* (2nd ed.). New York: The Guilford Press.

McGoldrick, M., & Garcia-Preto, N. (1984). Ethnic intermarriage: Implications for therapy. *Family Process, 23/4.*

McGoldrick, M., Garcia-Preto, N., Hines, P., & Lee, E. (1989). Ethnicity and women. In M. McGoldrick, C. Anderson, & F. Walsh (Eds.), *Women in families.* New York: W. W. Norton.

McGoldrick, M., Giordano, J., & Pearce, J. K. (1996). *Ethnicity and family therapy, 2nd edition.* New York: The Guilford Press.

McKenna, A. (1979). Attitudes of Irish mothers to child rearing. *Journal of Comparative Family Studies, 10*, 227–251.

Mukherjee, B. (1991). *Jasmine.* New York: Fawcett Crest.

Pinderhughes, E. (1998). Black geneology revisited: Restorying an African American family. In M. McGoldrick (Ed.), *Revisioning family therapy: Race, culture and gender in clinical practice.* New York: The Guilford Press.

Ramu, G. N. (1987). Indian husbands: Their role perceptions and performance in single- and dual-earner families. *Journal of Marriage and the Family, 49*, 903–915.

Rosen, E. J., & Weltman, S. (1996). Jewish families. In M. McGoldrick, J. Giordano, & J. K. Pearce (Eds.), *Ethnicity and family therapy* (2nd ed.). New York: The Guilford Press.

Rudd, J. M. (1984). Irish American families: The mother child dyad. Unpublished master's thesis, Smith College School of Social Work.

Scheper-Hughes, N. (1979). *Saints, scholars, and schizophrenics.* Berkeley, CA: University of California Press.

Schneider, S. W. (1985). *Jewish and female: A guide and sourcebook for today's Jewish woman.* New York: Simon & Schuster.

Segal, U. A. (1991). Cultural variables in Asian Indian families. *Families in Society, 72*, 233–241.

Sluzki, C. (1979). Migration and family conflict. *Family Process, 18*, 379–390.

Stack, C. (1974). *All our kin.* New York: Harper & Row.

Stevens, E. (1973). Machismo and marianismo. *Transaction Society, 10*(6), 57–63.

Wadley, S. (1977). Women and the Hindu tradition. *Journal of Women in Culture and Society, 3*(1), 113–128.

13

Single-Parent Families Across the Life Cycle

The Single-Parent Household

Chapter Overview

The single-parent household has become an increasingly common family form. The challenges faced by single-parent families are varied and many. These can include changes in the level of family stress, modifications in one's personal and family identity, and major alterations in how the household is managed. Household management can be severely affected by diminished or altered financial resources, changes in a parent's employment status, and alterations in the family's residence. Additional modifications are likely to occur in the family's boundaries and emotional environment. Parenting strategies may have to be modified, particularly those centered around issues of parental custody. Social relationships and sources of support (family, friends) are generally altered, and dating relationships may be initiated. Although these stresses typically affect men and women differently, their effect on the family system can be extensive. The accumulation of demands has the potential to outweigh the system's available coping resources, leaving the family vulnerable to crisis and disorganization. Successful adaptation will depend on the family's capacity to alter its existing strategies and establish new sources of social support.

The Single-Parent Household

Despite the structural diversity found within contemporary families, all families can be thought of as facing the same basic tasks. The single-parent household is no exception. Strategies and rules are required to organize family themes and individual identities, maintain boundaries, manage the household, regulate the

Taken from: *Family Interaction: A Multigenerational Developmental Perspective,* Fourth Edition, by Stephen A. Anderson and Ronald M. Sabatelli.

emotional climate, and manage family stress. In addition, as with any family system, adaptations will be required over time. The strategies adopted by single-parent families are influenced by their unique composition, structure, and circumstances.

However, it should also be apparent that the single-parent family system confronts a unique set of challenges and circumstances. The family's ability to adapt in the face of these challenges will depend, in part, on the ordinary and extraordinary stresses and strains it encounters and its available resources. Because of the prevalence of this family form, it is imperative that we develop an understanding of the single-parent family system and the unique challenges it faces.

Diversity within Single-Parent Systems

While single-parent families are all, by definition, headed by a single parent, families differ with respect to the factors that gave rise to the origin of the single-parent system (Hill, 1986). Single-parent systems can result from death, divorce, separation, or desertion. Others can occur as a result of out-of-wedlock births. Some single-parent-headed households result from single-parent adoptions. In still other instances, a single-parent-headed household results when parents remain separated for extended periods due to out-of-state employment. This diversity is important to note, because different origins produce different challenges that will influence the family's methods of coping, motivation, and ability to manage system tasks (Hill, 1986). For example, the single-parent system that originates as a result of divorce must deal with the stresses and emotional turmoil that separation introduces into the system while attempting to restabilize as a single-parent system. Although single-parent systems originating from the death of a spouse face many of the same emotional and systemic issues, social and community support is usually more readily extended to those dealing with a death than with a divorce. Similarly, the social support experienced by a widow with a young child is often considerably different from the support experienced by a teenage mother who gives birth to a child out of wedlock.

Consider, as well, the unique challenges confronted by those single-parent systems that result when one partner works away from home or goes on active military duty for extended periods (McCubbin, Dahl, Lester, Benson, & Robertson, 1976). These systems must develop two sets of strategies for the execution of system tasks— one set that applies when both parents are present and one set that applies when only one parent is present. As a result, these exits and entrances challenge the family to devise different strategies for the division of tasks, the equitable allocation of resources, and the distribution of power and authority within the system. This challenges the adaptability and flexibility of the family system. It should be clear that these unique demands have the potential to strain marital relationships and overburden the coping resources of the system.

Single-parent families differ not only in terms of their origin but also in terms of their composition. Researchers have tended to use simplistic terms in describing family structures, such as "two-parent," "one-parent," or "stepparent." However, many single-parent mothers and fathers live with other adults, such as a cohabiting partner, grandparents, other relatives, or nonrelatives, which makes these typical designations inaccurate and misleading (Bumpass & Raley, 1995; Eggebeen, Snyder, & Manning, 1996; Manning & Smock, 1997).

In sum, each single-parent system is the result of a unique origin and developmental history. Each must balance its own set of demands and stresses with its available coping resources. These differences must be acknowledged in any effort to understand the unique patterns of interaction found within single-parent systems.

Single-Parent Family Systems: Prevalence and Challenges

A sizable percentage of American families are headed by a single parent. In 1970, single parents constituted 13 percent of all family groups with children. By 2003, the proportion was 34 percent. Twenty-six percent of these were single-mother family groups and 12 percent were single-father family groups. These percentages have remained fairly level since 1996 (U.S. Census Bureau, 2004b).

Over half of all children born in the 1990s will spend some of their childhood in a single-parent household (Lamb, Sternberg, & Thompson, 1997). These children are five times more likely to live with their mothers than with their fathers. The likelihood of a child living in single-parent household also differs by race. Recent estimates suggest that 22 percent of white children live in single-parent households. However, 34 percent of Hispanic American and 62 percent of African American children live in a single-parent household (U.S. Census Bureau, 2005). The reasons for children living in a single-parent household also differ among racial groups. For instance, most white children are likely to find themselves in a single-parent household as a result of parental divorce (49 percent) or an out-of-wedlock birth (31 percent). In contrast, the majority of African American single mothers were never married (62 percent), and only 20 percent were likely to have been divorced (U.S. Census Bureau, 2004b).

Because roughly two-thirds of those who divorce eventually remarry, it has been suggested that the single-parent household is simply a "stepping stone" to another marriage. However, as Herz Brown (1989) has pointed out, roughly one-third of those who divorce do not remarry, which makes it clear that the single-parent household has become a new family form in contemporary society. Whether a remarriage occurs or not, the family headed by a single parent must undergo changes in its structure, the role definitions of its members, and the means by which it executes its basic tasks. In the next section, we will examine the unique demands that challenge single-parent families in their efforts to manage their basic tasks.

Challenges in Meeting Basic Tasks within Single-Parent Systems

Managing Family Stress

One of the most significant challenges to single-parent systems is managing the increased levels of stress within these systems. The ordinary demands of family life must be managed along with the challenges imposed by the demands of single parenthood. The potential for an accumulation of stress is apparent in that the demands on these systems may easily exceed their coping resources. This is particularly true given that coping resources such as finances, time, energy, and social support may be less available to the post-divorce and single-parent system (Anderson, 2003).

A critical challenge facing the single-parent system is the need to balance system demands with available coping resources. The demands on these systems, particularly those that result from the disruption of the nuclear family system (e.g., disruptions brought about by divorce, desertion, or death), can be thought of as expanding at a time when available resources for coping are generally declining. In addition, although not all families are adversely affected by these changes, this situation can easily challenge the resourcefulness and creativity of the system. Under these circumstances, novel strategies are required to meet even the most ordinary of system demands. It should be apparent, as well, that the expansion of system demands places families at potential risk. When stressed beyond manageable levels, coping strategies can become less adaptive, contributing to the stress experienced within the family system. The potential for both individual and family dysfunction is increased. In other words, the fine balance between demands and resources that is necessary for families to manage stress effectively can be disrupted by the additional challenges and demands facing the single-parent system. This increases the likelihood that less effective strategies will be employed to manage tasks and responsibilities.

Developing New Family Themes and Identities

As suggested earlier, themes represent a fundamental view of the "reality of the family." That is, they represent the critical images and identities of the family system that family members hold. Living according to a theme necessitates the development of various patterns of behavior that affect (1) how members interact with the outside world; (2) how they interact with each other; and (3) how they develop personally (Galvin & Brommel, 1991). Themes affect every aspect of the family's functioning. Individual identities, external and internal boundaries, and the establishment of priorities for the allocation of resources are all examples of issues that are influenced by the themes selected. That many forms of single-parent systems in our society are thought of as being non-normative, deviant, or dysfunctional adds to the difficulty that single-parent systems encounter when called on to alter or evolve constructive and positive family themes. For example, often the single-parent system that has come about as a result of divorce is thought of as a "broken family." Politicians routinely talk about the need for strengthening the family and, in the same context, discuss the prevalence of single-parent systems within the United States as an example of the deterioration of the family. The powerful and negative images and identities that are projected onto single-parent systems complicate the process that single-parent systems confront when evolving family themes. The single-parent system must grapple with the difficulties of constructing positive and adaptive themes in what might be fairly characterized as a "hostile societal environment." Adopting the view that the single-parent system represents a "broken family" makes the task of fostering a positive identity among family members as well as themes that facilitate a positive connection with outside systems more difficult.

Managing Maintenance Tasks in a Changing Family Household

Clearly, some of the most dramatic changes that occur in single-parent families are related to the alterations in their physical environment. Strategies for providing basic necessities such as food, shelter, and education can be adversely affected by the sometimes dramatic decline in the family's available resources. The resources most likely to be affected by the transition to a single-parent family are finances, employment status, sources of income, and residence.

Financial Stressors.   One of the most potentially disabling stressors faced by single parents, especially women, is the absence of financial security that accompanies single parenthood. For example, 44 percent of mother-headed households with children in the United States live in poverty. This figure contrasts with only approximately 9 percent of two-parent households (U.S. Census Bureau, 2000). Financial hardship is greatest for older homemakers and mothers with young children (Rowe, 1991). In addition, poverty is more common among non-white single-parent systems. For example, 54 percent of black single-parent families live below the poverty line (U.S. Census Bureau, 2000).

Further evidence of the financial stress experienced by single-parent systems comes from the research that has analyzed how divorce affects the financial well-being of women and children. In the aftermath of a divorce, research suggests that the average income of the mother-headed, single-parent household drops by 27 percent, in contrast to men, whose incomes increase 10 percent (Peterson, 1996). This is because the husband's salary provided the largest share of the family's income prior to divorce. Many women, especially those with younger children, have left paid employment to raise their children. A two- to four-year hiatus from paid employment can permanently lower the average woman's future earnings by 13 percent. A four-year hiatus will permanently lower her future earnings by 19 percent. Even when women have continued to work full-time, their salaries average 50 percent of their husbands (Rowe, 1991). This decline in earnings is in no way offset by other potential sources of income such as alimony, child support, or government assistance. At least initially, such a dramatic decline in income has a major effect on the family's ability to manage the household and its overall standard of living. Sacrifices must be made, and coping strategies become focused on day-to-day survival patterns rather than long-term plans for the future, at least until a more realistic appraisal of available resources and current living standards can be made (Anderson, 2003).

This dramatic decline in the overall economic well-being of women-headed households challenges the resourcefulness and creativity of the family system. At the same time, economic hardship reverberates throughout the family system and affects other aspects of family life. Chief among the other aspects of family life affected by economic hardship are the single mother's work status, the single-parent family's sources of income, and family residence.

Changes in Employment Status.   For women whose primary roles prior to divorce involved managing the household and caring for children, the reduction in the standard of living accompanying divorce may force her into the work force. These homemakers may be relatively unprepared for such a change. They may have few marketable skills, limited training, and large gaps in their employment record, which make competing for available jobs difficult. Furthermore, the jobs that are available to them tend to be low paying. For some, the costs of child care may be so high as to offset the economic advantages gained by working. Many will be forced to settle for less-than-adequate child-care arrangements or seek assistance with child care from relatives, friends, or neighbors. The mother's return to work may also leave children feeling that they have been abandoned by both parents (Hetherington, Stanley-Hagan, & Anderson, 1989).

The economic crunch experienced by single mothers is further exacerbated by the fact that the wages of women, in general, are lower than the wages of their male counterparts. Reasons for this again include a lack of job skills and experience, irregular work histories, and limited child-care options, as well as sex discrimination in hiring practices. Nevertheless, most displaced homemakers have been found to choose work rather than turn to other sources of support, like welfare assistance (Mednick, 1987). Such a choice, however, complicates the lives of single mothers by forcing them to balance the needs of their children and the demands of their work (Jackson, Brooks-Gunn, Huang, & Glassman, 2000).

Changes in Sources of Income. The decline in family income associated with single parenthood may be augmented by additional sources of support and assistance. Although most single-parent families receive their major source of incomes from wages, they also receive assistance from a variety of other sources. Some may receive government assistance in the form of welfare, foodstamps, or financial aid for job training. Many may receive child support payments from the children's father. Others receive alimony from their ex-spouses. Although any of these sources of income may mean the difference between sinking into poverty and adequately maintaining the household, each is fraught with potential problems. For instance, reliance on government agencies for subsistence may perpetuate feelings of insecurity, helplessness, and dependency, rather than a sense of competence and self-efficacy. Female single parents on some form of welfare have been found to have poorer social and emotional adjustment than those who are not receiving such assistance (Pett & Vaughn-Cole, 1986; Teachman & Paasch, 1994).

The problems with reliance on ex-spouses for child support are well documented. The average child-support payment women receive from their former husbands generally does not meet even half of the cost of raising a child (Rowe, 1991). Approximately half of all single mothers actually receive full child support, a quarter receive partial payments, and a quarter receive no payments at all (Peters, Argys, Macesby, & Mnookin, 1993). Clearly, the unpredictability of support payments can contribute greatly to an unstable and insecure financial situation.

Only approximately 15 percent of divorced women receive alimony payments from their ex-spouses. Those who do tend to be older, have been married longer, and have less employment experience (Kitson & Morgan, 1990; Rowe, 1991). These women are also less likely to be caring for young children. Recent legal reforms have resulted in most alimony awards changing from permanent to "short-term, rehabilitative" awards. The intent of these laws is to provide women time to find employment or gain the skills, training, or education necessary to become self-supporting. However, most of these awards are too short-term and the amounts are too small to cover the time and cost needed to complete training and find employment (Rowe, 1991).

Most states have now implemented "no-fault" divorce laws that emphasize property settlements instead of alimony. In such cases, assets are equally divided between ex-spouses at the time of divorce. Some have pointed out that this is actually unfair to women who typically retain custody of the children and most of the costs (Kitson & Morgan, 1990). Others have found that only half of all divorced women actually receive some form of property settlement. When they do, the average amount is small (Teachman & Paasch, 1994).

The small value of property settlements, the irregularity of child-support payments, the rare granting of alimony, and the minimal assistance offered by entitlement programs do relatively little to alleviate the financial tensions that permeate many single-parent systems. These systems must tolerate a great deal of financial uncertainty and ambiguity. Consequently, considerable physical and emotional energy is devoted to the management of financial tasks, leaving less time and energy for other aspects of family life.

Changes in Residence.   Single parents may also find themselves displaced from their homes. Women, in particular, are often forced to sell their homes and find a less expensive place to live in order to manage the downward mobility that comes with making the transition to a single-parent system. Selling the family home involves both an economic and an emotional rebalancing of the family system. Economically, selling the family home may be an important step in reorganizing the family's financial resources to meet necessary expenses.

However, selling the family home is also an emotional and symbolic event. Moving to a less expensive residence graphically symbolizes the changes taking place in the family's standard of living. It can also represent conflicting feelings of wanting to be rid of the past while still wishing to feel the security and stability of old and familiar surroundings (Bagarozzi & Anderson, 1989; Herz Brown, 1989).

Children may also view the sale of the family home as a major loss symbolizing the end of the original family and any lingering fantasies they may have had for it reuniting. Moving also means saying good-bye to old friends, changing schools, and investing energy in making new friends.

Maintenance Tasks in Father-Headed Single-Parent Systems

Most discussions of the issues confronted within single-parent systems focus on women-headed households, primarily because most single-parent systems are headed by women. At this point, relatively little is known about the stressors and strains experienced within male-headed single-parent systems, although as noted earlier, this family structure is becoming increasingly common.

Some initial findings suggest that single-father households are quite diverse in their structure and composition. For instance, only 25 percent of these households follow the popular stereotype of a divorced or separated father living alone with his children. In the majority, the single father shares the household with a cohabiting partner, his parents, or other extended family members (Eggebeen et al., 1996; Meyer & Garasky, 1993). Roughly one-half of single-parent fathers who live with a cohabiting partner were previously married and then received custody of their children following a divorce. The other half have never been married. This raises the possibility that many of the children living in these single-parent (i.e., unmarried) households were born to the cohabiting couple. Thus, they may never have experienced many of the family disruptions associated with divorce, such as the loss of contact with a parent or changes in residence. However, single fathers in a cohabiting relationship tend to be younger, less educated, and have lower incomes than fathers who gained custody of their children following divorce (Eggebeen et al., 1996). Clearly, the unique set of circumstances facing each father-headed single-parent system will determine how the family's maintenance tasks are managed.

By far, the most extensive attention given to fathers in the single-parent literature has emphasized how divorce affects fathers' financial status and their willingness to support their ex-spouse and children. Financial settlements following divorce and the need to contribute support to two households can tax fathers' financial resources, at least initially. That the father is expected to contribute to a household from which he no longer benefits also can make this as much an emotional as a financial issue for him. When the father did not initiate the separation, he may have even more resistance to providing support (Herz Brown, 1989).

However, in contrast to single-parent custodial mothers, most custodial and noncustodial fathers generally maintain or improve their standard of living following divorce (Arditti, 1992; Kitson & Morgan, 1990). For some, this may be because they refuse to provide child support. For others, it may simply be because they cease to be the primary support for the mother and children (Rowe, 1991). Even when they do provide continuous child support, the amount generally represents a small percentage of fathers' usable income (Hetherington et al., 1989). Some have estimated that fathers are capable of paying more than twice the amounts currently being awarded in child-support settlements (Kitson & Morgan, 1990).

It appears that the critical factors regarding single fathers' compliance with child support have to do with their overall level of income (the higher the income, the more likely he is to pay), the level of attachment they feel toward their children and former spouse, and the extent to which he and his former spouse agree on child-rearing issues (Arditti, 1992). Once again, it is the quality of the emotional relationships between former spouses and the father's level of personal involvement with his children (along with his own financial security) that determine his willingness to share his financial resources. However, it may well be the differences between the father's and mother's financial situations that exacerbate conflicts between them. Mothers may come to resent that fathers have more discretionary income, can afford more "extras," and can spend more of their money on themselves, while they must spend their money on their children (Fletcher, 1989). Such differences can severely tax efforts to redefine the boundaries between mothers' and fathers' separate households.

Boundary Tasks: Renegotiating Family Members' Roles and Responsibilities

Because many single-parent systems result from divorce and separation, these families in transition must confront critical parenting issues. Parents and children must adjust to the changes in family relationships that occur as a result of marital strife and divorce. While dealing with these issues, parents and their children must rework family roles and responsibilities to accommodate the reality of the single-parent system. This redefinition of relationships between parents and children takes on a whole new dimension that adds to the ordinary stresses and strains that parents experience. Chief among these challenges are those related to custody and the clarification of each parent's role with the children.

Resolving Custody Issues. One of the initial challenges to parents is resolution of child custody and co-parenting issues. Working through these challenges requires, first, that decisions be made about who will assume primary responsibility for the children. In this regard, even though **joint legal custody** (when parents share decision-making and economic support) has become more common, **joint physical custody** (residence) has not (Kitson & Morgan, 1990). Approximately 85 percent of children reside with the custodial mother following divorce (U.S. Census Bureau, 2003c).

Obviously, sharing joint legal custody can be difficult when one parent has sole physical custody of the children (Kitson & Morgan, 1990). Sharing legal (or physical) custody is sometimes further complicated in that both parents do not always live in the same community (Kelly & Lamb, 2003). The transition to a binuclear family, in which both parents share custody, is further complicated by the absence of prescribed societal norms, traditions, and rituals for divorced parents. McCubbin (1979) noted that the family's vulnerability to stress is increased when community expectations and norms are not clear. Finally, unresolved personal feelings between former spouses can interfere with their ability to share parenting responsibilities cooperatively.

Reworking Parenting Roles. Even when parents are able to work together to share the tasks of parenthood, divorce precipitates a movement toward greater separateness and autonomy, and a corresponding decline in the couple's level of interdependence. Each parent must establish new personal relationships with their children without the same kind of continuous input, support, or collaboration that was formerly available from the partner. Tasks that were once allocated to the partner must now be assumed by the single parent. For example, Father may have to become more involved in chauffeuring children to after-school activities or helping them with their homework when they visit him, even though it was Mother who "usually took care of these things in the past." Similarly, Mother may now have to establish her own methods of discipline rather than leaving some matters "until Father gets home." Therefore, even in the best of circumstances, divorced parents must contend with the task of redefining their parental roles and responsibilities. The family must contend with how some of the tasks that were formerly shared between two parents are now to be managed independently by each parent.

Managing the Family's Emotional Environment

The research literature suggests that the challenges posed by the transition to single-parenthood are rarely handled in an optimal manner. The accumulation of stressors brought on by changes in the family's household routines, financial changes, the mother's increased work demands, and unresolved feelings of loss and grief for the ex-spouse tend to increase the risks of psychological or physical dysfunction among parents and decrease the effectiveness of their efforts to attend to their children's evolving needs. Specifically, alcoholism, drug abuse, depression, psychosomatic problems, and accidents are all more common among divorced than nondivorced adults (Amato, 2000; Gringlas & Weinraub, 1995; Hetherington & Kelly, 2002).

In addition, parents coping with changes following divorce often exhibit marked emotional changes, alternating between periods of euphoria and optimism and periods of anxiety, loneliness, and depression, along with associated changes in self-concept and self-esteem (Hetherington & Kelly, 2002). Many custodial mothers report feeling overwhelmed at this time (Anderson, 2003), and a period of diminished parenting is common among them. Parental attention and discipline are often infrequent or inconsistent (Amato, 2000; Anderson, 2003).

In other words, the greater the accumulation of demands (work, expenses, unresolved issues with ex-spouse, younger versus older children) and the more limited the custodial mother's resources (financial, psychological, extended family, social supports), the greater the potential for ineffective parenting strategies to be established. The critical issue in this regard appears to be the extent to which the single mother is able to assume the role of **sole administrator** for the household. That is, the mother must accept that the single-parent household can no longer operate as it did before, when two parents were present. She must assume complete authority and responsibility, enlisting the help of others when needed without allowing them to take over for her (Anderson, 2003; Herz Brown, 1989). In structural terms, the parental hierarchy or executive subsystem must be clearly defined with the mother in charge. When others are sought for assistance (e.g., babysitter, grandparent, older child), they are given responsibility but not ultimate authority (Haley, 1987; Minuchin, 1974).

To the extent that the mother feels a gap in her own personal competency, she is likely to enlist her children, her parents, or the children's father into the coparent role, thereby inviting triangles or coalitions that may provide temporary assistance but long-term dysfunction (Anderson, 2003; Byng-Hall, 2002). One such triangle is when the oldest child (often a daughter) is called on to fill the role of **parental child.** Children in single-parent families are often expected to help out more around the home than children from two-parent families, and this can serve as a valuable resource for mothers (Kitson et al., 1989). There also is evidence to suggest that such increased expectations can contribute to children's heightened senses of independence and competence (Amato, 2000).

However, in other instances this can become problematic. The daughter who becomes a parental child may be given authority over younger children who may not accept her newly elevated status, thereby creating sibling conflicts. The mother may begin to treat the daughter as her confidante, sharing personal information with her about the other children, her dating life, or other aspects of her personal life. Such an arrangement may serve to strengthen the emotional bond between mother and daughter and provide each with a necessary measure of emotional support. However, the demands of this relationship and the parental responsibilities the daughter must fulfill may, over time, interfere with her own growth and development. For instance, responsibilities at home may curtail her own extracurricular activities after school or social interactions with peers, both of which are important to personal adjustment, especially during adolescence (Sabatelli & Anderson, 1991).

The mother may also pull her own mother into the vacuum created by the father's absence. She may move in with her parents, or live nearby, so that the grandparents can help care for the children while she works or goes to school. The more overwhelmed the single-parent mother is, the more domineering the grandmother may become. Put another way, the less successful the mother has been at individuating from her own mother, the greater the chances that the grandmother will begin to function as the mother. What may have started as an effort to cope with the pressures of single parenthood may end as an added stress, with increased feelings of failure, incompetence, or low self-esteem for the single mother.

On still other occasions a triangle may develop among the mother, the children, and the children's father. The mother may rely on the father for support payments, child-care responsibilities, or, in some cases, even continued discipline, while also resenting him for his intrusions. The children, too, may learn that they can undermine their mother's decisions by getting their father to agree with them. In each of these cases, the mother's role as sole administrator in her own home is undermined and ineffective, and inconsistent parenting strategies become established.

Managing the Emotional Environment in Father-Headed Single-Parent Households

For fathers, the parenting experience may be quite different than that experienced by mothers. As noted earlier, it has become more common for men to receive sole or joint custody of their children. These fathers experience many of the same parenting stresses that single-parent mothers face. However, they tend to cope with them differently. For instance, they, too, may seek out their own parents to fill in for the missing spouse when it comes to child care. However, men are less likely to view parents or a girlfriend as a competitor for their children's attention and more likely to view them as convenient child-care substitutes (Anderson, 2003).

In most instances, fathers become noncustodial parents, with custody awarded to the mother. As a consequence, men often experience a loss of a sense of home and family. Furthermore, with the loss of legal custody, many men also experience a loss of influence and control over their children (Arditti, 1992; Arendell, 1995). Their contacts with their children may be limited to court-defined visitation schedules. If these schedules are poorly defined (i.e., visits are allowed only at unreasonable times and places) or not closely adhered to by the custodial mother, the father's sense of loss and powerlessness can be even greater.

It may be this sense of loss of contact and control, coupled with feelings of guilt, anxiety, and depression and loss of self-esteem following the family break-up that may lead fathers to emotionally withdraw from their children. Numerous studies have documented that fathers tend to decrease the frequency and duration of their visits with their children over time (Amato, 2000; Arditti, 1992; Kelly, 2003). Of course, there are a number of other explanations for this, including unresolved conflicts with the former spouse, inability or unwillingness to continue with child support, the superficiality of the visitation experience, a lack of interest in parenting, relocation to another state, or remarriage and the establishment of a new family.

Take for example, a situation in which there are unresolved conflicts with the ex-spouse. Struggles may occur over keeping to the agreed-upon visitation schedule. Mother may "forget" Father was coming or neglect to have the children ready for the visit. Conversely, Father may be late returning the children after the visit or deliberately spend the time with them in an activity that was forbidden by Mother. In these instances, the children's visits with father simply become another battleground for unresolved feelings between the ex-spouses.

Adaptation to Single-Parenthood: Sources of Social Support

Both men's and women's social relationships are disrupted by divorce. The loss of one's supportive social network is a major reason for the stress that accompanies divorce and single-parenthood (Anderson, 2003). On the other hand, research also has consistently shown that the availability of social supports in the form of personal friendships, relationships with extended family, and new dating partners are positively related to adaptation to single parenthood (Edin & Lein, 1997; Pledge, 1992; Sutton & Sprenkle, 1985). Unfortunately, not all social relationships offer this positive benefit. Some can have the opposite effect and produce greater stress when they are not responsive to single parents' emotional or physical needs, or when they impose even greater demands on the single parent.

The Family of Origin

One's family of origin plays an especially important role in coping with becoming a single parent, especially for women (Kitson & Morgan, 1990). Relationships with one's family of origin often change as a result of becoming a single parent. Most women report increases in the amount of contact they have with family members (Leslie & Grady, 1985; Milardo, 1987). About one-fourth of divorced women live with their parents at some point after divorce (Hetherington & Kelly, 2002). However, the kind of contact will depend greatly on the overall quality of the relationship with the family, especially with one's parents. Parents and other family members can be emotionally and instrumentally supportive (running errands, babysitting, sharing information), but they can also be more critical than friends or other acquaintances (Milardo, 1987).

One spouse's parents may have been very fond of the ex-spouse and fail to see the reasons for the marital breakup. They may even hold the single parent responsible for it (Spanier & Thompson, 1984). Alternatively, parents may not have approved of the marriage and express pleasure that it has ended. This can be perceived as either supportive or unsupportive, depending on the meta-message received. For instance, a message such as, "I told you he was no good from the beginning, but you were too thick-headed to listen," may serve only to heighten feelings of incompetence and failure. On the other hand, a message such as, "We're glad that you had the strength and courage to end a relationship that was causing you so much pain," would probably be received very differently.

One's level of individuation from the family of origin plays an important role in determining the kinds of relationship changes that may occur. Some single-parent mothers, especially younger ones, move in with their parents following divorce. For those who have managed a "good enough" individuation, such an arrangement can provide the single mother with a host of resources such as financial assistance, help with child care, an easier reentrance into the work force, increased time for leisure activities, and a supportive emotional environment in which to resolve feelings about the divorce.

When individuation has been less successful, this arrangement can result in the single mother becoming overinvolved with her own parents, allowing them to take over her responsibilities and place her in an "incompetent" role. Others who have not yet successfully individuated may choose to separate emotionally from their parents to save themselves from criticism. In so doing, they isolate themselves further and lose a potential source of emotional and practical support (Anderson, 2003; Bowen, 1978). As a result, an important means of releasing emotional tension is lost. This can, in turn, intensify tensions and conflicts within the single-parent household or force the single mother to turn to her children or ex-spouse for emotional support (Bowen, 1978). In so doing, she may compromise her position as "sole administrator" for the household.

For men, the family of origin often plays a somewhat different role. Men tend to reduce their overall contact with family following divorce rather than increase it (Milardo, 1987). When contacts are maintained, they tend to be more emotionally distant, less personally disclosing, and more instrumentally based than those of women. For instance, fathers may rely on their own parents for help with child care, or they may help out around the parental home by doing such things as house repairs, yard work, or errands. These behaviors are in keeping with men's traditional socialization toward being objective (relying on facts, coping by trying to manage the physical environment) and functional (providing for others).

Friendships

Often a recently divorced single-parent mother does not seek new outside friends because of the financial and parenting stresses she is experiencing. She may feel overwhelmed by her many tasks and responsibilities or still be working through unresolved feelings toward the former spouse. She may still feel a sense of failure about her earlier marriage, which makes the prospect of beginning new relationships or seeking out others for support seem risky (Pledge, 1992). She may also not be able to afford either the cost of recreational activities or the expense of hiring support (child care, domestic work).

The friendships that she does maintain are generally those that have been her own personal friends rather than friends of the former couple. They are generally long-standing rather than recent acquaintances, and they tend to live nearby, generally within the same neighborhood or town (Leslie & Grady, 1985; Milardo, 1987). In contrast to family members, friends can be emotionally supportive without tending to be critical. A friend who is critical can much more easily be dismissed than a family member. Friends who are often the most helpful are those who can understand the reasons for the divorce, offer advice, and provide daily help with errands and tasks (Leslie & Grady, 1985).

As do most women, men experience a decline in the number of their friends, especially in the initial year following divorce. It has been estimated that both men and women decrease their friendship networks by roughly 40 percent following divorce. Friends who are lost are often those who were closer to the ex-partner or who were friends of the former couple (Milardo, 1987). The divorced man or woman may withdraw from former couple friends because he or she may think that they no longer have any overlapping interests with married friends (Milardo, 1987). Couple friends sometimes withdraw from the divorced individuals because they feel caught in the middle and forced to take sides. Others exclude the individuals from couple activities, thinking that they might be uncomfortable participating alone (Herz Brown, 1989).

However, beyond this similarity, men's experiences with friends are considerably different from women's. Men tend to interact less frequently with their remaining friends following divorce than do women (Anderson, 2003). They are more likely to become involved with social clubs and organizations in contrast to women, who affiliate more with family (Colburn, Lin, & Moore, 1992; Milardo, 1987).

Men also typically experience less support from their friends than do women. This again may be due, in part, to gender differences in men's and women's socialization. Men generally disclose less personal information to their friends than do women, and know considerably less about their friends' attitudes and opinions (Milardo, 1987). Overall, men tend to communicate through more active channels (i.e., doing something together) than verbal ones that require a greater amount of emotional sharing (Meth & Passick, 1990). It may be this difficulty that men have benefiting from potentially supportive relationships (along with losing contact with their children and having to leave the family home) that accounts for some research showing that men experience adjustment problems such as loneliness, anxiety, and depression following divorce (Amato, 2000; Emery & Sbarra, 2002; Hetherington, Cox, & Cox, 1976; Pledge, 1992).

Therefore, while women tend to increase their involvement with family and friends, men tend to experience a decline overall in these relationships. The relationships that men do maintain with family and friends are focused more on practical matters such as helping with child-care and sharing activities rather than providing emotional support. However, the one area from which men do appear to derive emotional support is dating relationships.

Dating Relationships

Men are likely to initiate new dating relationships sooner than women are (Price & McKenry, 1989). In addition, whereas women strive for greater independence and autonomy following divorce, men are more likely to redefine their identity in the context of another "love relationship" (Colburn et al., 1992). Although they may lack the intimate social supports of women, they are more likely to have an established network of acquaintances at work. This offers them a pool of eligible dating partners. They are also generally free of the role overload women may experience and more able to afford the expenses associated with dating. A divorced man may also be viewed as more of a "catch" by both younger and older women (Herz Brown, 1989). He may be more established in a career, have more financial resources, and be less likely to be part of a "package deal" that includes the full-time responsibility for children. Therefore, not only are men more likely to seek out new dating partners in an attempt to cope with the changes they are experiencing, but they are more likely to be supported in their efforts by a social context that promotes their efforts.

Differences in men's and women's social networks and socialization may also contribute to the likelihood of men dating sooner. Men, more so than women, may tend to rely on dating partners for their needs for intimacy and support. This may come about because men lack supportive social ties with others and the interpersonal skills necessary to elicit this support. It may be that contact with a regular dating partner provides men with a safer and more secure context within which to express feelings and disclose personal vulnerabilities. Dating relationships also offer men the opportunity to express themselves sexually. This is more in keeping with the prevailing social norms for how men express feelings of closeness and intimacy.

It is important to acknowledge that, despite the obvious differences between men and women, there are no right or wrong ways to establish supportive social relationships during the transition into single parenthood. What is especially important, however, is that social relationships are not static but change. For instance, when the stress of becoming a single mother is high, the need for stability in one's friendship network may be greater. Close-knit relationships with family and friends can provide stability at a time when many other aspects of the single mother's household are undergoing rapid and dramatic changes. Similarly, a single father may find stability by relying heavily on a new dating partner to alleviate many of the feelings of loss and uncertainty that come from leaving the family home and his children.

However, an emphasis on stability, predictability, and sameness can eventually lead to stagnation rather than growth. As noted earlier, one of the essential tasks of the single parent is to establish a new life, one that offers new opportunities and a greater sense of personal competence, self-esteem, and mastery. Such an adaptation will eventually require relinquishing one's newfound stability and again moving on. Establishing new relationships helps to reorganize one's social network such that it can be more responsive to the individual's changing needs. Social relationships introduce new experiences, options, and information into the system. Such a reorganization is an important indicator of how willing the single parent is to put the past to rest and move on toward the future.

Conclusions

It is apparent that both men and women experience stress during the transition to a single-parent household. Both must undergo dramatic changes in their personal and family lives. Both are likely to experience stress due to the unresolved feelings and conflicts that may remain following divorce. They are also equally likely to encounter disruptions in their social support networks at this time.

However, men and women also differ with respect to some of the other stressors that they must face. For women, divorce and single parenthood precipitate a dramatic decline in financial well-being and standard of living. This change is further compounded by a host of other potential hardships and stressors, including changes in work status, source of income, and residence. Further compounding the woman's overload is the likelihood that she will assume primary parenting responsibilities.

Most men do not experience the same levels of stress due to finances or parenting responsibilities. Men's financial stress is generally short-term, if it is a factor at all. In addition, with the exception of those fathers who assume sole custody or joint legal and physical custody for their children, most experience fewer parenting demands than their female counterparts. The major source of stress for men appears to be the sense of loss they experience both with regard to their children and with regard to the family home. Finally, men and women differ in the coping strategies they enact to adapt to single-parenthood. For men, this often involves engaging rapidly in new dating relationships and initiating a new "love relationship." For women, coping often entails reaching out to family and friends for both emotional and practical support. However, regardless of the form coping takes, both men and women rely heavily on supportive relationships with others to manage the stresses and hardships that accompany the transition to single parenthood. It is through these supportive relationships that both men and women attempt to redefine their own personal identities as single persons, gain a sense of mastery over their personal and family environments, and seek out new opportunities and experiences that propel their lives forward toward the future rather than backward toward the past.

Key Terms

Joint legal custody   When parents legally share responsibility for child care, parental decision-making, and economic support of their children following divorce.

Joint physical custody   When parents equally share the responsibility for providing their children with a residence. The term is used to distinguish between this arrangement and joint legal custody, which involves shared parental decision-making and economic support, and a situation in which children generally reside with one parent most of the time.

Parental child   A role assumed by a child (often a daughter or older child) requiring him or her to take responsibility for parenting other children (or the parent) in the single-parent family system.

Sole administrator   The role assumed by a single parent that involves accepting complete authority and responsibility for the household and all related tasks, and enlisting the help of others when needed, without allowing them to take over. That is, the parent accepts that the single-parent household can no longer operate as it did when two parents were present.

14

Remarried Families Across the Life Cycle

Remarriage and Stepparenting

Chapter Overview

Remarried families have a uniquely different structure than that found in traditional nuclear families. For example, the parental subsystem predates the establishment of the new marital subsystem. Also, most children have a biological parent living elsewhere. These and other variations suggest that remarried families will have to develop different strategies for managing basic tasks. Strategies also will vary at different stages of the remarried system's development.

The remarried family can be thought of as passing through four stages over time. First, there is a period of courtship and preparation for remarriage. This gives adults and children an opportunity to accommodate to the changes that are taking place. During the next phase, the early remarriage stage, identity tasks must be addressed. The middle remarriage stage involves the restructuring of the family's boundaries. During the late remarriage stage, attention shifts to strengthening the emotional bonds between family members.

Models of remarried family development offer an ideal set of guidelines against which a given family's adaptation can be compared. Not all families adapt equally well, and some will become bogged down in problematic interactional patterns that can constrain optimal development.

Remarriage and Stepparenting

Consider these facts: Approximately half of all marriages in the United States are estimated to be remarriages for one or both partners (Bumpas, Sweet, & Castro Martin, 1990). Almost two-thirds of these individuals have children from a

Taken from: *Family Interaction: A Multigenerational Developmental Perspective,* Fourth Edition, by Stephen A. Anderson and Ronald M. Sabatelli.

previous relationship, thus forming stepfamilies (Chadwick & Heaton, 1999). It has been estimated that over half of all Americans will be part of a stepfamily at some point in their lives (Visher, Visher, & Pasley, 2003). One-third of all children are expected to live in a remarried family for at least one year before reaching the age of eighteen (Bumpass et al., 1995; Field, 2001).

Remarriages tend to take place quickly after earlier marriages end. Thirty percent will remarry within one year after their divorce. Men generally remarry at higher rates than do women. However, African American and Hispanic men remarry at lower rates than white men. For divorced women, the likelihood of remarriage declines as they become older. Remarriage is most likely among women under age 25 at the time of their divorce (Bramlet & Mosher, 2002). Women who are more educated and employed are also less likely to remarry (Coleman, Ganong, & Fine, 2000). Remarriages are also more likely to end in divorce than first marriages (Bramlet & Mosher, 2002). As a result, children in these living situations may undergo numerous family transitions.

The remarried or step-family is not a single, clearly defined entity. Rather, step-families vary greatly in their structure and composition. The most common remarried family structure appears to be that in which a mother, her children from a previous relationship, and a stepfather are present. This undoubtedly reflects the fact that women are more likely to retain physical custody of children from an earlier marriage than are men (U.S. Census Bureau, 2005). A more complex stepfamily household might include a mother and father who both bring children from a previous relationship, plus offspring of the remarried couple.

However, remarriage rates are now beginning to decline except among older adults and an increasing number of adults are bringing children into cohabiting relationships (Coleman et al., 2000). In fact, cohabiting couples are more likely (48 percent versus 37 percent) to bring children into their new household than are remarried couples (Wineberg & McCarthy, 1998). Some of these cohabiting couples with children will eventually marry. Others will continue to reside together in a cohabiting arrangement (Coleman et al., 2000). Little is known about these permanent cohabiting households with children. Most of what we know comes from research on remarried families.

These data indicate how much step-family life has come to characterize our contemporary culture. They also indicate dramatically how the environment in which many young children are being raised has changed from that of earlier generations. When neither spouse brings children from an earlier marriage into a remarriage, the family closely resembles that of a first marriage, and many of the same norms apply (Goetting, 1982). However, numerous theorists, clinicians, and researchers have suggested that the stepfamily with children is profoundly different from the traditional nuclear family (Coleman et al., 2000; McGoldrick & Carter, 1999; Visher et al., 2003). Efforts to understand stepfamilies by applying traditional nuclear family values have been criticized for ignoring the diversity and complexity that characterize these systems. As will be shown throughout this chapter, these differences result in many stresses that are not shared by the traditional nuclear family.

The Unique Characteristics of Stepfamilies

It is important to understand the ways in which stepfamilies differ from the more traditional nuclear family. Along these lines, Visher and Visher (1982) noted that stepfamilies differ structurally from nuclear families in the following ways:

1. *All stepfamily members have experienced important losses* (e.g., parental death or divorce; loss of the single-parent family structure; changes in residence, income, and social and peer networks; changes in relationships with grandparents). Even though nuclear families may experience losses over the course of their development, the nuclear family is not born of numerous and repeated losses, as is the stepfamily.

2. *All members come with histories.* In a first marriage, the couple comes together with differing experiences and expectations based on their family of origin experiences. They gradually work out a shared set of strategies and rules for how their nuclear family will operate. Children are added gradually. In a remarriage, adults and children often come together more suddenly. Every strategy, rule, tradition, and preferred way of doing things must be renegotiated. Even the strategies for negotiating differences must be worked out.

3. *Parent–child bonds predate the new couple relationship.* That biological parent–child bonds predate the marriage relationship means that the couple does not have time to develop an intimate, clearly defined marital subsystem slowly before the arrival of children. Furthermore, in most remarried systems, the parent–child bond not only predates the remarriage but is more central than the marital relationship, at least initially. Failure to recognize this key distinction can lead stepparents to compete with their stepchildren for their new spouse's attention, as if the relationships were on the same level (McGoldrick & Carter, 1999).

4. *A biological parent exists elsewhere.* In stepfamilies, there is another parent elsewhere. Even if the other parent has died, his or her influence will remain. Memories linger and influence present behavior. When the parent lives elsewhere, strategies are required for how children will be shared. Children can easily become caught in the middle of unresolved conflicts between former spouses. Furthermore, developing a close relationship with a stepparent may be perceived by the other biological parent, the child, or both as a form of disloyalty to the biological parent. As a result, relationships between stepparents and stepchildren may be resisted and become characterized by conflict and stress.

5. *Children often are members of two households.* When children spend time in two separate households, they are generally exposed to two qualitatively different and contrasting family environments. They must learn to operate under two separate systems of rules. If the adults are willing to work cooperatively with regard to the children, children will be able to move in and out of both households easily. If, however, the relationship between the two biological parents continues to be governed by conflict, insecurity, and competitiveness, children will become caught between two warring camps and, once again, struggle with loyalty conflicts.

6. *Stepparents have few legal rights.* State laws give almost no recognition to the role of stepparents living with stepchildren (Mason, Harrison-Jay, Svare, & Wolfinger, 2002).

This can lead to confusion and awkward situations when stepparents have no legal or decision-making authority in day care centers, schools, or other important areas of their stepchildren's lives. These restrictions can be especially problematic in long-standing stepfamily households where stepparents and stepchildren have established lasting emotional bonds (Visher et al., 2003). The lack of legal rights for stepparents is part of what Cherlin (1978) referred to as the **incomplete institution**. This refers to a lack of norms and institutional supports for stepfamilies.

These differences are compounded by the boundary ambiguity that exists within stepfamilies. Stepfamilies cannot operate like nuclear families, which have a clearly defined boundary around the immediate family unit. Instead, a more permeable boundary is required to allow interaction between the remarried household (e.g., biological parent, stepparent, siblings, stepsiblings) and the metafamily system. The **metafamily system** includes the other biological parent's household (perhaps another stepparent, siblings, and stepsiblings), biological relatives (e.g., grandparents, aunts, uncles, cousins), and steprelatives (grandparents, aunts, uncles, cousins) (Sager, Walker, Brown, Crohn, & Rodstein, 1981).

Finally, traditional gender patterns that encourage women to take responsibility for the emotional well-being of family members may add stress to the remarried family system (McGoldrick & Carter, 1999). These traditional assumptions can create antagonism and rivalry between stepchildren (especially stepdaughters) and stepmothers, or new wives and ex-wives. Successful functioning in remarried families often requires placing more importance on the role of the biological parent in parenting his or her own children rather than on traditional gender role socialization. This means that each spouse, in conjunction with the ex-spouse, must assume primary, co-parenting responsibility for raising and disciplining his or her own biological children (McGoldrick & Carter, 1999).

These conclusions are supported by research that has found one of the most frequently reported problems in the remarried family to be in the relationships between stepparents and stepchildren (Bray & Kelly, 1998; Coleman et al., 2000). This is especially true for stepmother/stepdaughter relationships (Coleman & Ganong, 1990). Problems in stepparent/stepchild relationships also have been found to be a critical factor in the level of marital satisfaction reported between remarried husbands and wives (Brown & Booth, 1996; Coleman et al., 2000; Visher et al., 2003). Many of the marital difficulties that remarried couples report are related to tensions between stepparents and children (Bray & Kelly, 1998; Coleman et al., 2000).

Differences within Remarried Families

The focus on the many differences between remarried and traditional nuclear families often obscures the variations within remarried family systems. It is not surprising, therefore, that the research that has been conducted on remarried families has been criticized for assuming that all remarried families are alike. Inadequate attention has been given to the various family structures these families may assume. Some of these families may be binuclear, with biological parents sharing joint custody arrangements and children spending time in two households. In other families, one of the biological parents may be unavailable and uninvolved in child-rearing. In some families, one spouse brings children from a former marriage, whereas in others, both spouses bring children from a former marriage. In some families, all children were born before the remarriage. In yet others, some children were born before the remarriage and others were born to the remarried couple after the remarriage.

Furthermore, the issues faced by remarried families may be different depending on the stages of development of individual family members. For instance, the younger the children at the time of remarriage, the more likely they are to eventually accept the stepparent as a parent (Coleman et al., 2000; Marsiglio, 2004). Adolescent children may never accept a stepparent as a parent given their longer shared history with their own biological parents and their greater investment in individuating from the family. At a time when the remarried family is moving to establish greater cohesion and intimacy, adolescent children are focusing their attention toward peers and moving out of the family orbit.

Spouses, too, may be at different developmental stages. The tendency of men to remarry women younger than themselves can often produce a situation in which the wife is at the life cycle stage of wanting to bear children while the husband, having already passed this developmental phase, does not wish to raise another family (Whiteside, 1983). In general, the greater the discrepancy between the life-cycle experiences of a husband and wife, the greater the difficulty they will have managing the transition to a new family structure (McGoldrick & Carter, 1999).

A Developmental Model for Remarried Family Systems

As has been noted throughout this text, families continually change as they encounter and adapt to various stressors, transitions, and stages over the life cycle. The family's strategies for coping with each current stage or transition are dependent, to some extent, on the strategies the family has selected for coping with earlier transitions and stages. In this manner, each family develops a distinctive identity, coping style, and structure, within which its patterns of interaction are maintained. However, changes occur that can greatly alter the family's structure and its distinct interactional style. One such change is the merging of two family systems through remarriage. The merging of two families dramatically alters how the family manages its basic tasks. The family's identity, boundaries, household management, emotional climate, and level of stress all must be renegotiated while allowing each separate family system and individual member to maintain some sense of stability and continuity with the past.

In an effort to acknowledge the unique and diverse set of demands that remarried families confront, clinical researchers and theorists have articulated developmental models that take into account the experiences of families at different stages of establishing a remarried family system. These models generally offer an "ideal" set of guidelines against which a given family's adaptation can be compared. The models are flexible enough to account for the tremendous diversity that characterizes remarried family systems. They also acknowledge the differences between traditional nuclear and remarried families. These models are presented in this chapter because they can help identify how a given family may, or may not, be proceeding successfully along this alternative developmental path.

Courtship and Preparation for Remarriage

The transition to a remarried family system begins before the two adults actually marry. Later adjustment to remarriage and a stepfamily system (for those with children) can be greatly facilitated during the period of **courtship and preparation** for remarriage if several issues are addressed. These include the continued resolution of the previous marriage, the gradual modification of the single-parent household structure, and the anticipation of the remarried family structure (Whiteside, 1982, 1983).

Resolution of the Previous Marriage. As has been noted in earlier chapters, the resolution of personal feelings about the divorce and the establishment of an effective co-parenting relationship with one's former spouse can greatly facilitate adjustment to later family stages and transitions. However, it is not only "unfinished business" from one's first marriage that is brought into a new marriage but the sum total of all unfinished business with each important personal relationship (parents, siblings, former spouse) that makes us emotionally sensitive in the new relationship. When these conflicts are severe, there is a tendency to react in one of two ways. One way is to become self-protective, closed off, and afraid to make ourselves vulnerable to further hurt (i.e., we create barriers to intimacy). The other is to develop unrealistically high expectations and assume that a new partner will make up for, or erase, past hurts. To the extent that either or both remarried partners expect the other to relieve them of their past hurts, the relationship will become over burdened. On the other hand, if each partner can successfully resolve his or her own personal issues with significant persons from the past, the new relationship can start anew on its own terms (Golish, 2003; McGoldrick & Carter, 1999).

Gradual Modification of the Single-Parent Structure. Despite the overload and strain of the single-parent system, the stable patterns of interaction that have evolved within these single-parent systems are not easily altered. Many single parents, for example, develop a greater sense of personal independence as well as close, supportive relationships with their children (Afifi, 2003). Although a new courtship relationship may offer the prospects of adult intimacy, companionship, and security, it also threatens to alter the relationship changes achieved during the earlier single-parent period. Consequently, the courtship period offers time to adjust gradually to the change from a single-parent family structure to a remarried family system. In other words, a gradual period of transition allows the partners and children to maintain a sense of stability and predictability while gradual changes take place. It takes time to alter daily household routines, strategies for financial planning, and decision-making. This period also offers an opportunity for prospective stepparents and stepchildren to develop friendships without the pressures that accompany living together on a regular basis. Pleasurable activities that do not place heavy loyalty demands on family members can allow a sense of cohesion and unity to begin to develop (Adler-Baeder & Higgin-Botham, 2004; Bray & Kelly, 1998; Hetherington & Kelly, 2002).

Anticipation of the Remarriage. As the couple becomes more intimate and starts to anticipate remarriage, many new issues may begin to emerge. These can include concerns about changes in one's personal identity, the effect of the remarriage on financial and custody arrangements with the former spouse, the response of the former spouse to the remarriage, the role of the new partner with regard to the children, the reactions of the children to the remarriage, and each partner's expectations for the new marriage based on their previous experiences. The more attention the couple is able to devote to negotiating their expectations for such issues as finances, household rules, child-rearing values, custody decisions, or children's visitation schedules, the greater the likelihood that succeeding stages will proceed smoothly (Coleman, Fine, Ganong, Downs, & Pauk, 2001; Visher & Visher, 1996). Failure to address these issues early may indicate that the couple has unclear expectations about the differences between a first family and a remarried family structure, or that they are unaware of the complicated emotional issues they will face in a remarried family (Visher et al., 2003; Whiteside, 1983).

The Early Remarriage Stage: Defining Critical Identity Tasks

As Papernow (1993) noted, the remarried stepfamily begins with the stepparent as an outsider to a biological subsystem that has a shared history and preferred methods of relating that have been built over many years. This biological subsystem also includes an ex-spouse, dead or alive, with intimate ties to the children. From a structural perspective, such a system would be characterized as pathological due to its weak marital subsystem, an overinvolved parent–child alliance and a weak external boundary that allows frequent intrusion in the family from an outsider (biological parent). However, such a family structure is the starting point for normal stepfamily development.

In the **early remarriage** stage, the system typically remains divided primarily along biological lines. Research has found that this stage can be turbulent and disorganized and last an average of one to two years for most families (Hetherington & Kelly, 2002). However, some families can remain stuck in this stage for many years (Papernow, 1984). The key task that must be mastered during this period, if the family is to move on to the middle and late stages of development, is establishing an identity as a stepfamily.

Given the lack of clearly defined cultural norms for remarried families, stresses related to defining a clear family identity are almost inevitable (Visher et al., 2003). In fact, our society has not yet even decided what to call these families. Numerous terms have been proposed, including "blended family," "reconstituted family," "restructured family," "stepfamily," and "remarried family." The term **remarried family** has been chosen to acknowledge that one or both spouses have been married previously. A family in which one or both partners bring children into the new household is referred to as a **stepfamily** to emphasize the presence of both biological and nonbiological parents.

Further compounding the task of family definition are the expectations, fantasies, images, and myths that different family members bring to the remarried family. For example, because the nuclear family is still considered the ideal family arrangement, many adults continue to assume that their new family can replicate their previous one, thereby perpetuating the myth of "reconstituting the nuclear family" (Visher & Visher, 1982).

Another such myth is the myth of "instant love." This myth overlooks that new relationships take time to grow. Children cannot be mandated to love a stepparent. Expecting caring simply because individuals suddenly find themselves living together can easily lead to disappointment, insecurity, and anger. The first step toward developing positive relationships between stepparents and stepchildren is for stepparents to avoid trying to replace the biological parents. When adults relax and let children gauge the pace of the relationship, caring friendships and love are possible, especially when the children are young (Schulman, 1972; Visher & Visher, 1982).

A third common myth is the myth of the "wicked stepmother." Fairy tales such as "Snow White" and "Cinderella" inform children at an early age about the potential dangers of living with a stepparent. Stepmothers, too, have exposed to this cultural stereotype in their own development and may, as a result, carry this anxiety into their relationships with stepchildren. They may try too hard to be "perfect" parents. Such unrealistically high expectations can lead to frustration that, in turn, can perpetuate the very myth that they are trying to avoid (Claxton-Oldfield, 2000; Visher & Visher, 1982).

Family members also differ in the fantasies they bring to the remarried family (Papernow, 1984). One adult may enter the new family with fantasies of "rescuing children from a deprived background" or "healing a broken family." A biological parent may expect the new spouse (stepparent) to "adore my children." The stepparent might expect that the stepchildren "will welcome me with open arms." A struggling single mother may enter remarriage fantasizing that "I have finally found someone with whom to share my load." Her new husband may anticipate that he "can now have the intimate and caring relationship that he has been looking for." On the other hand, children may hold vastly different fantasies: "I really hoped that my parents would get back together," or "If I just ignore this guy, maybe he'll go away" (Papernow, 1993).

Such myths and fantasies are a natural element of the early phase of stepfamily development. However, these myths and fantasies can easily become stressors as they come up against the "reality" of the situation. The stepparent may find himself or herself on the outside looking in as the new partner's energy remains focused on the children rather than on the couple. The stepparent may reach out to the stepchildren only to find them indifferent or rejecting. The stepchildren's loyalty may remain with their own absent biological parent. They may even view the stepparent as the "cause of their parents not getting back together again." During this phase, the biological parent may interpret the stepparent's failure to engage the children as "a lack of desire to be a part of the family" or as "a refusal to share the burdens of parenthood." The stepparent may perceive the partner as "distant" or "uninvolved in the marriage." Such reactions may invoke fears of having entered into another "bad marriage" and of having "failed again" (Papernow, 1993).

It is also important to point out that the confusion experienced within the remarried family reverberates throughout the entire extended family system (Papernow, 1984, 1993). For instance, what is the relationship between the grandparents and their now ex-daughter-in-law going to be like? Will these grandparents be welcome in the new remarried family and continue to have a relationship with their grandchildren? In general, research has indicated that paternal grandparents are more likely than maternal grandparents to lose frequent or regular contact with their grandchildren following divorce and remarriage (Dunn, 2002). Finally, how are the stepchildren to be received by the stepparent's parents?

Families that successfully progress through this early stage will gradually clarify their confusion and begin to develop common expectations and a shared sense of family identity. This process also will involve clarifying each member's personal feelings and coming to some understanding of the primary strategies and rules by which the family has been operating. It is often stepparents who first become aware of the need for change in the family. This may be because their more peripheral position in the family allows them to see the situation from a more detached perspective. On the other hand, this may be due to the discomfort that comes from entering the family as an outsider. Since many of the new stepfamily's strategies and rules are determined by those inherited from the biological family, stepparents may come to experience the boundary between themselves and the rest of the family as a "biological force field" (Papernow, 1993).

However, the biological parent, too, must begin to clarify the stresses he or she is experiencing as a result of holding the central role in the family. This role includes nurturing and controlling children, maintaining a close and supportive relationship with the new spouse, and negotiating with the ex-spouse around financial and parenting issues. Biological parents naturally want to protect their children from further pain or from too much change. On the other hand, they must also begin to alter their previous strategies for managing the household, caring for children, and fostering the family's emotional climate to make room for the new spouse. The biological parent's position in the middle will be even more stressful if unresolved issues with the former spouse remain.

Although awareness of the major issues confronting the family may be heightened, the family's structure is not dramatically altered at this time. The biological parent–child subsystem remains the center of family activity. However, a supportive spouse appears to offer the best chance of moving smoothly through the early stage. Such a spouse appears to be able to empathize with the partner without imposing heavy expectations that the situation change (Papernow, 1993; Visher et al., 2003).

The Middle Remarriage Stage: Restructuring Family Boundaries

Movement from the early stage to the **middle remarriage** stage is often related to an infusion of support from someone or something outside the couple's relationship (Papernow, 1984, 1993). This might come from another stepparent who understands the situation, a self-help book for remarried families, a therapist, a support group, or a move out of the biological family's home to avoid the feeling of "living in someone else's house" (McGoldrick & Carter, 1999).

With this added thrust, the stepparent may begin to demand changes in the family's structure. The stepparent may want to spend more time as a couple, to set a clearer limit on the amount of contact between the partner and his or her ex-spouse, or to have a greater say in the disciplining of children. Alternatively, if the stepparent (especially a stepmother) has been expected to assume the traditional role of caretaker for the spouse's children, she or he may now demand that she or he be relieved of this excessive burden.

These bids to alter the family's structure may provoke a renewed period of stress and potential conflict as many highly charged differences are openly expressed for the first time. Although the fights that emerge at this time may seem trivial, they may actually reflect major struggles over whether the system is going to remain differentiated along biological lines or undergo change (Papernow, 1993). For example, a stepmother's temper outburst when ten-year-old Johnny leaves his dirty clothes all over the house may actually be about whether she has a right to discipline her husband's children and have a say in how the house is to be maintained. Similarly, an argument over how the stepfather sets the dinner table may actually be about whether sixteen-year-old Donna is losing the role of parental child that she assumed while living with her mother and siblings in a single-parent household. Each of these interactions can be viewed as an effort to loosen the boundaries around the biological subsystem (Afifi, 2003; Coleman et al., 2001; Golish, 2003).

As couples and children work together to resolve their differences, the structure of the family will gradually undergo change. This will require involving all family members in the process and insuring that each individual member's needs, expectations, and feelings are attended to (Whiteside, 1982). It is through mutual participation, open communication, shared empathy, and respect for individual differences that family cohesion and unity are developed (Golish, 2003; Visher et al., 2003). The most successful strategies that emerge from this process are generally those that leave some of the "old ways" of doing things intact while also creating new rituals, rules, and boundaries (Papernow, 1993; Whiteside, 1989). Thus, sixteen-year-old Donna may have to give up her responsibilities for caring for younger children in the family, although she and her mother may find other ways to maintain a special mother–daughter bond. The family may have to create new holiday rituals that respect the history and legacies of both families.

Clarifying the family's boundaries also entails defining the relationship that will exist between the custodial household and the other biological parent's household. This includes establishing a routine and mutually acceptable schedule of visitation, child support, and parental decision-making (Visher et al., 2003). For example, both biological parents may have to agree that children will be required to finish their homework before being allowed to play. However, it also is important to the adjustment of all family members, but especially for children who have loyalties to two families, that differences between the two households be openly accepted without connotations of right or wrong (Papernow, 1984). For instance, it may be permissible to eat dinner while watching television in one home but not in the other.

As was true in the early stage of the remarried family's development, changes in the family's boundaries during the middle stage also reverberate throughout the extended family system. For example, should the family change its rituals around Christmas or Hanukkah, these changes might alter how four sets of grandparents, aunts, and uncles (biological mother's, biological father's, stepparent's, and stepparent's ex-spouse's) celebrate their holiday rituals. Fulfilling obligations to each family's traditions and legacies while also redefining the present family structure can become exceedingly complex.

Nonetheless, by the time most families complete this stage, they have begun to function as a cohesive unit with more clearly defined boundaries and a shared sense of belonging. It appears that most families complete this stage after about three to five years (Hetherington & Kelly, 2002).

The Late Remarriage Stage: Strengthening Emotional Bonds

The **late remarriage** stage is marked by a greater sense of shared intimacy and authenticity in family relationships (Papernow, 1993). With the restructuring of the family's boundaries comes greater flexibility in roles and interactional patterns among family members. The family at this stage is characterized by a higher level of differentiation with dyadic personal relationships taking precedence over disruptive triangles and coalitions.

It becomes possible for stepparents and stepchildren to have more personal one-to-one relationships without interference from the biological parent. Although issues of inclusion and exclusion may periodically reappear because biological ties often remain more intense than steprelationships (Anderson & White, 1986; Coleman & Ganong, 1990), these issues by now have been essentially resolved. In some families, this may mean that members have agreed to accept a more distant relationship between a stepparent and stepchild. In other families, these issues may be resolved by the stepparent assuming a role of "primary parent" to the stepchild equal in authority to the biological parent. Whichever is the case, the role of stepparent has now been clearly defined.

The clearly defined stepparent role is defined by the following characteristics: (1) the role does not usurp or compete with the biological parent of the same sex; (2) the role includes an intergenerational boundary between stepparent and stepchild; (3) the role is sanctioned by the rest of the stepfamily, especially the spouse; and (4) the role incorporates the special qualities this stepparent brings to the family (Papernow, 1993). Whereas the stepparent's "differentness" may have been a source of conflict in the past, these qualities may now be appreciated for the diversity they bring to the family. For example, a stepmother's interest in clothing styles and fashion that may have been criticized as "extravagant" or "weird" during earlier stages may now be considered a resource by an adolescent stepdaughter who is more conscious of her appearance with her peers.

With the establishment of personal stepparent–stepchild relationships and the clarification of boundaries with extended family and the other parental households with which children are shared, the couple's relationship may now assume a more central position in the family system. The couple may now be able to turn their attention to "getting to know each other all over again" and experience their relationship in more personally supportive and intimate ways (Golish, 2003; Papernow, 1993).

As in any family, new stresses will continue to emerge for families at this stage of remarriage development. Decisions about childbearing, changes in children's visitation and financial arrangements, renegotiations of co-parenting decisions with biological parents, or routine stressors brought on by changes in employment, residence, or income can stress the family and precipitate changes in family interactions. When the stress becomes great, families may find themselves reexperiencing the entire remarriage developmental cycle. Periods of confusion or conflict, accompanied by alterations in the family's structure and perhaps polarization along biological lines, may all occur. However, these changes now occur within the context of a solid couple and stepfamily structure with a history of successful coping and problem resolution.

Problematic Family System Dynamics in Remarried Stepfamilies

Not all families will proceed through the various stages of remarried family development noted above. Some families will become stuck in an earlier stage indefinitely or for an extended period (Braithwaite, Olson, Golish, Soukup, & Turman, 2001). Others will end their remarriage through divorce. Divorce rates among the remarried tend to be even higher than for those in first marriages. Thus, it is clear that remarriage is fraught with potential complications that can interfere with successful adjustment.

Relatively little research has examined the system dynamics that foster or interfere with stepfamilies' adjustment and adaptation. The research that has been undertaken generally suggests that stepfamilies are less cohesive and slightly less effective than nuclear families at problem-solving and communicating. However, the differences between the two groups of families on these factors are generally small (Coleman et al., 2000; Hetherington & Kelly, 2002). This combined with the fact that members of stepfamilies and nuclear families generally report similar levels of well-being and marital satisfaction has led researchers to conclude that patterns of effective functioning in stepfamilies are different from those in nuclear families (Coleman et al., 2000).

One important factor in the patterns of interaction found in stepfamilies appears to be the extent to which triangles and coalitions form between family members. Although research has found that even well-functioning stepfamilies are more likely to have coalitions than well-functioning nuclear families, these coalitions are far more extensive and intense in dysfunctional stepfamilies (Afifi, 2003; Anderson & White, 1986). Given the complexity of the stepfamily system, there are a great many forms that these triangles and coalitions can take. Descriptions of some of the most common ones follow.

Triangles Involving an Ex-Spouse

When the former married couple has not succeeded in reaching an emotional divorce, these unresolved conflicts may produce stress for the remarriage. Remarried spouses may disagree over how to deal with the former spouse over child custody, child support, or other issues. In addition, the ex-spouse may frequently intrude into the new marriage by remaining dependent on the former spouse for emotional, practical, or financial support. The effect of this triangle is to interfere with the establishment of the remarried couple's identity and the creation of a clear boundary around the new marital relationship.

Another triangle that can occur when spouses have not resolved their earlier divorce involves one or more children. Here conflicts develop between the remarried couple and an ex-spouse over the care of a child. In this situation, the tension in the triangle is most often felt by the child, who begins to misbehave, develop problems at school, or asks to have custody shifted to the other biological parent. The remarried couple tends to unite in blaming the other parent or the child for the problem, while the noncustodial parent blames the remarried couple.

Successful resolution of both of these triangles will require the two former spouses to resolve their feelings toward one another regarding their separation and divorce. In the case of triangles involving a child, the management of the child should be placed in the hands of the biological parents. The new spouse can then assume a neutral position rather than siding against the child. The new remarried couple can then work toward individuating from one another in their own relationship so that differences and disagreements can be aired and the biological parent can have a personal relationship with the child without interference from the new spouse (Afifi, 2003; McGoldrick & Carter, 1999; Visher et al., 2003).

Triangles within the Remarried System

Sometimes the new wife is expected to assume the traditional role of primary caretaker for her new husband's children. The children will generally resent the stepmother's involvement, especially when they still have regular contact with their own biological mother. The resolution of this situation will generally require that the father assume the primary responsibility for enforcing discipline and providing support to the children. The stepmother then can have time to develop a trusting relationship with the children (Carter & McGoldrick, 1999a).

Another possible triangle puts the new husband in a stressful position in relation to his new wife and her children. The second husband may be seen as both "rescuer" and "intruder" (McGoldrick & Carter, 1999). He is expected to share the single mother's financial and parental burdens, but he may also be viewed as disrupting the close bonds that have become established between his new wife and her children during the single-parenthood period (Papernow, 1993; Visher et al., 2003). The stepfather's expressions of authority are then resented by the stepchildren, who go to their biological parent for support.

Here again, resolution will require that parental responsibility be assumed by the biological mother, with her new husband assuming a role that is supportive of his wife's efforts. Relationships between stepparents and stepchildren require time to develop. Unresolved issues with former spouses also must be addressed such that children are not caught in the middle, thereby reactivating stress in the remarried marital subsystem.

A third possible triangle involves the remarried couple, his children, and her children. In this triangle, the couple may report that they are "happily married" and that their only problem is that their two sets of children are "constantly fighting." In this instance, the children may be fighting out the unexpressed differences or disagreements between the remarried spouses (McGoldrick & Carter, 1999). These disagreements may involve unexpressed feelings about ex-spouses, about how to manage their own and each other's children, or about any of the myriad of tasks associated with establishing a new household. It is not uncommon for remarried partners to be cautious with one another, fearing that disagreements or conflicts may result in another failed marriage and loss (Papernow, 1993). However, the resolution of this triangle requires that spouses begin to communicate openly about their differences and implement problem-solving strategies that are mutually acceptable to both (Adler-Baeder & Higginbotham, 2004; Visher et al., 2003).

A fourth possible triangle involves one parent, instead of the couple, caught between two sibling subsystems. This triangle may appear on the surface to represent simple household conflict, with the parent caught between two "opposing camps" of children. However, the source of this conflict can be quite complex. It can represent a series of interlocking triangles including the children, the remarried couple, and the couple's ex-spouses (McGoldrick & Carter, 1999). Although it is quite common during the early stages of remarriage, when this arrangement continues over time, it can come to represent the system's failure to alter its structure toward a more cohesive, integrated, and flexible family unit.

Instead, the family remains divided primarily along biological lines. The children act out the unresolved issues of each spouse with their former spouses, or the children's own conflicted loyalties to their noncustodial parent and the new remarried system. Resolution of this impasse will require active efforts by both parents to establish clearly defined relationships with their own and each other's children. Open communication and sharing of parental responsibilities with the children's other biological parent also are essential.

Triangles Involving the Extended Family

Triangles with parents or in-laws are especially likely when the latter disapprove of the remarriage or when they have had an active role in raising their grandchildren (McGoldrick & Carter, 1999). For instance, the grandparents may remain loyal to the ex-spouse (their grandchildren's biological parent), thereby causing the new spouse to feel excluded. When the grandparents have been active in parenting their grandchildren, they may resent forfeiting this role to the new stepparent, thereby creating a triangle among the children, the grandparents, and the stepparent. This may force the children to take sides, leaving the stepparent again feeling excluded or forcing the grandparents to withdraw. The resolution of this triangle generally requires that each spouse take responsibility for clarifying the boundary between his or her parents and the remarried system. The other spouse must generally agree to stay out of it and to stop arguing or criticizing the in-laws.

Conclusions

Adults marry, divorce, become single parents, and remarry with great frequency in contemporary society. These events alter the family's developmental course in dramatic fashion. The structure of the family undergoes many changes in a typically short period. Members are added or lost to the system. Relationships undergo a series of changes as previous roles (e.g., marital partner) are redefined and new roles are created (e.g., ex-spouse, coparent, stepparent). The family is called on to alter continually its strategies and rules as it seeks to fulfill its basic tasks.

It is also important to emphasize that the changes in structure that accompany divorce, singlehood, and remarriage occur in conjunction with other typical and expected developmental changes in the family and its members. In the course of this text, patterns of change or stages through which families must pass have been discussed as basic or universal. For instance, one underlying assumption has been that individuals are continually individuating by negotiating and renegotiating their levels of individuality and intimacy with significant others over the entire life course. Another has been that the family system must continually alter its strategies and rules in response to individuals' changes so that an environment conducive to each member's growth and development is maintained. Still another has been that it is possible to anticipate the kinds of stresses that families will often face at each developmental stage and that certain coping strategies (e.g., effective communication, conflict—resolution skills) can ease the transition from one developmental stage to another.

However, it has been also repeatedly emphasized that expected developmental stages interact with each family's unique set of coping strategies, internal and external stressors (e.g., disability of a family member, unemployment, natural disasters), family background, and intergenerational legacy to produce untold complexity and diversity. No two families are alike. Families vary greatly in how they manage the stresses and strains of divorce, remarriage, or any of the other developmental stages examined in this text. Each family must ultimately be understood by examining its own unique context. In the final analysis, the theories and models presented here provide raw, primitive "snapshots" of the family's inner world. None of them, however, comes close to approximating the actual experience of being a member of a family.

Key Terms

Courtship and preparation   An initial stage in the process of remarriage that provides time to resolve issues related to the earlier divorce of one or both partners and a gradual introduction of the new stepparent into the present single-parent system.

Early remarriage   The second stage of the process of remarriage beginning immediately after the remarriage, during which the system typically remains divided primarily along biological lines.

Incomplete institution   A lack of norms and institutional supports for stepfamilies.

Late remarriage   The fourth and final stage of the remarriage process, marked by a greater sense of shared intimacy and authenticity in family relationships. Restructuring is now complete, and the family is characterized by flexibility in roles and interactional patterns. Personal one-to-one relationships take precedence over disruptive triangles and coalitions.

Metafamily system   A remarried family system that includes the households of both biological parents (perhaps other stepparents, siblings, and stepsiblings), biological relatives (e.g., grandparents, aunts, uncles, cousins), and steprelatives (grandparents, aunts, uncles, cousins).

Middle remarriage   The third stage of the remarriage process during which the structure of the family will gradually undergo change.

Remarried family   A family in which one or both spouses have been married previously.

Stepfamily   A family in which one or both partners bring children into the household, resulting in the presence of both biological and nonbiological parents.